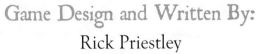

· HAIL CAESAR ·

™

Game Design and Written By:

Rick Priestley

Photography:

Alan Perry, Michael Perry, Dr Phil Hendry
Kevin Dallimore, Duncan Macfarlane,
Eric Hagen and Wargames Illustrated

Cover Artwork:

Peter Dennis

Design and Layout:

Paul Sawyer and Tim Vincent

Editing:

Steve Yates and
Duncan Macfarlane

With Special Thanks To:

Drew Will, Alessio Cavatore,
Sean Turtle, Mark Sims and
Great Escape Games

ISBN: 978-0-9563581-1-0

www.warlordgames.co.uk

Artwork by Peter Dennis   © Warlord Games Ltd 2011

CONTENTS

FOREWORD

Hail Caesar is a game for those whom the gods have marked for glory – for men who do not quail at the sight of barbarian hordes nor quibble with what fate decrees at the roll of a dice. It is unashamedly a game of model soldiers, fought with miniature armies representing warriors of ancient times, be they the tramping legions of Rome, bronze-clad Greeks, the clattering chariotry of Egypt, or whatever age or subject happens to inspire our interest and endeavours. Our ambition is to breath life into the warriors and tales of former days; to paint a picture that lacks nothing of the colour and splendour of an era long past; even if imagination alone must paint the hue and cry of battle, the whistling flight of arrows, and the flash of plunging spears.

So let us consult the oracles and make ready to meet with destiny upon the tabletop battlefield. Be sure that our battles will be as dramatic and hard fought as those of our forebears. And though our efforts may never topple tyrants nor change history's long run course, let us summon forth the ghosts of Hannibal, of Xerxes, Alexander and even Caesar himself, to stand at our shoulders, watch and – hopefully – approve.

Before the din of battle drowns out all other voices let us finally recall that we stand as comrades in arms: united in purpose, led by the same enthusiasm for the world of ancient battles and for the companionship of our fellows.

HAIL CAESAR

This book is about recreating the warfare of ancient times upon the tabletop using armies of model soldiers to represent the forces of ancient Egypt and Rome, of Greece and Persia and all the colourful warriors of former days. Our armies will strive for victory in the game of war just as their real-life counterparts strove to defeat their enemies so many years ago. We, the players, take the roles of the commanders and generals whose task is to drive our armies to victory whether by tactical guile or personal valour.

The greater part of this volume is taken up by the rules of play as well as accounts of battles played by the author and illustrated with models from our own collections. Our game aims to recreate something of the challenges faced by ancient warriors as well as the romance and heroism of former days, and it attempts to do so in a manner that we hope is both entertaining and engaging. The rules themselves have been devised for our own use – amongst friends and in our own homes– and are presented with the intention of inspiring others to their own efforts as much as to win converts to our cause. We therefore present our game for the enjoyment and interest of those who either share our sensibilities, or who value such things, and who are broad minded enough to consider our method upon its merits.

There are many hundreds if not thousands of players who already collect model armies and fight battles set in the ancient world. Many reading this book will be perfectly aware of how games are played, of the various types and styles of models available, and even of the various rulesets that are commonly used at competition and inter-club level. Our rules are not intended to compete with such – but are a deliberate attempt to produce a more friendly style of game with a strong element of role-playing by the participants. It is true that we do expect our players to put some effort into arranging and running games – and the examples of battles shown later give a good idea of how our own games are organised and run. This is not a set of rules that is ever likely to be adopted for strict competitive play, and those whose preference is for games of that kind will probably prefer to look elsewhere.

In putting together Hail Caesar we have drawn extensively upon what is known of warfare in ancient times, the writings of ancient authors, the scholarship of modern researchers and the delvings of archaeologists. Naturally we wish our game to be a credible account of its subject within reason. We would not be attempting to re-enact games set in ancient times were we not also keen enthusiasts of ancient history, culture and archaeology, and our game will undoubtedly appeal to those of similar mind. First and foremost though;

"Romans, remember that you shall rule by your authority, for this is to be your skill, to make peace the custom, to spare the conquered, and to wage war until the haughty are brought low."

Virgil

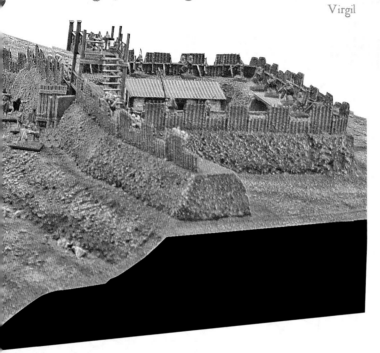

the rules of play have been developed so that our own group of players can spend an evening – or occasionally a long weekend – fighting battles with model soldiers amongst kindred spirits. As such the rules aim to convey a sense of drama to the action, to present the players with nerve-racking decisions, and to reward and punish risk taking in equal measure.

Finally, for those who are interested in the ideas and aims behind the rule set and its development we have added a section of Designer's Notes at the end of the book.

HOW THE RULES ARE CONSTRUCTED

The rules of our game can be readily adjusted to suit different sized battles, different numbers of players, and differing levels of complexity. This reflects the fact that the game has evolved amongst a core of players, but also has to accommodate friends and occasional visitors who may not be familiar with the course of play. As it happens this is a useful basis for a broadly based set of ancient rules, as it also allows us to easily adapt the game to represent the specific considerations of warfare throughout the ancient era.

With this in mind it will help to think of the game as a core set of rules for command, movement and combat. The basic values and ratings assigned to the armies facilitate these core mechanics: they define how troops move, how effectively they fight in different situations, and how they react to casualties suffered. In addition, the specific qualities of troops, technologies and cultural traditions are represented by means of additional or special rules that we apply according to our tastes and the type of game being played. These special rules have been largely improvised through play, and they can be readily extended or changed as the occasion demands. Often they were devised as part of a specific scenario and not necessarily used regularly. We leave it up to the players themselves to decide how much of this kind of representational detail to apply. Our aim is to provide an adaptable framework, plus a suggested 'kit' of additional rules that can be altered or expanded at will. To illustrate how this works we have included seven examples of quite different games that demonstrate the rules as applied to specific battles and eras.

WHAT IS NEEDED TO PLAY

We mostly play games with two or more players on each side and certainly prefer to do so wherever possible, but games can be just as enjoyable when fought between two opposing players. Whatever your preference you will need at least one opponent to fight, and both sides will require a model army to command. It will be necessary to find a good-sized table and preferably some model trees and terrain. For now let us indulge ourselves and imagine that we already possess two forces eager to do battle.

Players will also need a number of ordinary six sided dice – a dozen should just about do, but the more the better. A tape measure marked in inches will be needed to determine distances for movement and ranges for shooting. It is preferable to have several such tape measures, especially if two or more players are taking part on each side

Although it is not a strict requirement, where possible we play with the benefit of a third party, or umpire, whose job is to interpret the rules where necessary, impose his own should he feel the need, and otherwise help out to ensure the game proceeds at a pace. We find games far more entertaining when fought in this way and heartily recommend it.

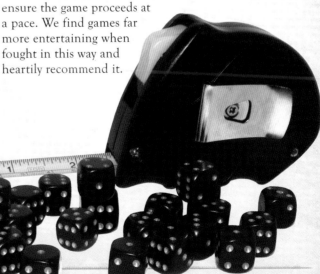

THE ARMY

Before it is possible to play a game it will be necessary to muster an army in miniature. Many prospective players will undoubtedly already own model armies, whilst a player contemplating starting a collection will find a bewildering choice of subjects from the earliest Egyptians through Greeks and Romans to medieval times.

The Hail Caesar game provides rules that cover more than 3,000 years of the history of warfare, so it would obviously be impractical to describe detailed rules for every nation and era from the get go. For now we shall confine ourselves to matters that affect all armies equally.

If you are about to start a new army the most important consideration of all is finding an opponent to play against. If you already have friends who own ancient armies, then you might wish to collect one or more armies to oppose them; for example, the Carthaginians of Hannibal's day beg to be opposed by the Romans of Scipio Africanus and his contemporaries. Some players like to collect both sides of a conflict, especially if they have a keen interest in – say – the era of Rameses the Great, the Peloponnesian War, or the Roman Civil Wars of Caesar and Pompey.

Either way, be aware that most players prefer to play games between armies that actually fought each other in history. However, there are a significant number of gamers who, quite cheerfully, fight battles between armies that never met

or which are separated in time by hundreds or even thousands of years. Although this latter approach is often frowned upon by purists, the relatively stable technology, and broadly comparable effectiveness of armies over hundreds of years, does mean that such games can be perfectly satisfying as 'games'. Our own preference is to play within a historical setting and all the games described in this book are of that kind. We shall let those who take pleasure in the strict recreation of historic battles do so. Equally we shall let those who prefer to conjure with the past enjoy doing just that. Our game is perfectly suited to either approach and happily embraces all aspects of collecting and gaming with model soldiers of the ancient era.

MODELS

The game can be played with models of any size or scale, but for the most part we have settled upon models that are 28-30mm tall to illustrate this book. This is the most popular size amongst serious collectors of model armies because the individual pieces are sufficiently large and detailed to reward careful painting. However, there are other sizes available, all of which have their advocates and all of which can be used to play our game should you wish to do so. Our choice is for models of the size stated, but players who prefer to collect 6mm, 10mm, 15mm or 1/72 (20mm) models – to list the most popular alternatives – may wish to refer to the appendix on page 174 for more about using these smaller warriors.

ROMAN FIELD ARMY OF THE FOURTH CENTURY

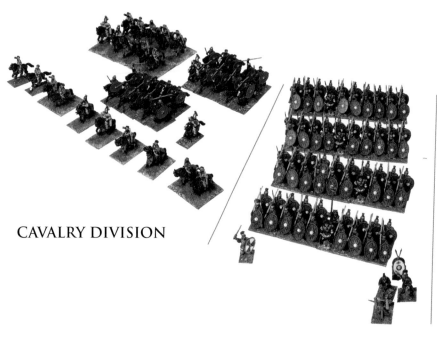

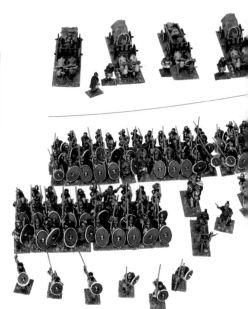

DIVISION OF BAGGAGE AND GUARDS

CAVALRY DIVISION

INFANTRY DIVISION

The majority of collectors purchase models as metal castings or plastic kits, which they proceed to assemble and paint before mounting the finished pieces onto bases for ease of handling. For those that do not wish to go to all this effort, it is possible to buy models that have already been painted. Some will gladly pay a professional artist to paint their collections for them; though they will need deep pockets, for such skills are not purchased cheaply. Models painted to the highest artistic standards are always in demand amongst serious collectors of whom there are a growing number. At the other end of the scale there are some gamers to whom building the army takes second place to the game itself, and they are happy to make use of unpainted models, being content to let their imagination alone colour the spectacle before them. It must be said that the majority of players prefer to build collections of models they have painted themselves, and most enjoy doing so. There is undeniably something satisfying about completing each new band of warriors and adding it to the growing army.

ORGANISING THE MODELS

Whatever army the player chooses to collect, it will be necessary to organise the troops into bodies of men, which we shall henceforth refer to as 'units'. These units are in turn formed into larger groups called divisions or brigades; we tend to use either term according to personal preference. A number of divisions make up our army.

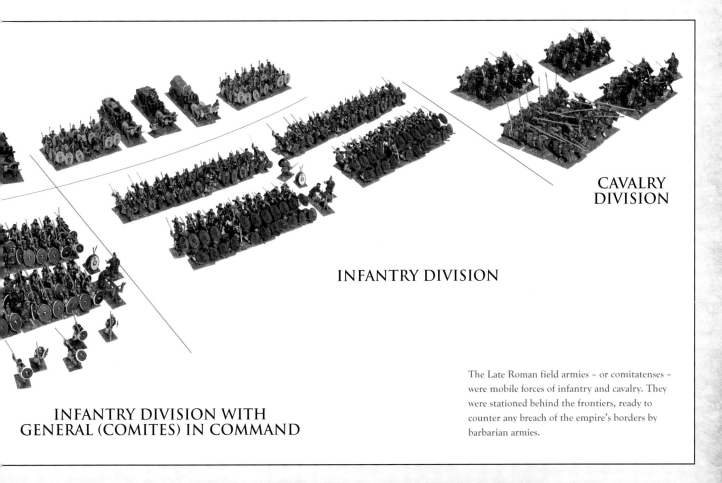

CAVALRY DIVISION

INFANTRY DIVISION

INFANTRY DIVISION WITH GENERAL (COMITES) IN COMMAND

The Late Roman field armies – or comitatenses – were mobile forces of infantry and cavalry. They were stationed behind the frontiers, ready to counter any breach of the empire's borders by barbarian armies.

THE UNIT

Each unit of model soldiers represents a typical fighting formation of its day, for example a cohort of Romans or taxis of Greek Hoplites. The term 'unit' is admittedly a rather bleak piece of jargon; however, it has the advantage that it allows us to devise rules in an even-handed manner without distinguishing between the varied military terms used in different armies. Of course, the language - let alone the military terminology – of many ancient peoples is now lost to us; so it is convenient to resort to a generic cover-all term for purposes of describing the game.

Naturally, we are mindful that a real formation of warriors would typically number some hundreds of fighting men, but the need to accommodate our battles on a tabletop means our units must be scaled down to something like a few dozen models. None-the-less, our band of model soldiers shall stand for a whole formation complete with its officers, troopers, standards, horn players and supernumeraries where appropriate.

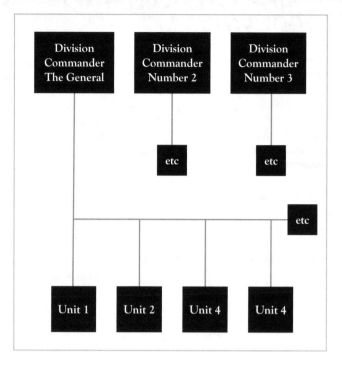

DIVISIONS AND COMMANDERS

The army's various units must be properly organised into divisions and each division assigned a model commander to lead it. A typical division might comprise a handful of units up to about a dozen. There is no limit, but the more units a division contains the harder it will be for its commander to control its movements. It is up to each player to allocate his units into divisions in a manner that he believes will be effective and which reflects actual practice where this is known. We shall return to the rules for organising and commanding divisions shortly.

Our armies need an overall commander or general: a Julius Caesar, Alexander the Great, or Boudicea to rise above the nameless throng of history. One of the army's commanders is therefore nominated as general. The general fulfils two roles: he is both a commander in change of a division and the army's overall leader.

A whole army consists of a number of divisions each comprising a number of units of troops. A commander leads each division. One of the commanders is also the army's general.

TROOP TYPES

For purposes of describing our game we divide our units of troops into easily recognisable and distinct types as follows.

▶ **Infantry** – warriors fighting on foot are the most numerous part of many armies. Infantry units are further subdivided into heavy infantry, medium infantry, light infantry, and skirmishers.

Cavalry – mounted warriors form an important arm in many armies and the most numerous part of nomadic armies. Cavalry units are further subdivided into cataphracts, heavy cavalry, medium cavalry, light cavalry and horse archers. Although cavalry are generally mounted on horses we also count camel mounted warriors as cavalry in armies that include them.

Artillery – artillery has an important role to play in siege warfare and also appears on the field in some armies. Artillery units are subdivided into light artillery, medium artillery and heavy artillery.

◀ **Chariots** – chariots are common only in armies of the ancient Near East such as Egyptian and Hittite, but continue to have a role in later times in some armies. Chariot units are subdivided into light chariots and heavy chariots, with the latter often pulled along by four horses.

Elephants – elephants are an important part of Indian armies and played a significant part in many battles of Alexander's Successors. We shall make do with the one category – elephants.

▼ **Wagons and Baggage** – all armies required a huge amount of logistical support, which we represent with these units. Once again a single category is all we need – wagons and baggage, sometimes referred to simply as baggage.

Within these standard troop types, units can be better armed or motivated, they can carry different weapons and may have different capabilities. The broad definitions described are useful basic types that enable us to ascribe core abilities and rules to our troops. A complete list of standard troop types, together with game values and a wide variety of different armaments is included in the Troop Types section of the rules on page 86.

FIGHTING QUALITIES							
Unit	Combat				Morale Save	Stamina	Special
	Clash	Sustained	Short Range	Long Range			
Legionary Heavy Infantry armed with pilum	7	7	3	0	4+	6	Testudo, Drilled

We attribute appropriate fighting qualities to each of our units by allocating game values that best reflect their abilities. These values determine how effectively each unit fights in different combat situations. By way of example, the values for a unit of Roman Legionaries of Trajan's Dacian Wars are shown above.

Unit

The name of the unit and its type and armament where appropriate – in this case Legionary troops who are heavy infantry armed with pilum.

Combat

Four different values are used for combat depending upon the situation and range. The first two values are clash and sustained – used for fighting hand-to-hand combat. The clash value is used in the first round of a combat engagement and the sustained value is used in subsequent rounds. The second two values are short ranged and long ranged. Long ranged attacks are used for shooting at distances of greater than 6". Short ranged attacks are used for skirmishing at short range, and also for supporting other units in hand-to-hand combat.

Morale Save

A unit's morale save indicates its ability to shrug off the debilitating effects of combat. This value is expressed as the minimum dice score required to withstand enemy attacks. A

value of 3+ is therefore excellent, as a roll of 3, 4, 5 or 6 will succeed. A value of 4+ is good, 5+ average, 6+ poor, and a value of 0 indicates the unit is very fragile and no dice roll is permitted. This is explained at length under the rules for ranged and hand-to-hand fighting.

Stamina

A unit's Stamina value shows how many casualties it can take before it is 'shaken' at which point it becomes vulnerable to destruction or collapse. Casualty markers are used to represent reduction of stamina. Most units can suffer 6 casualties before they are 'shaken'. Once again, this is explained under the rules for ranged and hand-to-hand fighting

Special

Any special rules that apply to the unit will be listed here. Such rules may reflect tactical doctrine, weaponry, cultural inclination or special skills of one kind or other. This need not concern us for the moment – various special rules will be discussed in due course.

THE UNIT'S LEADER

During the game we will have recourse to arrange formations, measure distances or calculate targets from the centre of a unit's front rank. Where practical it is a good idea to place the unit's leader model in this position to mark the middle of the unit's front edge. The rules that follow often refer to this centre-front or leader position.

It is left to the players to include leaders, standards, officers, horn blowers and such-like to represent their chosen subject. Naturally we would recommend that units include such figures where they would have had them in reality, as this contributes greatly to the appearance of the units in play.

The centre-front or 'leader' position – during play many measurements are made from the centre of the unit's front rank as shown here.

A MUCH TRAVELLED MAN

Ammianus Marcellinus was a general of the fourth century during the reigns of the emperors Constantius II and Julian. Although he wrote a Roman history covering from 96AD onwards, only the section relating to the years 353 to 378 survives. He served both in Persia and in Gaul, where he was part of the army led by Ursicinus against the usurper Claudius Silvanus. He accompanied Julian in his disasterous expedition against the Sassanid King Shapur II, and took part in the retreat of the surviving Roman army under Jovian. He describes the Persians as follows:

> *"The Persians opposed us serried bands of mail-clad horsemen in such close order that the gleam of moving bodies covered with closely fitting plates of iron dazzled the eyes of those who looked upon them, while the whole throng of horses was protected by coverings of leather."*

Ammianus Marcellinus

These very heavy cavalry were known as cataphracts or, in the case of the most heavily armoured of all, clibanarii; a word that may mean something like 'camp oven men' – perhaps a reference to what it must have been like wearing enclosing metal armour under the desert sun!

INFANTRY

Infantry mounted on bases 20mm per man (Celts) and 15mm per man (Hittites) – 20mm per man is the usual size

CAVALRY

Cavalry mounted on bases 25mm per rider – this is the usual size

BASE SIZES	
Type of Troop	**Individual Base**
Infantry	20 x 20mm
Cavalry	25 x 50mm
2 Horse Chariot	40 x 80mm
4 Horse Chariot	80 x 80mm
Elephant	80 x 80mm
Light Artillery	40 x 60mm
Medium/Heavy Artillery	60 x 100mm

Depths for chariots, elephants and artillery must be adjusted to fit the models as these tend to vary a great deal in overall size.

"I am dying from the treatment of too many physicians."

Alexander the Great

BASES FOR THE MODELS

The models shown in this book have been mounted onto rectangular card, wooden, or plastic bases and suitably decorated. This makes the models easier to handle without knocking them over or damaging them, and also allows us to more easily arrange the units into neat blocks. It is not strictly necessary to mount the models onto bases in this way, but amongst collectors who intend to take their troops into battle it is the usual practice.

Some players like to mount every individual model onto its own small base. This has the advantage that it allows a unit to adopt any kind of formation simply by rearranging the models themselves. On the whole it is preferable to mount several infantry or cavalry models onto a larger multiple base as this makes it quicker and far easier to move an entire unit. For example, single infantrymen are normally mounted onto a square base 20mm x 20mm, so a single rank of three infantry could be mounted onto a multiple base 60mm x 20mm. Artillery models, chariots and elephants are best based individually, either with their crew or with the crew separate.

The table on the left shows the sizes of bases used in the majority of photographs in this book. These are the sizes we'd recommend. The depths for chariots, elephants and artillery in particular must be adjusted to suit the models where necessary and are not critical to the game.

We should stress that our game is perfectly suited to playing with models whatever sized bases they happen to have. Some of the models shown in this book are based to narrower frontages (usually 15mm for infantry and 20mm for cavalry). As it happens these are mostly older and 'slighter' models than many currently available, but we find no problems in using them alongside models based as described above. The important thing is that units should be more-or-less the same width when deployed for battle as noted on page 16.

CHARIOTS

A chariot mounted on a 40mm wide base
– 50mm is also common – both work just fine

COMMANDERS

Commanders can be based to suit – many players like to put their
commanders on round bases to distinguish them from ordinary troops

BASES FOR COMMANDERS

Our commanders are represented by either individual models or small groups mounted onto a single base. Ideally, these pieces should be readily distinguishable from the troops they command. We do not feel the need to specify base dimensions for these models – players can adopt a size and shape they find serviceable – numerous examples are shown throughout the book.

Just as our units of a few dozen models are understood to represent formations of hundreds of men, so a commander is taken to represent not just the great man himself but his bodyguard, runners, soothsayers, secretaries and such personal servants as the exercise of command plainly demands. A commander can be mounted onto a larger base and include such individuals if you please. This can be fashioned to look suitably imposing!

SIZE OF UNITS				
Type Of Troops	Standard Size	Large	Small	Tiny
2 deep Infantry	16 to 20 models	32 to 40	8 to 12	5 or 6
3 deep Infantry	24 to 30 models	48 to 60	12 to 15	5 or 6
4 deep Infantry	32 to 40 models	60 to 80	20 to 24	Not Allowed
Cavalry	12 to 16 models	24 to 32	6 to 8	3 or 4
Light Chariots	4 or 5 models	8 to 10	2	1
Heavy Chariots	2 or 3 models	4 or 5	1	-
Artillery	2 or 3 models	4	1	-
Elephants	1 model	-	-	-

SIZE OF UNITS

Units of troops are categorised into one of four arbitrary sizes: large, standard, small, and tiny. We should emphasise that the majority of close fighting units in the army always conform to the standard size. Skirmishers and other units that habitually operate in open order are usually fielded as small units. Tiny units are reserved for scouts, foragers and the like. Large units are employed only in the biggest games where barbarian hordes can be conveniently represented by double-sized formations.

The sizes we generally prefer are given on the table above. Note that it really doesn't matter too much if units are a little over or undersized on the day, so long as it is clear whether they are standard size, large, small or tiny.

Players are free to set unit sizes with fewer or more models as they please, these just happen to be the sizes we use and which suit our collections.

In setting these sizes our intention is that all units present a frontage that is more-or-less the same for their size and type when arranged in their usual fighting formations. Small units will be a little narrower, large units a little wider. This is why infantry deploying three or four ranks deep have more models: they have extra ranks to fill.

The table below summarises the frontages in millimeters for units based as described above and deployed in their usual fighting formations. As tiny units don't have strict formations these have been left off.

UNIT FRONTAGES TABLE				
Type Of Troops	Formation	Standard	Large	Small
2 deep Infantry	2 deep battle-line	160-200mm	320-400mm	80-120mm
3 deep Infantry	3 deep battle line	160-200mm	320-400mm	80-120mm
4 deep Infantry	4 deep warband/phalanx	160-200mm	300-400mm	100-120mm
Cavalry	2 deep battle-line	150-200mm	300-400mm	75-100mm
Light Chariots	1 deep battle line	160-200mm	320-400mm	80mm
Heavy Chariots	1 deep battle line	160-240mm	320-400mm	80mm
Light Artillery	1 deep battle line	80-120mm	160mm-240mm	40mm

As you can see from the Unit Frontages table, our units have a comparable frontage when arranged into a typical fighting formation. Artillery units are significantly shorter, but as these are not close fighting troops we don't worry about it too much.

Incidentally, we enjoy the mass spectacle of our armies and so arrange our battle lines two or more ranks deep. Some players may prefer to reduce the number of ranks simply to lessen the number of models required for each unit and this is entirely up to the players. It is the width of the unit that plays a major part in the game, the depth is far less important and can be adjusted to suit. For example, on occasions we would deploy cavalry units one deep either because we want to field more units, or because a player has built his collection round units with fewer models; this makes no difference, and units of one or two depth can both be used alongside each other.

CASUALTY MARKERS

The fighting effectiveness of troops declines during the heat of battle due to breakage of weapons and armour, bodily fatigue, failing morale, and men or officers falling wounded or killed. We represent all these factors by means of casualty tokens or markers placed beside or behind the units. The maximum number of casualty markers a unit can take is referred to as its 'stamina' and depends upon the unit's size:

most standard sized units can suffer 6 casualties, large units 8, small units 4 and tiny units only 1. This is explained together with the resultant effects later in the game rules.

SIZE OF UNITS				
Unit Size	Large	Standard	Small	Tiny
Typical Stamina Value	8	6	4	1

Any kind of markers can be employed to record casualties, such as actual models of dead or wounded, discarded shields, or basic card or plastic tokens. Players are welcome to use whatever method they feel most comfortable with, and can resort to pen and paper to record casualties if that is their preference.

LEADERSHIP RATINGS

In the ancient world commanders frequently had to lead from the front. They had to be fighters as well as leaders. This is true in our game too. Commanders will often find themselves in the thick of things! Sometimes they will intervene to lead units in person, or rush to rally units that are flagging. Most of the time their job will be to direct the army by issuing orders to units under their command.

We assign a value to all commanders to represent their effectiveness within the army's overall command

structure. This leadership rating can vary from army to army, and from commander to commander, but for most purposes it is assumed to be 8. We'd recommend that players stick to a value of 8 at least until they have a fair grasp of the rules.

Note that commanders who are killed in battle will be replaced by subordinates whose leadership rating will usually be one lower, i.e. a commander with a rating of 8 will be succeeded by another with a rating of 7. This is described in the section on Commanders page 80.

LEADERSHIP RATING	
Leadership Rating	Description
10	**Military Genius.** A natural born leader, impossibly handsome, beloved of the gods, worshipped by his men, adored by women, highly organised, courageous, with an instinctive feel for battle.
9	**Great.** An extremely capable, trustworthy, forthright, pious and popular commander.
8	**Good.** An able and confidEnt leader respected by his peers.
7	**Average.** An honest sort and a capable, if uninspired, leader.
6	**Poor.** An indecisive or reluctant commander, prone to dithering.
5	**Fool.** A feckless blustering imbecile, cursed by the gods, justly despised by his men, and a prime target for assassination at the first opportunity.
4 and less	**Unfit for Duty.** We shall not rate any of our commanders below 5 for all that the Praetorian Guard might mark this fellow out for the purple.

FORMATIONS

Before our troops are ready to take part in a battle we must decide how to arrange them into fighting formations. For the most part, ancient warriors fought in simple linear formations and, although hints of how this worked in practice can be gleaned from surviving commentaries, it is far from certain how troops fought in any detail.

Despite the necessary uncertainties imposed upon us by the passage of time, the general similarity in weapons and the universal constant of the human body make it reasonable to assume warriors fought in comparable ways in comparable circumstances. This is a broad assumption of course, but for the purposes of playing battles with model soldiers it seems a not unreasonable one.

BASIC FORMATIONS

The following are all formations that are either used by all armies or often employed by specific but relatively common troop types. For example, the pike phalanx formation won't interest those whose inspiration is drawn from the legions of Rome or the chariotry of Egypt, but it is basic to all the Hellenistic armies of Alexander the Great and his Successors, so it is worth consideration from the onset. Some very specific and unusual formations are dealt with separately, for example the Roman Testudo and enigmatically named Pigs Head (see page 103).

We sometimes refer to **formed** bodies of troops, by which we mean troops arranged in any formation aside from 'open order', where models are spaced apart with gaps between as explained below. This is a useful distinction to make because some rules apply only to formed units and other rules apply only to units in open order.

BATTLE LINE

This is the basic fighting formation for most units whether they are infantry, cavalry, chariots, artillery or even elephants. A battle line is a straight line of troops deployed as shown.

A standard battle line of infantry and cavalry is represented in the game by a unit arranged into two ranks of troops. This represents a real unit arranged something like four to six men deep in the case of infantry and perhaps two to four deep in the case of cavalry.

We arrange some of our close fighting infantry battle lines into three ranks, representing a real life formation in the order of eight to ten men deep. We do this mostly for the look of the thing and also because our units happen to be fairly sizeable. It makes no difference in play. In reality deeper formations tended to be distinct of specific armies and troop types, and we provide the option for players whose collections reflect this.

A battle line of chariots and artillery is arranged one deep as this looks more convincing and provides a more playable depth given the size of the models. Elephants are fielded as a battle line of a single model and cannot adopt other formations.

Battle in the Holy Land – Turkic horsemen ride past a desert oasis as they prpare to do battle with the infidels

This is a unit in a battle line formation – in this case Assyrians with a front made of spearmen and a rear rank of archers

This is a unit in a column formation – note how the crusaders are mounted on to 40mm x 40mm bases for ease of movement

COLUMN

A column is a unit arranged for moving quickly, and generally speaking for marching, but also for deploying into position, and potentially for making a rapid advance over the battlefield. It is an extremely poor formation for fighting purposes, and troops attacked by the enemy whilst in column are likely to suffer badly as a result. An infantry column must be between two and four models wide and must have more ranks than files (i.e. the formation must be deeper than it is wide). All other columns must be one or two models wide and must have more ranks than files, aside from elephants as already noted.

A column of troops need not necessarily be a perfect rectangle, but can be arranged to flow around obstacles or follow a curving track, for example. Columns will often be marching along roads or tracks, or between buildings or around other troops, and must obviously be free to follow the necessary path.

Note that a unit of elephants is represented by a single model in a battle line, but even so the elephant can still enjoy the benefits of moving as a column on a road or track as noted under Elephants on page 99.

OPEN ORDER

Open order formation is a dispersed fighting formation where individual models or their bases are spaced apart. Units in open order are often distinguished from 'formed' units for rules purposes, as will become apparent.

Skirmishers, horse archers and all tiny units are restricted to open order or column formations and cannot adopt other formations.

Light infantry, light cavalry and light chariots can adopt open order as an option during the battle. These troops can operate in column, battle line or in open order as the occasion demands.

Other infantry and cavalry can only adopt open order when moving in situations where they could not otherwise move at all, or where they could not move without incurring some penalty. This usually happens when operating in wooded land, moving over rough ground, and crossing rivers or other kinds of obstacles (see Terrain page 38). Such units must revert to a battle line or other

formation as soon as possible once they are out of the woods, rough ground, etc.

Other units – heavy chariots, artillery, elephants and baggage – cannot adopt open order at all. This will restrict their ability to move through some kinds of terrain such as woods and rough ground.

When a unit adopts open order the models' bases are spaced up to 1" apart so they form a chain or loose mass.

Pikemen deployed 4 models deep in 'pike phalanx' formation. These models have been fielded to a slightly smaller size than we'd normally use, but such things are easily accomodated within the game

PIKE PHALANX

This formation is unique to troops armed with the long pike or sarissa. This is a spear-like weapon somewhere between sixteen and twenty-four feet long with a long spearhead at one end and a counterweighted butt-spike at the other. These troops fought in very deep formations and so we arrange our model pikemen to fight in a pike phalanx four models deep. This represents sixteen ranks of real warriors. The phalanx is the usual formation for such troops when deployed for battle. It is the

equivalent of a battle line, and we do not allow pikemen to form into battle lines three or two deep.

Not surprisingly, the pike phalanx was an unwieldy formation that demanded a very high degree of training and discipline to operate effectively. Consequently we will require special rules to deal with pikemen as well as a distinct formation – see page 102.

WARBAND

An infantry warband is a mass of loosely ordered warriors - generally speaking barbarians – lacking much in the way of formal organisation and training. Infantry warbands are arranged into formations four ranks deep. This is their usual fighting formation and the equivalent of a battle line for such troops, they are not allowed to form into a two or three deep battle line as described above.

If composed of light infantry they may not form open order except in the same way as medium or heavy infantry.

A Celtic Warband

SQUARE

We use the term square to cover a number of very closely ordered defensive formations. In reality such formations were often circular or rectangular rather than literally square, but we shall make do with a single formation that represents all.

Only heavy, medium or light infantry can form a square. The unit is arranged into a roughly square shape with each side the same width as near as possible, and the models facing outwards where it is practical for them to do so.

Assyrian infantry in a square formation

TESTUDO, PIG'S HEAD, AND WEDGE

These are rather unusual formations that are only allowed to specific troops as a special ability. They need not concern us for the moment. The rules for these are included under the section A Selection of Useful Rules on page 98.

A Roman Testudo – in this case represented by a bespoke model

TUCK IN –
PLENTY FOR ALL!

No wargame is complete without suitable refreshments and what could be more appropriate than a quick delve into the Roman cookbook of Apicius.

Milk-fed Snails
(adapted somewhat) from *Apicius' De Re Coquinaria*

Ingredients
>   4-5 snails per person
>   A quantity of milk
>   Olive oil
>   1 clove of garlic per person
>   1 tablespoon of red wine per person
>   Garum – fish sauce

First catch your snails – make sure these are nice big ones that haven't been anywhere near anything nasty such as ivy or other poisonous plants, pesticides, or practically anything else you might typically find in your garden. Starve for two days to cleanse thoroughly. Put snails in closed container and cover with milk. Leave for two or three days – but be mindful to remove the snail excrement every hour and change the milk completely twice a day.

After two or three days take the fattened snails and remove them from their shells. Heat the olive oil in a frying pan and add the garlic, finely chopped. Add snails and fry for about five minutes. Add wine and heat until the whole thing is reduced by about half. Serve with garum, which – as we all know – is a kind of salty sauce based on rotted fish.

Sadly garum is no longer available – probably due to some namby-pamby food hygiene regulation – a strong soy sauce or similar will have to do.

CHANGING FORMATION

Generally speaking, changing from one formation to another requires a specific instruction when orders are given. We shall address the rules for giving orders and resultant moves in the following rules section. For now we shall simply establish the procedures for changing from one formation to another.

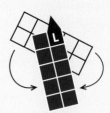

When changing formation from column to battle line, phalanx or warband or from any of these formations back to column, begin with the model or base in the centre-front or 'leader' position (see The Unit's Leader page 13). Turn the model on the spot to so that it faces the desired direction. Rearrange the rest of the unit around the leader so the model or base is as near as possible in the centre-front position of the new formation. This manoeuvre takes the unit one move.

In the case of an open order formation the approximate 'middle' of the formation is used as the fixing point for changing formation (left). Place the leader model in the middle of the open order formation and rearrange the unit into a new formation around him (right). To change from another formation to open order simply reverse the process. This takes most troops one entire move, but in the case of skirmishers, horse archers, light infantry, light cavalry, and light chariots the change in formation to or from open order can be followed by a normal move all counting as 'one move'. For example, a unit of skirmishers in column can form open order and move 6" as one move, a unit of light cavalry in open order can form a battle line and move 9" as one move, and so on. See Moving Units page 33 for more about rates of movement.

In the case of a square we use the same principle as for open order units, calculating the unit's position from the middle of the square. Thus when a unit forms a square from a battle line the centre-front position of the battle line becomes the middle of the square (left). Alternatively, it is acceptable to form a square from the leading edge of the unit as shown on the right if the terrain or proximity of other troops makes this a more practical option. We would use the same principle in the case of a testudo or wedge as described in A Selection of Useful Rules on page 98.

FORMATION AND TINY UNITS

Tiny sized units don't have proper formations as such – consequently they are always represented in open order or as columns. In this respect they are restricted in the same way as skirmishers and horse archers. Tiny units cannot be reorganised into other formations.

FRONT, FLANK, AND REAR

The areas to the front, sides and rear of a formation form its front, left flank, right flank, and rear quarters. This is a useful concept as it allows us to define how troops move, what they can see and react to as a body, how they shoot, and so on. This idea underpins many of the rules that follow so it's worth nailing this one down straightaway. These quarters, areas, or zones are most readily demonstrated by means of a diagram (right).

Units in open order are sufficiently dispersed for troops to face whichever direction they wish, and therefore they have no flanks or rear as such. Units in open order are treated as having one continuous front that extends all the way around their edge.

Units in a square formation still have four distinct quarters in the way illustrated below but have no flanks or rear. Each face of the square is treated as a separate front.

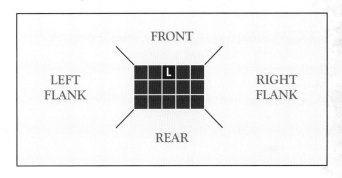

DIVISIONS

An army consists of a number of divisions. Each division consists of one commander plus a number of units. We make no limit on the number of units in a division or to the mix of troops that they contain. For example, a division could consist of its commander, some heavy infantry, some skirmishing infantry, a cavalry unit, and an artillery piece. Where in reality it would be organised along ethnic or other lines we leave it to the players to arrange such matters to their satisfaction.

Units from the same division do not have to remain within any specified distance of each other during the game.

However, if they are to be directed by means of a single order, divisions must form a loose body with no unit separated by more than 6". This is described in detail in the Command rules that follow. Broadly speaking, divisions operate more efficiently when forming a close group as described.

Commanders must remain within a move's distance of at least one unit under their command. The closer they are to the units in their division the easier it is for them to issue orders. Note that commanders can't normally be shot at in the game and cannot be attacked except when fighting combat – so there is rarely any need to worry about their safety as they move.

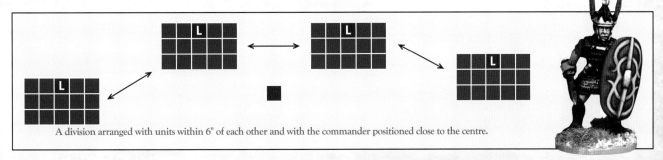

A division arranged with units within 6" of each other and with the commander positioned close to the centre.

GAME RULES

For purposes of explanation we shall assume that the game is played between two opponents. This makes it easier for us to describe the rules and procedures, and, in any case, this is a common and perfectly good way to play.

In practice we firmly hold to the view that our game of war – much like a Roman banquet – is for a host of friends to enjoy together. Stuffed Dormice and Larks' Tongues may rarely grace the menu, but food, drink and camaraderie are ingredients as much a part of the feast as the model armies and the battle itself. Our ideal game is played with two, three or more players on each side and frequently includes an umpire to reign over all. This arrangement usually allows each participant to take command of a single division of troops. So, in each side's turn each player rolls dice for his own division, moves his own units, and tries to achieve whatever aims the players have – hopefully – agreed as part of their battle plan.

When more than one player represents each side one player must take on the role of the General and his division. This is up to the participants to agree amongst themselves in whatever manner they prefer.

PREPARING TO PLAY

Before the game can begin it is necessary to set the scene of battle using whatever model terrain and miniature scenery best depicts our imagined landscape. Ancient battlefields are often represented as flat, featureless plains – and open, level terrain was certainly the arena of choice for many large, well-ordered armies of the ancient world. Our historians rarely take the trouble to describe raids, ambushes, and smaller encounters in detail – but it does not take a great deal of effort to imagine a conflict amongst the mountainous landscapes of Spain, the Balkans or Armenia – nor the dense woods and marshes of Germany and Central Europe.

For now we shall not concern ourselves too much with the terrain – we will be discussing such matters together with appropriate rules later on. The moment will come to consider fording rivers, tramping through dank woods, and occupying towns and villages. To begin with it is not unreasonable to assume our game takes place upon the unadorned and level surface provided by a tabletop or floor.

A battle can begin with two armies lined up on opposing sides of the table. Many large battles of our era began in just such a way, with troops marching out of camp and deploying to face each other. Some battles are known to have started with chance encounters between opposing troops, followed up by reinforcements, until whole armies became unexpectedly committed. That is to say nothing of ambushes and raids upon exposed baggage or foraging parties. It is not for nothing that Legions campaigning in enemy territory took the trouble to build a fortified camp at the end of each march. To begin with it is convenient to assume our armies have simply marched from their respective encampments to face each other across the full width of the playing area and at least 3 feet apart if possible. With both forces fully deployed the battle is ready to begin.

SEQUENCE OF PLAY

The game proceeds in turns. In each full turn both sides take an individual turn – first one and then the other as shown below.

BLUE
1. Blue Command – Blue moves his units starting with *initiative* moves.

2. Blue Ranged Attacks – Blue units make ranged attacks.

3. Blue Hand-to-Hand Combat – both sides resolve any hand-to-hand fighting.

RED
4. Red Command – Red moves his units starting with *initiative* moves.

5. Red Ranged Attacks – Blue units make ranged attacks.

6. Red Hand-to-Hand Combat – both sides resolve any hand-to-hand fighting.

We have dubbed our opposing armies 'blue' and 'red' for ease of reference. As you can see each full turn comprises a blue turn followed by a red turn – after which the sequence just repeats itself blue, red, blue, red, blue, and so on until the game is fought to a conclusion. Note that during the hand-to-hand combat part of the turn both sides fight regardless of which side's turn it is.

To begin the battle you will need to decide which side has the first turn – which side is to be 'blue' in our sequence. Although it might seem there is a great advantage in going first, in practice these things tend to even themselves out over the course of a game. Indeed, it is often beneficial to go second as it gives you a chance to take advantage of any partial or failed moves made by your opponent. Sometimes the kind of game will dictate who goes first – an ambush for example – but in most cases it is entirely adequate to roll a dice for both sides and the highest scorer decides whether to go first or second.

MEASURING DISTANCES

During the game players will find it necessary to measure distances when issuing orders, moving units, shooting at the enemy and in other situations too numerous to mention. Players are free to measure distances at any time they wish, whether it is their own turn or not.

Generally speaking, distances between models are always measured from the edges of the bases on which the models are mounted rather than from the models themselves. The notable exception to this is in the case of commanders. It is usual to measure from the head of the commander model rather than from his base edge when determining the distance between the commander and a unit he wishes to give an order to. This is because commanders might be riding chariots or elephants – which have correspondingly huge bases – but measuring from the head of the commander ensures all is fair.

VISIBILITY

Before we proceed further it is necessary to introduce a fairly basic concept: namely what a unit of troops can or can't see. This is quite an important distinction because troops have to be able to see an enemy unit to shoot at it, or charge, and in various other circumstances. So what do we mean by 'see' as our model warriors are but dumb tin or plastic and unhelpfully uncommunicative on such matters?

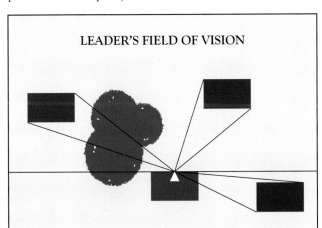

LEADER'S FIELD OF VISION

In the diagram the blue unit cannot see the left hand enemy because the wood blocks the unit leader's view. The centre unit can be seen perfectly clearly. The blue unit's leader can't see through his own troops, so anything behind the unit's frontage isn't visible – such as the right hand enemy unit.

In principle, when we talk about what a unit can 'see', we mean something that a body of troops could clearly identify and take appropriate action in respect of in real life. Whether individuals can actually see other individuals is not important in this sense. If a hill or wood lies between shooters and their target then the target cannot be seen because the hill or wood is in the way. Where the enemy is obscured by topography, by buildings, or by the formations of other units, then it is not possible to see in the sense described. These matters require

judgement and players are encouraged to rely on good sense rather than be slavish about such things.

For convenience of play a unit's ability to 'see' is always judged from the centre-front or leader model position. The unit sees what the leader sees, and if the leader cannot see the unit cannot see either.

At his stage it's worth pointing out that models representing the army's general and other commanders are simply ignored when it comes to deciding what a unit can see and which enemy is closest. Just imagine they are not there. Commanders represent a small number of mobile individuals who would largely go unnoticed amongst the hurly-burly of battle.

Note that aside from artillery (which will be considered in due course) units are not permitted to see through or over the heads of other formations even where some models might be on slopes or occupying ramparts overlooking others. This applies even if the intervening troops are in open order and therefore have gaps within their formation. Any units in the way automatically block line of sight through or over their formation.

LEARNING THE GAME RULES

It will be necessary to learn the rudiments of the game before committing your troops to their first battle; however, this need not be too daunting a task. There is no need to memorise every rule before you can play – but it is a good idea to read through the rules once to get an idea of how things progress. The best way to learn is to play a small game with a single division on each side and then add more as you get used to handling your army.

The rules are presented with *command* first, in which we explain how orders are issued and how troops move across the tabletop. Next come the rules for *ranged attacks*, which includes shooting with bows, slings and javelins. After that we deal with the rules for hand-to-hand combat – which is to say close quarter combat with swords, spears and such-like. Finally we'll introduce some of the more detailed rules covering specific troops types and unusual weapons and formations. This running order seems the most logical as battles usually begin with manoeuvre, followed by a discharge of missiles as the armies close, and finally end with *hand-to-hand* combat.

AN IMPORTANT PRINCIPLE

Battles with model soldiers are supposed to be enjoyable affairs. All questions of victory and defeat pale to nothing before this objective. Our rules of play have been formulated for our own games, and our aim in presenting them here is purely to explain, entertain and hopefully inspire other enthusiasts. We make no pretence that our game is superior to others and invite the reader to adopt whatever portion of our game happens to please. Different players find interest and satisfaction in different things, so there is plenty to be gained by amending, or otherwise improving, aspects of the rules that fail to meet with approval.

COMMAND

In the command part of his turn the player gets a chance to move his army. Sometimes troops are allowed to move automatically, but in most situations they must be issued orders to do so. Orders are issued on behalf of the army's commanders to the units in their divisions. Broadly speaking, to give an order the player first nominates a commander to issue the order, then he indicates which unit he wishes to move, and finally the player describes what he wants the unit to do before rolling dice to determine if he is successful or not. This is the basic method by which troops are moved in the Hail Caesar game.

ORDERS

Giving orders is one of the most important parts of the game and also one of the most entertaining aspects of play. When framing orders participants are encouraged to imagine themselves as proud consuls, brave warlords or merciless despots according to their inclination.

Players should endeavour to state orders aloud, in good time, and in a straightforward, robust fashion without conditions or vagaries. Orders must always be stated **before** making the requisite test for success. Failure to state an order before rolling the dice is considered an affront to the gods resulting in a *blunder* as described later. A generous opponent may choose to forgive such a fundamental error – though it is questionable whether it is worth a player so indebting himself to his adversary!

Units don't need orders to make ranged attacks or to fight when they find themselves in hand-to-hand combat – they do these things automatically. In most situations units *do* need orders to move in the Command part of the turn, although there are some situations where units are able to move without orders, as we shall see. There are also situations

where units can or must move during other parts of the turn: for example, following hand-to-hand combat when defeated units are often obliged to give ground and victorious units have the opportunity to press forward or fall back.

The order must explain where a unit is to move to and by which route in cases where there is room for doubt. A unit must also be given a specific order if the player wishes it to change formation: for example, to rearrange its ranks into a column or disperse into open order. Finally – and importantly – if you want a unit to move into hand-to-hand combat with an enemy then you must specifically state that you want the unit to *charge*, and you must indicate which enemy unit or units you intend the chargers to contact. If you want a unit to charge then you **must** say so when giving the order.

Units will always attempt to obey their orders in so far as they are able and in the most direct and straightforward way they can. If a unit's move proves inadequate to fulfil an order in its entirety, then the unit will follow its instructions to the best of its ability in so far as it can. For example, if a unit is ordered to charge an enemy but has insufficient movement to do so, then it will move as far as it can towards the intended target.

TEST FOR SUCCESS

To determine if a stated order is successfully formulated and received, a test is taken as follows. Roll two dice, add the scores together to get a result from 2-12 and check the number against the commander's leadership rating:

- If the score is greater than the commander's leadership rating then the test is failed and no order is issued. The unit cannot move unless it is entitled to a 'free move' in which case it makes one move (see Free Moves page 31).

Sumerian spearmen advance behind a screen of skirmishers

- If the score is equal to the commander's leadership rating or 1 less, the order is issued and acted upon in due course – the unit can make one move.

- If the score is 2 less than the commander's leadership rating, the order is speedily issued and acted upon immediately – the unit can make two moves.

- If the score is 3 less than the commander's leadership rating or lower the order is issued in anticipation of events and hurriedly obeyed – the unit can make three moves.

For example: rolling against the standard leadership rating of 8: a score of 9 or more is a failure, a score of 7 or 8 gives 1 move, a score of 6 gives 2 moves and a score of 5 or less gives 3 moves. Statisticians will note that the chances of rolling 1, 2 or 3 moves varies depending on the leadership rating and is not a linear progression. Often a result of 3 moves will be more likely than a result of 2 or even 1. Before anyone writes to us about this we'd just like to say – we know. This is one of the reasons why it is often worth going for a long move, as the odds often favour aggressive and ambitious play. On the other hand, this has to be balanced against the chances of not moving or of moving only once or twice.

As you can see a unit might not move at all or may have one, two or three moves to complete its order. Often a single move will enable only part of an order to be fulfilled. Sometimes it will be possible to complete an order in a single move even where more moves would otherwise be available. Such things are matters to consider when formulating orders. Remember also that orders must be unconditional and cannot therefore be dependent on the results of the dice or the number of moves available.

For example, Ludicrus Sextus gives an order to a Legionary Cohort to move to the crest of a hill – the dice roll is 1 and 2 = 3 which gives 3 moves compared to Ludicrus' leadership rating of 8. The Legionaries make one move as instructed and reach their destination – the remaining two moves are wasted in this case. Next Ludicrus orders his cavalry to make a sweeping move around the enemy's flanks – keeping a good distance from the enemy to avoid being caught up in combat. Once more the dice are rolled this time scoring 5 and 4 = 9 a failure! The cavalry stay put, having failed their order. Ludicrus' orders are now complete, although he still has a unit of archers and some skirmishers who have not received orders at all and which are therefore unable to move this turn.

COMMANDERS, UNITS AND ORDERS

A unit can only be issued **one** order each turn. If its order is passed then the unit obeys the order in so far as it can, but cannot then be issued any further orders. If its order is failed then the unit cannot be issued another order. In some cases units are allowed to make a single move even if they fail their order – this is generally referred to as a *free move* see Free Moves (page 31).

A commander can only give orders to units belonging to his **own** designated division. Refer back to the section on The Army for a description of divisions (page 10).

If a commander issues an order successfully then he can continue to issue further orders to other units in his division. He can issue any number of orders so long as he continues to do so successfully, and so long as his division has units able to receive them. If a commander fails to issue an order then he cannot give any more orders that turn. This can sometimes result in some units moving and others staying where they are, or even for entire divisions to not move at all in some cases.

Each commander must finish giving **all** of his orders before another commander can begin to do so. It is not permitted for one commander to give an order, then a second commander, and then the first commander again. Where several players are playing on one side, it is usual for them all to issue orders and make moves at the same time as this is only sensible, but each player must finish giving orders from each of his own commanders one at a time.

CHARGE ORDERS

It is necessary to give a specific order if you want troops to move into hand-to-hand combat against an enemy. This is the *charge* order. It is not necessary that the intended opponent be in sight of the charger when the order is given. Nor do we worry whether it is possible for a unit to mount its charge successfully at this point. The important thing is that the unit has been given a clear order to engage the enemy – charge!

Charge orders can be framed in as specific or general a manner as the players deem appropriate. For example, 'charge the elephant!' and 'advance to the ridge and charge any enemy that appear!' and 'charge the enemy to your front!' would all be perfectly good orders. In the last two examples given, the player might also indicate which units he expected his troops to discover if only for the sake of clarity. Players should not give orders that are unclear or ambiguous, and where the umpire considers this to be the case he is encouraged to interpret such orders in as devious and disastrous a manner as possible. Units will always try and fulfil their orders in the most direct and straightforward way they can, so a unit simply instructed to 'Charge the enemy!' would naturally take the shortest route towards the closest enemy within sight.

We will return to charges later on when we come to the rules for fighting hand-to-hand combat (page 52). There we will discuss how units interpret charge orders and attempt to fulfil them. We need not worry about such things for purposes of explaining how orders are issued and received.

DIVISION ORDERS

So far we have assumed that an order is given to a single unit. This is a perfectly good and often useful way of issuing orders as it allows a commander to exercise precise control over the unit concerned. However, it is often more practical to issue the same order to a group of units at the same time. This is called a *division order*.

A commander can issue the same order to any or all of the units in his division so long as all the units form a group and so long as none of the units in the group have already moved that turn. To qualify as a group none of the units must be separated by more than 6" from other units in the group when the order is given. Similarly, once the units have moved none can be more than 6" from other units in the same

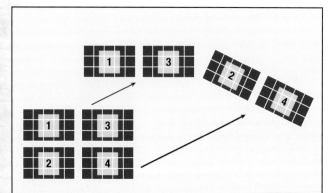

Units given a division order must form a group at the start of their move and must complete their move as a group with no units separated by more than 6". In this example the division has advanced to form a line – but as no units are separated by more than 6" this is fine.

group. In short – the group has to remain together in a group as it moves.

It is important that the division order is essentially one order which all units can follow in broad terms: for example, all moving forward, all moving back, all moving to engage the enemy, or deploying into position as a body. This is why units are obliged to stick within 6". This 6" rule overrides any order issued – so if a mixed formation of infantry and cavalry were ordered to 'advance at maximum pace!' then the cavalry would not be allowed to leave the infantry behind but would be obliged to advance along with the infantry and stay within 6" of them.

Where you want units from the same division to do different things then it is necessary to give them separate orders: for example, if you wanted units to move apart, one going left and the other right so they become divided by more than 6". This allows divisions to be split apart where necessary: for example, one unit occupying a building whilst another forays towards the enemy.

To issue a division order, the player indicates which units will receive the order and tests in the usual way. If successful *all* units are in receipt of the order and will attempt to carry it out. If he fails then *all* the units have failed to receive an order and will usually remain where they are. When wishing to move a whole division, or a substantial part of a division, this is the usual means of doing so.

Example: Our player wishes to move a division consisting of three cohorts of legionaries, a unit of auxiliaries, and a unit of cavalry. He gives the order as follows. "Ludicrus Sextus commands the division to advance and seize the ridge with the

Roman Legionaires advance upon a Celtic village in Testudo formation, the close ranks and interlocked shields protecting them from the missiles of the villagers

legions taking the centre, the cavalry the right flank, and the auxiliaries breaking into open order formation to occupy the wood on the left flank". Our player banishes any lurking doubts as to his intentions by carefully indicating where he imagines his troops will deploy. This is a perfectly reasonable order. The player rolls two dice to test his success. Ludicrus Sextus has a leadership rating of 8 and rolls 4+1 = 5. With a result of '3 under' the division has 3 moves to complete its orders. The auxiliaries leading the advance have to expend a move to change formation but manage to take up the indicated position with their third move. The two cohorts immediately behind also manage to reach the positions indicated without any trouble, leaving the third cohort just short of its desired position but well placed for the following turn. The cavalry with their longer move also manage to get close to where they are needed despite starting at the rear of the formation. Overall it is a pretty successful manoeuvre – the ridgeline is firmly defended and the position affords a good view of the approaching enemy.

DISTANCE MODIFIERS

We assume orders are relayed by messengers who form part of every commander's staff or bodyguard, although there is no need for these individuals to be represented on the tabletop. It can readily be imagined that messengers might be killed or captured, delayed, or distracted in some fashion. To represent this we apply a penalty to the commander's leadership rating if he is a long way from troops he is trying to give an order to. Note that skirmishers, light cavalry and horse archers in open order are exempt from these penalties as explained below.

Measure from the commander model to the closest point on the unit being ordered. If a commander wishes to give a division order to several units at once, measure to the unit that is farthest away. If the distance is more than 12" then deduct –1 from the commander's leadership rating for every full 12". For example: at 19" deduct 1, at 38" deduct 3, at 48" deduct 4, and so on. Measurements are normally made from the commander's head, as this frees us to mount our models on bases of any size, thereby facilitating models riding chariots or elephants and the use of scenic dioramas to represent individual commanders.

Regardless of any modifiers that may apply, including bonuses afforded by special rule of one kind or other, no commander ever has a leadership rating of better than 10 or worse than 5. 10 is the best possible value and 5 is the worst.

No distance modifiers apply when orders are issued to skirmishers in open order, light cavalry in open order or horse archers in open order. However, in the case of a division order, distance modifiers apply if they would normally apply to any other units included in the order. For example, a division order to a unit of skirmishers and a unit of horse archers both in open order would attract no distance penalties; however, a division order given to a unit of skirmishers in open order and a unit of heavy infantry in battle line formation attracts the penalty for heavy infantry.

THE BATTLE OF EMESA

The following graphic account of a battle between a Roman army and that of the rebel Palmyrenes comes form Zosimus' New History. It was written in the early sixth century in the time of the Byzantine Emperor Anastasius I, but refers to events of the mid-third century and is regarded as a compilation of earlier writings. It is interesting to us wargamers because it describes a cavalry action in some detail, and also the subsequent attack of Roman auxiliaries armed with 'staves' that they wield to notable effect against the exhausted Palmyrene cataphracts.

'Finding the Palmyrene army drawn up before Emesa, amounting to seventy thousand men, consisting of Palmyrenes and their allies, he opposed to them the Dalmatian cavalry, the Moesians and Pannonians, and the Celtic legions of Noricum and Rhaetia, and besides these the choicest of the imperial regiment selected man by man, the Mauritanian horse, the Tyaneans, the Mesopotamians, the Syrians, the Phoenicians, and the Palestinians, all men of acknowledged valour; the Palestinians besides other arms wielding clubs and staves.

At the commencement of the engagement, the Roman cavalry receded, lest the Palmyrenes, who exceeded them in number, and were better horsemen, should by some stratagem surround the Roman army. But the Palmyrene cavalry pursued them so fiercely, though their ranks were broken, that the event was quite contrary to the expectation of the Roman cavalry. For they were pursued by an enemy much their superior in strength, and therefore most of them fell. The foot had to bear the brunt of the action. Observing that the Palmyrenes had broken their ranks when the horse commenced their pursuit, they wheeled about, and attacked them while they were scattered and out of order. Upon which many were killed, because the one side fought with the usual weapons, while those of Palestine brought clubs and staves against coats of mail made of iron and brass. The Palmyrenes therefore ran away with the utmost precipitation, and in their flight trod each other to pieces, as if the enemy did not make sufficient slaughter; the field was filled with dead men and horses, whilst the few that could escape took refuge in the city.'

Zosimus – The New History

BLUNDERS

We would suggest that anyone reading or playing for the first time ignores the rules for blunders until they have a good idea of how the game works. Indeed, players who abhor the lack of control that often results from blundered orders are entirely at liberty to ignore the following rule – no harm will be done!

If a commander rolls a double 6 when giving an order this signifies that the unit has gone out of control in some fashion. We call this a blunder. Either an order has been misunderstood or perhaps warriors are overcome by exceptional eagerness or timidity. The consequences are determined by making a test. Roll a dice and consult the blunder table below. The result is the unit's order for that turn and the affected unit must endeavour to obey as best it can. If a division has blundered the same result applies to all the units given the original order. A unit in open order has no defined front, so for these purposes assume its front is

the part of the unit closest to the enemy or the opposing player's table edge as seems most appropriate.

As you can see a blunder cannot override the rules that forbid some units from charging others: for example, skirmishers are not allowed to charge infantry in battle line formation. A blunder can sometimes contradict a rule that otherwise obliges troops to face their enemy. Similarly terrain, enemies, or the position of friends may make it impossible to act as instructed. In all these cases the unit will try and obey the instruction it has been given in so far as it can, in the most direct and straightforward manner, and to the umpire's satisfaction.

Non-combatant units such as messengers, scouts, civilians and baggage are not normally subject to blunders, but umpires should feel free to improvise in such cases. There is certainly no harm in rolling a few dice, contemplating the score sagely, and remarking what awfully thirsty work all this adjudication business is.

BLUNDER TABLE
1   **Uncontrolled flight!** The unit turns round to face its rear and then makes two full moves into its facing quarter. The unit will move even further if necessary to clear the position of friends. Once it has moved, the unit suffers 1 casualty to represent loss of life and equipment suffered during the ignominious stampede.
2   **Back!** The unit moves backwards one move to its rear quarter whilst continuing to face the same direction.
3   **Drift left.** The unit makes one move to its left quarter.
4   **Drift right.** The unit makes one move to its right quarter.
5   **Forward!** The unit makes one move to its front and will charge if facing enemy within one move's distance and which the unit is otherwise allowed to charge.
6   **Uncontrolled Advance!** The unit makes three moves to its front. The unit will charge if facing enemy within three move's distance and which the unit is otherwise allowed to charge.

Bronze Age warriors attack a lake-side settlement, somewhere in Northern Europe

INITIATIVE MOVES

Units that are within 12" of the enemy at the start of the Command part of their turn are allowed to use their initiative to move **instead** of receiving orders. This represents the leaders of these units taking matters into their own hands or acting according to some prearranged plan or signal. The important thing to remember is units that move using their initiative **cannot** also be given orders that turn – the two are mutually exclusive.

All units wishing to move using their initiative must do so **before** any orders are issued. Thus, during the Command part of his turn, a player always moves units using initiative first and then issues any orders for remaining troops as required. In practice there is no need to be rigid about applying this rule should a player prove forgetful, or where the field is a large one and the action widely scattered. However, in situations where the outcome of a move would otherwise be affected it is important to stick to the proper sequence and make all initiative moves before issuing orders: for example, it would affect the normal course of game play if an ordered move created a space that another unit was subsequently able to move through on initiative.

We do not concern ourselves whether a unit can see the enemy entitling it to an initiative move. For our purposes it is enough that there is an enemy within 12" for the unit to use its initiative. The umpire may override this principle in cases that merit it; for example during ambushes where enemy are lying 'hidden'. All enemy units count for this purpose including artillery, baggage and civilians, but enemy commander models *do not* count. Commanders represent individuals or small groups whose presence otherwise goes unnoticed, and they are therefore ignored for purposes of triggering initiative.

All units using initiative are considered to be automatically in receipt of an order and can make **one** move. The player states the order in the usual way before making the move.

Note that units are not obliged to use initiative just because they are within 12" of the enemy. Units can always be issued orders instead. Whether it is better to take the certainty of an initiative move or go for an order with its attendant risk of failure is a matter of judgement for our players. Much will depend upon circumstances.

FREE MOVES

In some situations units are entitled to make **one** move even though their order has failed as noted below, and assuming they have not blundered. In some unusual situations units may be entitled to a free move even where no order is issued.

- A unit in *column* formation moves once if it fails its order.

- All *tiny units* representing scouts, working parties, civilians and such will move once if they fail their order.

- All *baggage, carriages, wagons* and such like will move once if they fail their order so long as they are on a road or track. In this instance wagons moving along a road are treated as if they are columns.

- Some units have a special rule that entitles them to move once when an order is failed. See the section A Selection of Useful Rules on page 98 for more about these.

- Units from *broken divisions* can move once if they fail an order or if no order is attempted. However, such units are obliged to attempt to leave the battle where possible as described in the section on Victory and Defeat (page 84).

A division order might encompass some units that are entitled to a free move and others that are not. In such a case those units entitled to a free move can move as described whilst other units cannot. For example, if a division consisted of a mix of units in column and units in battle line then only the units in column would get the free move. Bear in mind that if a division order has been issued units must still remain within 6" as a group, even where some units have a free move whilst others do not.

ORDERS TO UNITS IN COMBAT

Units that are engaged in combat, whether fighting or supporting as described in the Hand-to-Hand Combat rules, cannot be given orders and cannot use their initiative. They must stay where they are whilst the combat continues. See the Hand-to-Hand Combat rules on page 52.

Note that an exception is made to this rule as a special ability – allowing some fast, highly mobile troops to move out of combat, either feigning flight or taking advantage of their speed to escape their enemy. See A Selection of Useful Rules on page 98.

DETERMINED MEN

The term 'cataphract' is often used to describe very heavily armoured cavalry of the kind used by the Parthians, Armenians, and later by the Persians. The word itself is Greek and means something like 'covered' or 'fenced' – the same term can also describe galleys that have their decks planked over, for example. The original cataphracts, such as the cavalry of the Parthians who defeated the Romans at Carrhae in 53BC, wore armour that covered them from head-to-toe and rode horse, likewise protected by metal armour. Over time the term came to refer to almost any armoured cavalry; for example, Late Roman and Byzantines who wore relatively little armour and whose horses were either unarmoured or only lightly so. Having usurped the word 'cataphract' for armoured cavalry in general, the old-fashioned very heavily armoured cavalry became known to the Romans as Clibanarii – especially as employed by their enemies the Sassanid Persians. Ammianus describes the Sassanid cavalry as follows:

"All the companies were clad in iron, and all parts of their bodies were covered with thick plates, so fitted that the stiff-joints conformed with those of their limbs; and the forms of human faces were so skilfully fitted to their heads, that since their entire body was covered with metal, arrows that fell upon them could lodge only where they could see a little through tiny openings opposite the pupil of the eye, or where through the tip of their nose they were able to get a little breath."

Ammianus Marcellinus

ORDERS TO OFF-TABLE UNITS

There are two situations where units can be off the table but can still be given orders. These are: if the units began the battle off table and are allowed to enter during the game; and, where units are obliged to leave the table during the game for whatever reason.

Units that begin the game 'off-table' are usually allowed to enter at a point designated by the umpire or agreed by the players before the game. Units that leave the table during play can re-enter at the same point they left the battle unless they are *shaken*, in which case they are gone for good and cannot return. In both cases a unit's first move is to place it on the table edge and no more than 6" onto the table regardless of its formation or usual speed of movement.

Orders are given to units that are off-table in the same way as to units already on the table, except that the distance between the commander and unit is always measured to the designated entry point on the table edge. If the commander is also off the table with his troops then he is assumed to be within 12" of his whole division and no penalty is applied to his leadership rating for distance.

Where a division or part of a division is being ordered onto the battlefield all units are assumed to form a group, and a single order can therefore be given to all the units at once. Sometimes a division will be unable to deploy all of its units at the same time because it's impossible for them to fit in the space available: for example, in the case of a marching column of several units. In this case we simply place the lead unit on the table and declare that the rest of the units are deployed *following behind*. Those following behind can move straight onto the field at their full speed in subsequent turns so as to keep up with the rest of the division.

DISORDERED UNITS AND ORDERS

There are various circumstances when a unit can become *disordered* during the game. This represents a temporary loss of formation and control. Disorder often follows from enemy shooting, from hand-to-hand fighting, and sometimes as a result of movement through other units or difficult terrain. Disordered units are always indicated with a suitable marker so their status is obvious to all. For more see Disorder on page 74.

Units that are disordered cannot be given orders of any kind in the Command part of the turn. Disordered units cannot normally use their initiative to move either. However, disordered units in open order formation can use their initiative specifically to move away from or avoid the enemy, or towards their own rear, table edge or encampment where this is appropriate for units trying to avoid their foe.

Units otherwise entitled to a free move cannot normally make their free move if disordered. However, units from *broken divisions* can and must attempt to leave the battlefield even where disordered, as described in the rules for Victory and Defeat on page 84.

MOVING UNITS

A unit in receipt of orders can potentially move up to three times in a single turn depending upon the result of the test when issuing orders. The total distance a unit moves during the Command part of the turn therefore varies: for example, an infantry unit could potentially move 18", a heavy cavalry unit 27", and a light cavalry unit in open order 36".

Strictly speaking, if a unit is entitled to move three times then it makes three separate and distinct moves – but plainly

it would be rather tedious to demand that players move their models three times where it is perfectly simply and sensible to make all three moves at once. So, for most purposes an infantry unit with three moves can be moved 18". However, there will be situations where it is necessary to break moves down, in which case it is usually sufficient for a player to move a token base and then to reassemble the whole unit in its final position.

The table to the left shows the standard move distances for units in inches. This is generally very straightforward: less mobile troops such as infantry, elephants, and baggage move 6" at a time, faster troops such as cavalry and light chariots move 9", whilst light cavalry and horse archers in open order are allowed a move of 12".

When a unit moves the individual models or bases are free to move in any direction or orientation so long as the unit retains the same formation as a whole and no model moves further than the distance allowed (except where specifically permitted in the rules, e.g. during a charge). This enables a unit to swing about, to reverse its facing, move to its right or left, move at an angle, go forwards or backwards, or make any comparable manoeuvre the player might wish. This rather free and easy method of moving is quite different to many sets of gaming rules and can take some getting used to – it is a 'no nonsense' method that gets the game moving at a good lick!

MOVING UNITS TABLE	
Infantry, Elephants, Wagons and Baggage, Man-portable Artillery, Cataphract Cavalry, and Heavy Chariots.	6"
Light Chariots and other formed Cavalry.	9"
Light Cavalry in open order and Horse Archers	12"

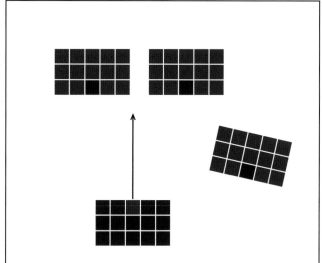

The enemy unit to the right is within 12" of the red unit and lies partially to its front. Red must therefore face an enemy when he moves. He can face any of the units opposing him, even though the two distant enemies are more than 12" away (but within 18"). If red moves so that he is facing any of the enemy units within 12", he is then obliged to move towards or away from that unit as already noted.

PROXIMITY OF ENEMY

We impose a common-sense exception upon our free and easy approach to movement that most players will tend to apply instinctively. In most cases, once a unit has enemy within 12" we oblige it to face the foe. We call this the *proximity rule* or 12" rule. For purposes of explaining how this works we shall forget about units in open order as various exceptions apply to them, we shall only consider formed units in 'proper' formations.

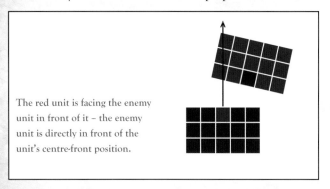

The red unit is facing the enemy unit in front of it – the enemy unit is directly in front of the unit's centre-front position.

A unit is said to be **facing** its enemy if at least part of the enemy unit lies directly in front of the unit's centre-front or leader position.

Once a unit is facing an enemy within 12", the unit can only move either towards or away from the opposing unit whilst continuing to face towards it. This obligation overrides – or governs – any actual order the unit is given. This means that units cannot attempt to move round an enemy or step sideways in the face of the foe. The proximity rule obliges units to 'face off' as the opposing armies close upon each other.

If a unit is not facing an enemy as described above, but has enemy within 12" and to the front, even if only partially so, then the unit must face towards an enemy within no more than three moves distance as it moves. For example, an infantry unit must face towards an enemy within 18", and a heavy cavalry unit must face towards an enemy within 27".

We make a general exception for enemy commanders, artillery, tiny units, non-combatant units including wagons and baggage, and units in fortifications or buildings. None of these enemy units count for the proximity rule for reasons that should be self-evident.

PROXIMITY AND OPEN ORDER TROOPS

Units in other formations can choose to ignore enemies in open order when it comes to the proximity rule. If a unit chooses to ignore open order troops that are 'masking' another enemy, then the unit must take account of the masked enemy as if the open order troops were not there. For example, just because it is acceptable to ignore a skirmisher screen does not mean you can ignore the huge hoplite formation advancing behind it!

Units in open order are not affected by the proximity of enemy unless there are enemy within 6" of any part of the unit. Whilst there are enemy within 6", open order troops can only move either towards the closest enemy or away from the closest enemy whilst facing the opposing unit. No other rules regarding proximity apply to units in open order.

MOVING THROUGH ENEMIES AND COMBATS

Units are not allowed to move through opposing units although they can move over opposing commanders freely. Commanders moved over in this way are obliged to move as described in the section on Commanders on page 80.

Units cannot normally move through friends if they are engaged in hand-to-hand combat, but are allowed to do so if moving to join the engagement either as supports or by charging. This exception is necessary to allow for multiple charges in some situations, see Charging Two On One on page 58.

MOVING THROUGH FRIENDLY UNITS

Aside from units engaged in hand-to-hand combat as noted above, units from the same side can move through each other where it is possible for the moving unit to completely clear the position of the unit or units moved through. It does not matter whether it takes one, two or three moves to clear the position of friends, so long as their position is cleared once the unit has finished its movement. If it is not possible for a unit to clear a friend in this way then it may not move through. Note that it is harder for deep units such as warbands and phalanx to move through friends, as two or three moves will often be required to clear their position, and we do not hold this to be unreasonable.

Units can move through friends without penalty if either unit is skirmishers or other infantry in open order, or if both units are light cavalry, light chariots or horse archers in open order. Other units can also move through friends without penalty if only a minor portion of both units is moved through. This is generally determined as shown below, although unusual and marginal cases will obviously attract the judgement of the umpire. Where a unit can move through another without the centre-front position of either unit passing over the other then no penalty is applied.

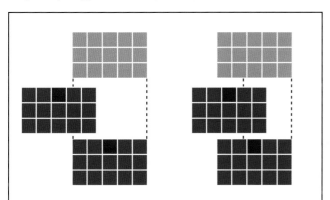

Left – these two units can pass through as shown without penalty – the centre-front 'leader' position' of both units its not touched as the rear unit moves through. Right – these two units can pass through as shown but both must take a test and risk becoming disordered.

If the centre-front position of either unit moves over the other then it will be necessary to test for both units to determine if they become disordered as a result. Roll a dice for each unit. If the result is a 4, 5 or 6 the unit retains good order and there is no penalty. If the result is a 1, 2 or 3 the unit becomes **disordered**.

Disordered units suffer penalties for ranged attacks and in hand-to-hand combat, and any disordered unit that has not already moved will be unable to do so. Disorder does not usually affect units from turn to turn unless they are engaged in combat, so this is not an insufferable penalty in most situations. See page 74 for more about disorder

ROOM TO FIGHT

Ancient warriors fought in fairly dense ranks – if not quite shoulder-to-shoulder then certainly pretty close. In fact, they fought with almost exactly the same spacing of ranks and files as did all troops right up until rigid formations were finally abandoned by modern armies at the end of the nineteenth century. Perhaps this is not surprising – as the need to manoeuvre troops on the battlefield and the size of the human body would be more-or-less the same. Similarly, whether armed with a spear or a musket and bayonet, a man needs about the same room to fight. This is what Asclepiodotus has to say upon the matter:

'The needs of warfare have brought forth three systems of intervals: the most open order (araiotatos), in which the men are spaced both in length and depth four cubits apart, the most compact (pyknotatos), in which with locked shield (synaspiskos) each man is a cubit distant on all sides from his comrades, and the intermediate (messon), also called a 'compact formation' (pyknosis), in which they are distant two cubits from one another on all sides.'

Asclepiodotus (4.1) *Loeb translation – quoted in Hellenistic Infantry Reform in the 160's BC by Nicholas Sekunda.*

A cubit is equivalent to about one and a half feet or eighteen inches – that's 45 cm for those who are metrically inclined – or the distance from a man's elbow to his fingertips (try it!). There were slightly different standards for the cubit in different places and at different times – leading to some lively discussions amongst academics about the size of Noah's Ark and the length of a Macedonian sarissa – amongst other things. Blissfully unaware of these future conundrums Asclepiodotus goes on to add:

'I have stated that of the two spacings the one of two cubits is called pyknosis and the one of a single cubit synaspismos. The former is used when we are marching the phalanx upon the enemy, the latter when the enemy is marching upon us.'

Asclepiodotus (4.3)

Ceremonial Bronze axe head c. 900BC Iran
(Perry Collection)

MANHANDLING ARTILLERY

Artillery can range in size from the smallest man-portable bolt-throwing machines to huge static siege engines. Here we are concerned only with mobile field artillery of different kinds.

The lightest types of man-portable machines move at infantry rates – i.e. at 6" per move. A machine of this kind can move once in the Command part of the turn and still shoot in the Ranged Attacks part of the turn. If a machine moves more than once it cannot also shoot that turn.

Heavier types of field machine can still be carried by their crew and, in some cases, have wheels to enable them to move more easily. Such machines can only move once in any Command part of the turn and cannot move and shoot in the same turn.

FORMATION CHANGES

Formation changes must be stated when giving orders and it is necessary to do so even where a formation change would be obligatory to fulfil an order. For example, a heavy infantry unit would have to form into open order to enter a wood.

A formation change takes an entire move except in the case of skirmishers, light infantry, light cavalry, horse archers and light chariots. In these cases a unit can change formation to or from open order and then move counting this as a single move in all. However, these units are not allowed to change formation in this way and charge as a single move, their move must be a non-charge move. See Charge Moves page 54 for more about charge moves.

A unit can only make one formation change in each Command part of the turn. No matter how many moves a unit has, it can only make one formation change. For example, a heavy infantry unit with three moves could not adopt open order, move through a wood, and form a battle line all in the same turn.

SQUARES

Squares are essentially static defensive formations. A square cannot move and the only order it can be given is to change formation. A square cannot change to another formation and move further that turn. Regardless of the number of moves a square is allowed it can only change formation.

UNITS LEAVING THE TABLE

Units can leave the table in several circumstances, most commonly following a blunder or as a result of a break test. A unit is adjudged to have left the table once any models pass the boundaries of the tabletop or playing area, or if a model would otherwise 'fall off the edge' having completed its move. Such units are removed at once, but can potentially return to the battle as already described (see page 32)

Note that a unit cannot return to the battlefield if it is shaken or if it belongs to a broken division. Units become shaken once they have casualty markers equal to their stamina value as described later. Such units always retire from the battlefield for good once they leave the table. Divisions become broken once a proportion of their units are destroyed or deemed lost as described under Victory and Defeat (page 84).

COMMANDERS

Commander models are treated a little differently from units of troops. Commanders are ignored for purposes of determining initiative, proximity of enemy, when calculating targets for ranged attacks, and in other circumstances as described throughout the rules. Commanders can move through units from their own side freely unless they are engaged in combat, and similarly units can move through their own side's commanders as they wish. If a unit ends its move on top of a friendly commander then the commander model is moved sufficiently far to allow the unit to take up its position.

A commander who is moved into by an enemy unit must immediately join a friendly unit within a move's distance – otherwise he is deemed to have been captured, and is removed as a casualty. Note that commanders cannot force enemy commanders to move in this fashion – only units can do so. See page 82 Risk to Commanders.

MOVING COMMANDERS

Each commander is allowed to make one move as soon as he has completed issuing any orders that turn, or once all orders have been issued if he has not moved already. There is no need to be strict about this rule – it is included to help players remember to move their commanders rather that to penalise those who forget! Commanders do not require orders to move – they move automatically.

All commanders move 24" regardless of whether or how they are mounted. We assume that commanders riding horses, chariots or elephants have the sense to dismount where necessary and so impose no restriction upon them in respect to terrain and their mounts (see Terrain page 38). Players may wish to provide both foot and mounted models to represent their commanders to avoid the insensitive spectacle of chariots plunging through woodlands, elephants standing upon ramparts, and other incongruous situations of that kind.

A commander can join a unit in his division by moving into touch with it. The player should also declare that the commander has joined the unit for clarity's sake and position him in the unit's formation if this is practical. Once a commander has joined a unit he becomes a constituent part of and moves along with it until the start of his following turn.

Commanders are also allowed to join friendly units that are fighting in hand-to-hand combat within 12". It does not matter which side's turn it is, but commanders must join the combat before any troops fight – they are not allowed to join half-way through. For this and more about commanders see the separate section Commanders on page 80.

Sassanid Persian Elephants prepare to advance – these creatures carry bowmen in the howdah on their backs

Greek hoplites advance behind a wall of overlapping shields

TERRAIN

To complete our rules for movement we shall deal with battlefield terrain of various kinds.

We usually agree upon the rules for different kinds of terrain before the battle, or the umpire or player who has devised the scenario will work out the rules for terrain at the same time. So, we quite commonly improvise the rules as suits our purposes and expect others will wish to do the same. Summaries of the rules we have found most useful and practical are given here.

WOODS

By woods we mean areas designated as being reasonable dense woodland or forest and covering an area that justifies representation on the tabletop. The boundaries of our miniature wood need to be delineated in some fashion: for example, by a row of tree models or by a scenic base covering the entire wooded area. Individual model trees can be positioned within this area to stand in for the mass of trees and tangled undergrowth that practicality dictates must otherwise be left to our imagination.

It is usual to assume that woodland can't be seen through or into by our troops, apart from those positioned along the edges who can see out and who can likewise be seen. We often allow for troops to lie in hiding at the edge of woods, in which case they remain unseen until they move or until the enemy approach within a specified distance, but such matters are up to the players or umpire to determine as part of the game scenario.

Infantry in open order, cavalry in open order, commanders or other models representing individuals can move through woods. Other troops cannot move through woods at all. The movement of cavalry in woods is reduced to infantry speed – i.e. 6" per move – for each move that begins within the wood.

Players are at liberty to run roads or tracks through woods if they wish - in which case movement via road is treated as completely accessible if preferred. Make sure this is clear at the start of the game.

ROUGH GROUND

This covers all manner of broken or difficult ground including scrub, marshes, soft sand, steep or rocky slopes, areas of ruinous or tumbled down building, and heavily irrigated or flooded fields. Such areas need to be designated in some fashion: for example, by arranging appropriate scenic features to mark a boundary.

Apart from infantry in open order, cavalry in open order, and commanders and other individuals, units moving over rough ground are restricted to a maximum of one move. A unit moving into rough ground completes its move and moves no further that turn, whilst a unit already in rough ground is limited to a maximum of one move. Open order infantry and open order cavalry can make up to three moves as usual.

As with woods, players are at liberty to run roads or tracks through rough ground if desired, in which case movement will be via road or treated as completely accessible if preferred.

LINEAR OBSTACLES

A battlefield might include any number of fences, ditches, boundary walls, streams, narrow rivers and such-like, and on the whole we simply treat these as decorative or use them to delineate the boundaries of rough ground, settlements or fortifications. On occasions we will want to attach some significance to a dried up stream or riverbed, wall, or some such feature, in which case we have found the following rules useful.

Infantry in open order, cavalry in open order, and commanders or other individuals can cross linear obstacles without penalty to their movement. All other units can cross an obstacle giving up one entire move. So, with one move a unit can move up to the obstacle without crossing, in the second turn the unit surrenders a move and moves whatever distance is required to cross the obstacle, in the third turn the unit continues moving.

Alternatively, where they are substantial, obstacles can be judged to be impassable to chariots, wagons and wheeled vehicles of all kinds except by gates or gaps. This is up to the

umpire to determine prior to the game – or by dice roll during the game should he be feeling mischievous.

RIVERS

If a river is of such width that it can be crossed by infantry in a single move, then it is best treated as a linear obstacle. Otherwise rivers can be assumed to be either completely impassable, or fordable along their whole length, or crossable only at designated fording or bridging points.

Where a river is fordable it is necessary to represent the fording point and to decide whether the ford can be crossed by a unit in battle line formation or whether it will be necessary to form column. On the whole we find it best to assume fords are wide enough to allow a unit to cross without restricting its formation.

Any unit can cross a river at a bridge. The width of the bridge will naturally restrict the formation of the unit to a column – though for gaming purposes it is often easier to simply assume a unit can cross in any formation so long as the front centre/leader model moves over the bridge itself. We leave this up to the players to arrange as convenient.

BUILDINGS

It is usual to represent farmsteads, settlements and forts by means of either a single large model building, or by a roughly rectangular group of smaller buildings and yards covering an equivalent area. The total area must be sufficient to allow an infantry unit to be placed inside with a little room to spare, up to a maximum size of about 12" x 12". The size can be reduced or increased if you wish to use units that are substantially smaller or larger than those described in our game. Larger settlements and fortifications can be represented by several such 'building blocks' placed together or next to each other, or designated as able to hold two, three or more units and correspondingly bigger. Conversely small forts and watchtowers may be designated as capable of holding only tiny or small units.

At the start of the game it is a good idea to make sure the extent of all farmstead, settlement or fort areas is clear and understood, as such areas are likely to play a major role in the game. The edges of a settlement can be partially defined by walls, barricades or similar barriers, in which case they serve only to indicate the edge of the building and are not treated as obstacles as described above.

Only infantry can enter or assault buildings, except that artillery pieces can be included as part of a building's defence if set up at the start of the game. Aside from a light artillery bolt-thrower, artillery deployed in this way cannot be moved during the game. A single building block can hold one unit of infantry, plus up to one tiny unit of infantry, and up to one artillery unit with crew. We assume troops take up a position around the perimeter, within houses, outbuildings and so forth. For this reason troops occupying a building

don't have a specific formation in the game, and artillery pieces can be mixed amongst troops to cover more than one direction if required.

To enter an unoccupied building a unit moves into touch with the perimeter and then expends one full move to move inside. Once a unit moves into a building its movement automatically ends for the turn. A unit cannot move into a building and then continue moving out the other side. If a unit reaches the perimeter but does not have a move remaining then it cannot enter. Once the unit moves inside the models are arranged within the designated area as the player wishes. It doesn't matter that the unit has no formation or that the models become separated. The models simply serve to indicate the building is occupied. Don't worry if there isn't quite room for all the models, rather than risk damage by cramming figures together just leave some off the table

To leave a building one move is required. Begin by declaring the unit is leaving the building, then measure a normal move from the edge of the building and place the unit's leader model on that spot. The rest of the unit is then arranged into a suitable formation around its leader. A unit leaving a building in this way can make up to three moves if issued orders, but the first move is always to leave the building and reform in the manner described. This first move can be a charge if enemy are within reach.

On occasions we will specify that troops can only enter or leave a building at particular points - usually the gateways of forts or fortified settlements. Once again this is up to the players to arrange as best suits the model buildings and the circumstance of the battle.

IMPASSABLE TERRAIN

Before the start of the game players can agree to treat any terrain features as impassable if that seems appropriate. A scenario might sometimes specify that some terrain is impassable. Features that are typically represented in this way are very steep gullies or ravines, cliffs, and open water – unless you plan on staging an amphibious operation of course. Buildings can also be treated in this way if they are essentially decorative and you don't want troops to occupy them during a game.

EMBELLISHING THE TABLETOP

As you can see from the accompanying photographs we do very much enjoy creating a scene for our warriors to fight over. A scatter of lone trees, winding tracks, low hedges, growing crops, farmyard carts, grazing cattle, locals going about their business – all such things help to create a sense of occasion. There is no need for such decorative features to hinder the movement of troops in any way. Indeed, we do not consider it unreasonable for the odd tree, farmyard animal or curious spectator to wander a few inches as necessitated by military manoeuvres.

RANGED ATTACKS

The term *ranged attacks* serves to describe all combat that takes place at range including skirmishing. It therefore covers missile fire from bows and slings, thrown javelins or spears, and – in some cases – a combination of thrown missiles and individual combat.

SHORT AND LONG RANGED ATTACKS

We divide ranged attacks into two types with two separate values: **short** range attacks and **long** range attacks. The short range attack value is used for targets up to 6" distant. The long range attack value is used against targets more than 6" away.

Many units have a short ranged attack that represents thrown weapons such as javelins, light spears and weighted darts. In appropriate cases, the short range attack value also represents individual warriors, or small parties, skirmishing to the front of a unit's position.

Long range attacks represent shooting by bows, crossbows, slings and various kinds of artillery. If troops have long ranged attacks their short ranged attacks value represents shooting at close range using the same weapons.

WHO CAN MAKE RANGED ATTACKS?

Units with a *Ranged Attack Value* can make ranged attacks and they commonly do so during the Ranged Attack part of their turn after Command and before Hand-to-Hand Combat. Formed units automatically make all of their attacks against the closest visible enemy to their front quarter and within range. Units in open order count their entire perimeter as 'front' and therefore make their attacks against the closest visible target regardless of direction. If two or more enemy are equally close then attacks are divided as equally as possible, or as seems most equitable. See page 23 for explanation of unit facing, page 25 for more about visibility and page 48 for further details on open order ranged attacks.

Units are not allowed to make ranged attacks if they are already engaged in hand-to-hand fighting. Note that units are considered engaged whether they are *supporting* or *fighting* combat as defined in the section on Hand-to-Hand Combat (page 52).

Units armed with long-ranged weapons can sometimes shoot in the opposing side's turn, or at other points in the game, by means of closing and traversing shots. Closing and traversing shots allow for units to shoot where common sense dictates they should be able to do so: for example, at an enemy charging towards them.

RANGE

All short ranged attacks have a maximum range of 6" whether they are made by thrown weapons such as javelins or by warriors dashing forwards of their positions to hurl spears or exchange blows with the enemy. Long ranged attacks vary depending upon the weapon used as indicated on the following table.

RANGE	
Javelins, Darts and other thrown weapons	6"
Bows, Crossbows and Staffslings	18"
Slings	12"
Light Artillery	24"
Medium Artillery	36"
Heavy Artillery	48"

We have allotted a tactical range relative to the movement distances in the game allowing what we feel to be appropriate opportunities for shooting. For these purposes we rarely find any benefit in differentiating between different kinds of bows – for example – although that option always remains available of course. Where such differences reflect genuine historical advantages to one side or the other we would happily adjust the ranges accordingly and suggest that others do the same.

MEASURE DISTANCE

For formed units, the distance to the target is measured from the unit's centre-front or leader model to the closest visible part of the target unit. It doesn't matter whether other parts of the unit are in range or not, distance is always measured from the base edge of the leader model to the nearest base edge in the target unit. If the target is found to be within range then the whole unit is adjudged to be within range and can shoot.

Units in open order measure the range from the closest model to the closest part of the target. See Ranged Attacks and Open Order on page 48.

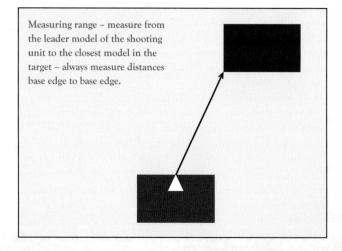

Measuring range – measure from the leader model of the shooting unit to the closest model in the target – always measure distances base edge to base edge.

THE BATTLE OF CANNAE

By the time the Carthaginians faced the Roman legions at the Battle of Cannae they had met and defeated the Romans twice already. After their victory at Trasimene, the vast quantity of arms and armour taken as spoils had been sufficient to re-equip Hannibal's army. Livy reports the Carthaginians' appearance so:

> To look at them, one might have thought the Africans were Roman soldiers – their arms were mostly Roman, having been part of the spoils at Trasimene, and some, too, at the Trebia.

The battle itself is often described as Hannibal's masterpiece, serving as a model of warfare that has been copied by other commanders right up until today. Recognising the strength of the Roman legions Hannibal deployed with his weaker troops – Gauls and Spaniards – in the centre of his army. These were arranged in a crescent shape bulging outwards in the middle. At the tips of the crescent Hannibal placed his strongest African infantry and beyond those his cavalry. Although the Roman army had the greater numbers overall, the

Carthaginians had the most and strongest cavalry. As the Romans came on they met the Gauls and Spaniards, and soon pushed into their ranks so that the Carthaginian centre was first flattened into line with the wings and then pushed beyond them. Hannibal encouraged his centre to give ground until the Romans had passed the Africans, at which point the trap was sprung and the Africans fell upon the Romans' flank and rear. Livy describes the attack upon the Roman centre:

> Recklessly the Romans charged straight into it, and the Africans on either side closed in. In another minute they had further extended their wings and closed the trap in the Roman rear.

Bronze short sword c. 1300 BC. Middle Eastern
(Perry Collection)

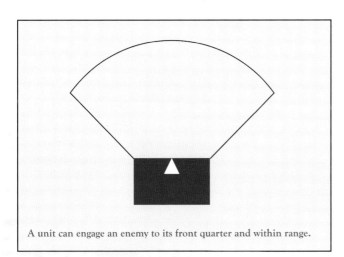

A unit can engage an enemy to its front quarter and within range.

NOMINATE TARGET

Formed units are obliged to direct their ranged attacks against the closest enemy unit to their front quarter measuring from the centre-front or leader model position. Units in open order direct their ranged attacks against the closest enemy regardless of direction as noted later (page 48). Players are not usually in a position to 'pick' a target as such, but there are situations where players are allowed to divide their attacks as described below.

Units in hand-to-hand combat are not eligible as targets whether they are fighting or supporting. Such units are ignored when it comes to working out ranged attacks, excepting that they can in some cases block line-of-sight to other targets.

A formed unit makes ranged attacks to its front quarter as shown on the diagram below. Note that as range is measured from the centre-front of the unit, the area covered by a unit's ranged attacks will have a shape something like that shown here, with a greater projection towards the centre of the unit.

In most cases a unit must direct its ranged attacks to a closer enemy in preference to a more distant one. Occasionally a number of enemy may be equally close – or as near as the players feel makes no difference – in which case it is usual to divide the number of attacks between the two as near equally as possible.

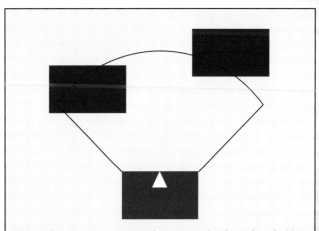

Here we have two enemy units within range and within sight – the blue unit must shoot at the closest.

HANNIBAL'S DEPARTURE FROM ITALY

After the battle of Cannae the people of Rome awaited the appearance of Hannibal and his army – for surely nothing now could prevent the Carthaginian general from advancing upon the capital. Yet he did not. For whatever reason he chose to rest his troops – and the moment was lost. Livy puts these words into the mouth of Hannibal's cavalry commander Maherbal.

> *Assuredly, no one man has been blessed with all God's gifts. You know, Hannibal, how to conquer, but you do not know how to use your victory.*

Ah – if only! Whether or not Hannibal really had much choice in the matter is a moot question. His army had taken a battering and was in no position to undertake a siege of Rome whilst much of the surrounding land still lay in Roman hands. The Romans, meanwhile, had learned a thing or two and never gave him another chance to flaunt his generalship on Roman territory. Soon Hannibal was leaving Italy to defend Carthage in Africa where he would meet defeat at Zama. This is how Livy describes his departure.

> Seldom, we are told, has any exile left his native land with so heavy a heart as that of Hannibal when he left the country of his enemies. Again and again he looked back at the shores of Italy, accusing gods and men and calling down curses upon his own head for not having led his armies straight to Rome when they were still bloody from the victorious field of Cannae.

CHOICE OF TARGETS

There are some situations where we allow a choice of targets, and these are mostly common-sense situations where to do otherwise seems pedantic or petty. In all these cases we maintain that the closest enemy is either partly obscured or otherwise not a clear target of attack. Attacks against such units are made with a penalty to the dice roll, so it might be better to choose a more distant but clear target instead.

If a unit is partly obscured or otherwise not a clear target then it can be ignored in favour of the closest unit that presents a clear target of attack. The following are all units that are not considered clear targets.

- Units in open order formation.
- Artillery units.
- Wagons, carts, baggage and such like.
- Units that are only partly within the attacker's front arc as shown below.
- Units that are only partly in the attacker's sight as shown below.
- Units occupying buildings or cover.
- Units that can only be seen through narrow gaps as shown below.

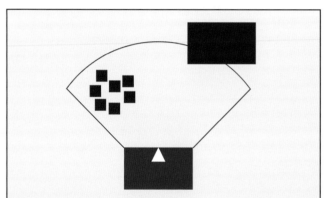

Here the closest enemy is a unit in open order, which can therefore be ignored in favour of the more distant unit beyond. Remember that line of sight is calculated from the attacking unit's centre-front position so the new target must be clearly visible as in the situation here.

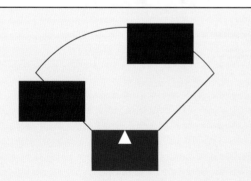

Here the closest enemy is partly outside the unit's front quarter. If less than half the enemy unit lies within the attacker's front quarter then it can be ignored in favour of the more distant unit beyond. The fact that the distant unit lies partly out of range doesn't matter – range is always measured from the centre-front of the attacker to the closest part of the target.

In this situation the closest enemy is partly behind a wood. If less than half the target is visible, the unit is not a clear target and can be ignored. In the example the target is not a clear target and can be ignored in favour of the more distant but fully visible target.

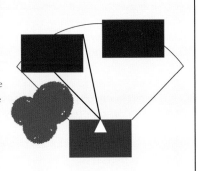

Sometimes an enemy will be visible only through a gap between other units or terrain features. Where a gap is at least as wide as the unit's own formation then no penalties are applied. If a gap is narrower than the unit's formation then we apply a penalty for an *obscured* target (-1 to hit) and the number of attacks is reduced in rough proportion of the unit's frontage relative to the gap. For example, if the gap is equivalent to a third of the unit's frontage then its attacks are reduced to a third also.

In the case of artillery units, a gap must be at least 3" wide to shoot through at all, but otherwise the same guidelines apply. We impose this minimum because artillery units are often relatively narrow and it is important not to confer too great an advantage when it comes to shooting through gaps.

As always we defer to the common sense of the umpire in all cases where a shot looks a bit marginal.

In this situation the closest enemy unit is partly behind a friendly unit and less than half is visible as a result. The target is therefore not a clear target and can be ignored in favour of the more distant but fully visible target.

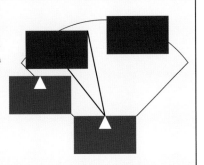

Here the closest enemy unit has taken up position in a farmhouse – units occupying buildings and comparable cover are not clear targets. In this case the unit occupying the farmhouse can be ignored in favour of the more distant but fully visible target.

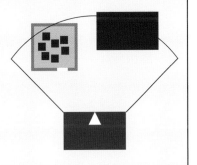

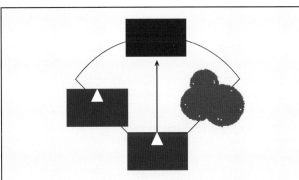

In this situation the archers at the bottom of the diagram wish to shoot at the enemy in front of them. The gap between the friendly unit to their left and the wood to their right is slightly less that the unit's own frontage so a dice penalty is incurred because the target is obscured. As the gap is only just narrower than the unit itself no penalty is applied to the number of shots allowed.

Infantry formed the backbone of most northern European armies during the Dark Ages

ATTACK

As many ranged attacks and all long ranged attacks are due to shooting we'll sometimes refer to such attacks as 'shots' and attackers as 'shooters', but bear in mind that short range attacks are not always down to shooting but can include skirmishing in a broad sense.

Dice are rolled to work out the effects of a unit's ranged attacks. The number of dice rolled equals the unit's Short Ranged Attacks value at up to 6" and the unit's Long Ranged Attacks value at ranges of greater than 6".

UNIT SIZE MODIFIERS FOR RANGED ATTACKS	
Ranged Attack Value	Unit Size Modifiers
+1 Dice	**Large Unit.** The attackers are a large unit.
-1 Dice	**Small Unit.** The attackers are a small unit.
1 Dice	**Tiny Unit.** Tiny units roll only one dice – their Range Attack Value is always 1.

If the unit is a tiny, small or large unit by the standards already discussed, then the indicated adjustments are made to the unit's fighting qualities. These adjustments are generally made when calculating the unit's fighting qualities in the first place, and are already included in the statistics for example units as given elsewhere in this book.

Units in column, testudo or square formations, or occupying buildings can only make ranged attacks in a very limited way. In these cases ranged attack values are automatically reduced as shown below. Such formations are not ideal for shooting or skirmishing, but sometimes troops are obliged to do the best they can.

Roll the appropriate number of dice. Any dice scoring 4, 5 or 6 indicate that the attackers have inflicted a hit on their target. For example, three dice scoring 1, 5 and 6 = 2 hits; 4, 5 and 5 = 3 hits; and 2, 3 and 3 = 0 hits.

In addition – except as noted below – if any of the dice rolled score a 6, then the target must take a **break test** once any casualties have been calculated. The rules for conducting this test are given on page 72. If the score required to hit is 6 then a break test is only required if **two or more** 6s are rolled. These 6s can be from the same or different units.

FORMATION MODIFIERS FOR RANGED ATTACKS	
Ranged Attack Value	Formation Modifiers
None	**Column or Testudo.** Units in column or testudo cannot make ranged attacks.
1 Dice	**Square.** Attacks in square are limited to a maximum of one dice only.
2/face	**Buildings.** Units occupying buildings are limited to a maximum of two dice from any face up to their ranged attacks value in total – see the rules for buildings.

In some situations it becomes easier or harder to score a hit. This is represented by adding or subtracting to the dice rolls as noted. For example, if shooters are *disordered* they suffer a penalty of –1 and therefore require scores of 5 or 6 to score a hit rather than 4, 5 or 6. Regardless of these modifiers, a roll of 6 always scores a hit, whilst a roll of 1 always misses. There is no such thing as an automatic hit or miss.

QUALITY AND QUANTITY

The highest principle of the Byzantine art of war, as the Strategikon makes clear, was economy of force.

"A ship cannot cross the sea without a helmsman, nor can one defeat an enemy without tactics and strategy. With these and the aid of God it is possible to overcome not only an enemy force of equal strength but even one greatly superior in numbers. For it is not true, as some inexperienced people believe, that wars are decided by courage and numbers of troops, but... by tactics and generalship and our concern should be with these rather than [with] wasting our time mobilizing large numbers of troops."

Bronze sheild decoration. Middle East c. 1200BC Iran
(Perry Collection)

'TO HIT' MODIFIERS FOR RANGED ATTACKS	
Dice Score	Situation
-1	**Attackers are shaken and/or disordered.** This applies if the attacking unit is either *shaken*, *disordered*, or both. These states are explained in due course and affect units in various deleterious ways.
-1	**The target is partly obscured, in open order, artillery or baggage.** This applies if the target is partly obscured as already explained, or in open order, or artillery or wagons and other baggage. Note that these are the same conditions for ignoring the closest target as described on page 42.
-1	**The target is formed heavy infantry being attacked by enemy to their front quarter, or formed cataphract cavalry regardless of the direction of attack.** This applies to heavily armoured targets and, in the case of heavy infantry, applies only when attacked from the front due to their shields and tight formation. Note that some unusual formations count as *front* all round in which case the penalty applies all round too, for example the testudo as described on page 105.
-1	**Closing Shots.** This applies to units shooting at enemies as they charge home as described for Closing Shots page 48.
-1	**Traversing Shots.** This applies to units shooting at enemies as they traverse their front as described for Traversing Shots page 50.
-1	**Long Range Shots.** This applies to all shots at ranges of over 12".

Auxiliaries lead the assault as legionary cohorts pour from their encampment to join the battle

MORALE SAVES

Every unit has a Morale value as part of its fighting qualities. This value is a measure of a unit's ability to stand firm in the face of ranged attacks or hand-to-hand fighting. It is both a measure of our troops' resolve as well as their physical protection. Morale therefore reflects how heavily armoured the unit is as well as how determined. The two factors often go together for obvious reasons: troops lacking armour are both more likely to suffer casualties and less inclined to stand up to their enemy. As the value is a composite of factors, there may be troops who are well-armoured but still have relatively poor morale, or troops that are less well-armoured but whose morale is extraordinarily good for other reasons.

Morale values vary from one type of troops to another, and a list of standard types can be found under Troop Types on page 86. Standard values vary from 4+ (good), to 5+ (average), 6+ (poor) and 0 (heaven help us!).

To test morale, a player rolls one dice for each hit inflicted on his unit. So, if a unit has suffered three hits the player rolls three dice, and so on. If a dice scores equal to or better than the unit's morale value then that hit is disregarded or

'saved'. Dice scoring less than the unit's morale value indicate that the hit is not saved and a casualty is inflicted. For this reason we commonly refer to morale checks as 'morale saves' or just as 'saves', i.e. the test is made to see if you can save your unit from taking casualties.

Casualties inflicted on a unit must be recorded, usually by means of a marker placed beside or behind the unit itself. See Casualties on page 48.

If a unit is attacked by two or more enemies, it is often convenient to roll all the attacks in one go and then roll all the saves at once. However, bear in mind that different modifiers can apply in which case it will be necessary to either roll separate batches of dice or use different coloured dice to differentiate between these attacks. Where there is any room for confusion it is always clearer to roll for each attacking unit separately.

For example: a unit has a morale save of 5+ and suffers three hits from enemy bow fire. Three dice are rolled scoring 4, 5 and 6. The roll of a 4 is a fail and the rolls of 5 and 6 are both successes – so two hits are saved and one casualty inflicted.

There are some situations where we allow a modifier to the unit's morale save as noted on the table below. These modifiers allow for a greater chance of saving for units that have adopted defensive positions or formations, but reduce the chance of saving for units that are in column and unprepared for combat. Modifiers are applied to the dice score rolled, but note that no penalty can reduce a save to worse than 6 if it started out as 6 or better, and no bonus can improve a save to better than 2+. In other words, a roll of 1 is a failed save regardless, and troops that start off with a save always save on at least a 6. Troops that have no morale save still benefit from positive modifiers: for example, with a +1

bonus a morale value of 0 becomes 6, with a +2 it becomes 5+, and so on.

If a unit is only partly within cover, then consider what proportion of the target appears to be within cover from the attackers perspective, and allow the bonus to the same proportion of dice throws in so far as possible. For example, if about half the unit is behind cover then allow the bonus to about half the dice throws. We normally err on the side of the player throwing the dice when it comes to making these calls, but players can adopt whatever convention they prefer when deciding such things.

MORALE SAVE MODIFIERS

Dice Score	Situation
+1	**Square** or **Wedge.** Troops in square or wedge formation derive extra protection from their overlapping shields, whilst their close mass makes it practically impossible for individuals to shy from the fight. Add +1 to the morale value of such troops.
+1	**Cover.** The unit is within woodland, behind hedgerows or low walls, or in other situations where it is felt it should rightly benefit from the physical protection and reassurance of cover. Add +1 to the morale value of such troops.
+2	**Testudo.** Troops in testudo formation derive extra protection from their overlapping shields and the rigidity of their ranks prevents flight. Add +2 to the morale value of such troops.
+2	**Buildings.** If a unit is occupying a substantial building it benefits further from cover. Add +2 to the morale value of such troops.
+3	**Fortification.** If a unit is sheltering behind even more considerable fortifications it will be protected from missile fire. Add +3 to the morale value of such troops.
-1	**Hit by Light Artillery.** If a unit is hit by light artillery then deduct –1 from its morale value to represent both the penetrating power and demoralising effect of artillery fire.
-2	**Hit by Medium or Heavy Artillery.** If a unit is hit by medium or heavy artillery then deduct –2 from its morale value to represent both the penetrating power and demoralising effect of artillery fire.
-2	**Column.** If a unit is attacked whilst in column formation it is unprepared for combat and will quickly fall into disarray. To represent this deduct –2 from the morale value of such troops.

Ancient Briton armies included a fair number of slingers. Piles of sling stones were found, ready to use, by archeologists excavating the remains of Maiden Castle, Dorset

CASUALTIES

Casualties represent men killed or wounded as well as other factors that affect a unit's ability to fight, such as exhaustion and loss of nerve. Casualties can be recorded in any fashion the players wish, but our preferred method is to use markers. For each casualty taken place a casualty marker besides or behind the unit. Models of dead or dying combatants make the most pleasing markers. We sometimes resort to using shields as more practical where many casualties have been suffered. Card or plastic chits or similar tokens will do at a push, although our own preference is to avoid anything so mechanical. The advantage of using markers, rather than simply noting down how many casualties a unit has taken, is that its status is visually obvious to both players – which we consider to be an important element of play!

SHAKEN UNITS

Once a unit has taken casualties equal to its Stamina value it is described as *shaken*. This value varies from unit to unit but is usually 6 for close-quarter fighting infantry, meaning that once the unit has taken 6 casualties it is deemed shaken. A unit can suffer more casualties than its Stamina value up to a maximum of double (i.e. usually 12) but casualties in excess of the Stamina value are only recorded for purposes of taking break tests as described later. Once any such tests have been taken all excess casualties are removed – for example if a unit's Stamina is 6 and it has suffered eight casualties then the excess two are removed after tests are taken leaving six markers in place.

Units shaken by ranged attacks must take a break test and can be forced to retire or may even rout and flee from the battle altogether. Units that are already shaken must take a break test if they suffer further casualties. Shaken units also suffer additional penalties as indicated throughout the book and summarised together with the rules for Break Tests on page 72.

SHATTERED UNITS

Units that accumulate casualties to a total of double their Stamina value are automatically broken. The unit has been shattered by missile fire. It is considered to have been destroyed and its warriors slain or irretrievably scattered. The whole unit is removed from the game immediately. No dice are rolled for the break test that would otherwise be required; the unit is simply removed.

DISORDER

Disorder often results from a break test, or a test for moving through friendly units. Disorder represents a unit losing its cohesion either because of panic or more likely due to its ranks becoming disorganised or thrown into disarray. A disordered unit suffers various penalties the most significant of which is that it is not allowed to receive orders or use its initiative in the Command part of the turn.

The rules relating to disordered units are indicated throughout the book and summarised together with the rules for Break Tests on page 73.

RANGED ATTACKS AND OPEN ORDER

Units in open order can direct their ranged attacks in any direction. Unlike formed units, which shoot to their front, open order units can see and shoot all round. Range is therefore measured from the closest model in the unit to the closest part of the target.

Units in open order are obliged to target the nearest enemy they can see in a comparable way to other units. However, an open order unit will often be spread out in such a way that a proportion of its models are closer to different enemies. Indeed, sometimes a large portion of the open order unit may be 'out of range' of the nearest enemy entirely. In such cases we deem it appropriate to divide the unit's ranged attacks against all of its potential targets in what seems the most proportionate manner.

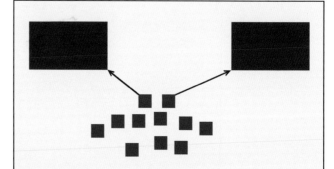

This unit of skirmishers is about 4" from the left red unit and 5" from the right unit – the left hand unit is therefore the closest target. However, a large proportion of the skirmishers are out of range of the closest target (6") although many are within range of the other enemy unit on the right. The player has three attacks to make and recognises that both enemy are practically as close – so he takes one attack against each and rolls a dice to decide where to allocate the second attack – a very fair thing to do! Some are happy to leave the choice to the player, and either convention works just as well in practice.

COLUMNS

Units arranged into a column are not permitted to make ranged attacks. A column represents a unit prepared to move and manoeuvre rather than fight, so we do not permit such units to use ranged attacks. On the whole, columns are vulnerable formations and must be used with care; infantry in particular will suffer very badly if caught whilst unprepared to fight. Cavalry can be luckier, as they are allowed a broader range of response moves when charged as described in the rules for Charge Responses (page 60).

CLOSING SHOTS

When a formed infantry, cavalry, elephant, chariot or light artillery unit that is armed with **long ranged** weapons is charged to its front it is allowed to shoot at its enemy as they close. Units in open order armed with long ranged weapons can make closing shots against a charge from any direction. These are called closing shots. These shots are worked out immediately after the chargers move into contact and before making any more moves with other units. As such, closing shots are worked out in the opposing player's turn or whenever a charge is made. Note that units that have short-ranged attacks, and which don't also have long ranged attacks, cannot shoot in his way: any throwing of missiles at close range is subsumed into the **Clash Combat** value for both sides.

Medium and Heavy artillery units are not allowed to shoot closing shots at their enemy as their rate of fire is assumed to be too slow to do so effectively. Light artillery units can shoot closing shots as described.

Shooting in this way is described as a *charge response* and a unit making closing shots cannot make another charge response as well: for example, a counter charge or evade. The rules for charge responses are covered as part of the Hand-to-Hand Combat rules on page 52. Note that troops with the special rule Parthian Shot are an exception in that they can both shoot and evade. See Parthian Shot (page 102).

Calculate the effect of closing shots as follows. Roll a dice for each long ranged attack. Apply the –1 penalty for closing shots to represent the limited time available for the shooters to employ their weapons. Calculate casualties as described for other shooting and make any break tests required if 6's are thrown or if the chargers become *shaken*. Note that the long

ranged attack value is always used when working out closing shots even though the enemy are in contact when the test is made. Shots are assumed to take place as the units close, even though it is convenient to work out the results once the charge move is complete.

If a missile break test is required this is taken immediately and can potentially result in the chargers becoming disordered, or even forcing them to retreat. If forced to retreat they are driven off before fighting hand-to-hand combat, so in such a case no hand-to-hand fighting takes place. Assuming chargers are not driven off, any casualties inflicted are recorded onto the unit as usual, and any excess casualties are removed once the break test has been taken. Casualties inflicted by closing shots *do not* count as having been struck in combat when it comes to working out which side has won the fight.

A unit can potentially fire closing shots more than once during the turn if it succeeds in driving away or destroying one enemy and is then charged by another.

If a unit attempts to charge more than one enemy at the same time, then it is possible it will take closing shots from two or more units. In such cases work out the closing shots from all the units charged, calculate casualties, and take any missile breaks test required.

Dig faster Marcus! Roman Legionaries entrench at the end of a long day's march, under the supervision of Centurion Cedo Alteram

TRAVERSING SHOTS

Sometimes you will get a situation where an enemy unit moves across the front of one of your missile armed units thus presenting a target as it passes. This is similar in concept to closing shots, except that it occurs as the enemy moves past your unit's front rather than into hand-to-hand combat with the shooter.

Shooting at a traversing target is a *response* to an enemy move and therefore usually takes place in the Command part of the opposing side's turn. It can also take place following combat during a *sweeping advance* as described on page 78.

As with closing shots, only infantry, cavalry, elephant, chariots or light artillery armed with **long ranged** weapons can make traversing shots. Units with short ranged attacks and which don't also have long ranged attacks cannot make traversing shots. Medium and heavy artillery units are considered insufficiently mobile to make traversing shots.

A unit can shoot at an enemy traversing its front that crosses half or more of the shooter's frontage and which comes within 12" range as it does so or within the unit's maximum range for its weapons if this is less than 12". Range is measured from the centre-front or leader position in the usual way. This is shown in the diagrams below.

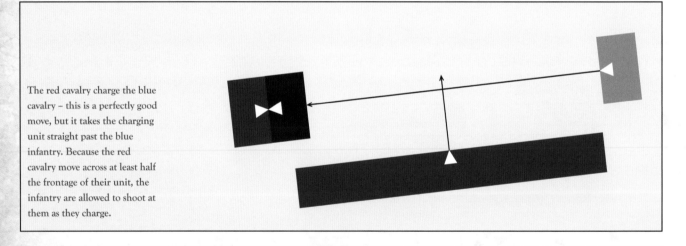

The red cavalry charge the blue cavalry – this is a perfectly good move, but it takes the charging unit straight past the blue infantry. Because the red cavalry move across at least half the frontage of their unit, the infantry are allowed to shoot at them as they charge.

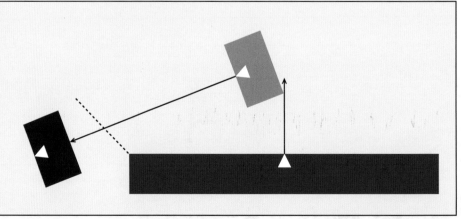

The red cavalry unit moves across the infantry unit's front and out of its front quarter. This diagram shows the position where the cavalry move across exactly half of the infantry unit's front – if the cavalry had started further to the left, it could have moved without attracting the infantry unit's fire.

Make the shots once the enemy unit has completed its move. Roll a dice for each long ranged attack, applying the –1 penalty for traversing shots to represent the limited time available for the shooters to employ their weapons. Work out casualties and take any break test required if 6s are thrown or the target is *shaken*. Note that, as with closing shots, units making traversing shots always use the long ranged attack value even if the enemy approach to within 6".

Traversing shots quite often occur where a bow or other missile armed unit has taken up a position in a building, as such a unit is able to shoot at enemy moving past their position. Note that the number of shots in such cases will be limited to the number normally allowed from buildings (see page 44).

ARTILLERY

Artillery includes all team operated long ranged stone and bolt throwing engines. In antiquity such weapons were invariably torsion powered, and engines of similar design were often employed to throw stones, bolts or darts. We distinguished between light, medium and heavy types. 'Light' typically describes a man-portable scorpion, 'medium' an onager, and 'heavy' a stationary weapon requiring assembly on-site and therefore restricted to assaults upon, and defence of, fortifications.

Artillery units have the same arc of fire to their front as other missile armed units. Unlike other missile armed units artillery **are** allowed a free choice of target if no targets present themselves within half maximum range. This enables artillery units to pick a target where enemy remain distant, and this is a useful ability in siege and assault situations. Where one or more targets presents itself within half range, the artillery unit is obliged to shoot at the closest in the same way as for other shooters.

Light artillery can move once and shoot, but cannot move further and shoot in the same turn. Other artillery cannot move and shoot in the same turn. This has already been covered in the rules for Manhandling Artillery (page 36) but is worth repeating whilst we consider the effect of artillery shooting.

Unlike other shooters, medium and heavy artillery units have no short ranged attacks and therefore cannot bring

their weapons to bear at ranges of 6" or less. Where the closest enemy to their front are within 6" they cannot shoot at all. Note that this also means they are unable to act as *supports* in hand-to-hand combat, as a short ranged attack value is required to do so (see Supports page 66). This doesn't apply to light artillery units, which have a short range attack values being assumed to shoot with a flat trajectory much as a crossbow.

Note that artillery hits impose a –1 or –2 modifier to the target's morale save and are therefore especially to be feared by heavily armoured troops and those placing their faith in fortifications.

SHOOTING OVERHEAD WITH ARTILLERY

Artillery units can shoot over the heads of other units or terrain if the artillery is positioned on high ground or elevated on fortifications, and where it is possible to draw a line of sight to the target. The only way to determine if this is so is to get down over the table for a model's eye view. The unit must be able to draw line of sight to the target from the centre-front of the unit just as for any other shooter.

As well as being able to see the target as described, an artillery unit can only shoot over the heads of intervening units or blocking terrain that is both further than 6" from the artillery piece and further than 6" from the target. This 6" represents 'dead ground' – too close to either the artillery or the target to afford a shot.

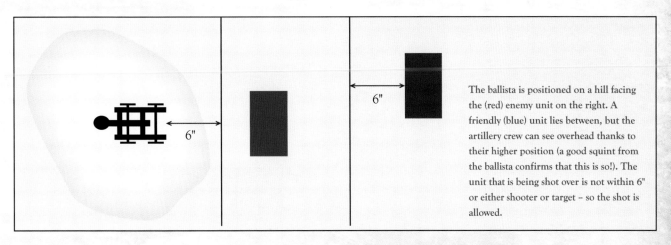

The ballista is positioned on a hill facing the (red) enemy unit on the right. A friendly (blue) unit lies between, but the artillery crew can see overhead thanks to their higher position (a good squint from the ballista confirms that this is so!). The unit that is being shot over is not within 6" or either shooter or target – so the shot is allowed.

HAND-TO-HAND COMBAT

Close quarter fighting is what ancient battles are all about. This is where it comes to determining victors and vanquished. When we speak of combat we also tend to use the terms 'hand-to-hand' combat, 'close' combat and occasionally 'melee' combat to describe exactly the same thing. Whatever term falls to hand, it represents decisive man-to-man fighting with spears, swords, and such-like weaponry, and the exchange of missile fire at very short ranges and especially during the moments before contact.

HOW COMBAT WORKS

Units begin hand-to-hand fighting by charging their enemy in the Command part of the turn as described below. Once opposing units have moved into touch they exchange blows as described in the rules that follow.

Once both sides have struck blows and casualties have been determined, the side that has inflicted the most casualties is deemed to have won. The units on the losing side must then take a *break test* to determine if they hold, give ground or break altogether, in which case they are destroyed. The resolution of break tests and resulting moves are covered in the separate section Break Tests page 72.

WHAT IS AN ENGAGEMENT?

A combat engagement consists of opposing units that are fighting each other plus all those adjoining units judged to be supporting. The role of supporting units is described in depth later. For now the important thing to remember is that both **fighting** and **supporting** units form part of the same combat engagement as shown in the example below.

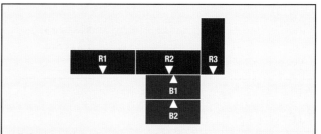

All the units shown here constitute a single engagement – Red 2 and Blue 1 are fighting (they are aligned face to face) and all the other units are supporting as described later.

In situations where more than one unit is fighting on each side, all units that are mutually fighting form part of the same engagement together with any associated supporting units.

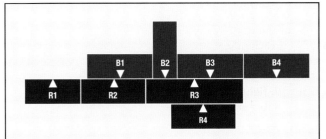

This is two combat engagements. Blue 1 is fighting Red 2 supported by Red 1. Blue 2 and Blue 3 are fighting Red 3 supported by Red 4. Blue 4 is supporting Blue 3.

FIGHTING UNITS

A unit is defined as fighting in a hand-to-hand combat engagement where its centre-front or leader position is either touching the enemy, or an enemy's centre-front or leader position is touching it. Basically, where the leader position touches an opposing unit both units are deemed to be fighting.

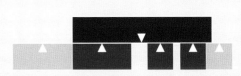

Although this is a somewhat extreme example, it serves to show what we mean by fighting units. The centre-front or leader position of all units is indicated. The red unit has been engaged by five enemy units. The three blue units are all fighting as their centre-fronts are touching the red unit. The red unit is fighting all three blue units because their centre-fronts touch it. The beige units are not fighting as neither their centre-front nor the enemy's centre-front touches either unit – these units are engaged as supports.

ENGAGED UNITS, COMMAND AND SHOOTING

Units that are engaged in combat at the start of the Command part of the turn cannot move either using their initiative or by means of an order. The only exceptions are units that have a special rule entitling them to move out of combat, but these are rare exceptions and are covered in A Selection of Useful Rules on page 98.

Units engaged in combat cannot make ranged attacks in the Ranged Attacks part of the turn, nor may they be targeted by ranged attacks in the enemy's turn. Such units are not eligible as targets and are otherwise considered pre-ocupied with their hand-to-hand opponents.

THE SPANISH SWORD

The sword carried by the Roman legionaries is called the gladius or gladius hispaniensis – Spanish Sword – perhaps because it was adopted from the Spanish tribes encountered by the Romans during the Punic wars. The gladius varied somewhat in style and method of manufacture but was essentially a short sword with a blade in the region of 50-60cm. The earliest weapons – those employed during the wars against Carthage – were somewhat longer and more slender than later types, and were always finely tapered with a leaf-shaped blade. In the days of the Empire the gladius developed into a heavier and shorter weapon, sometimes with a leaf-shaped blade (known as the Mainz pattern after examples found there) and sometimes with straight blades and short, triangular points (referred to as the Pompeii type after examples uncovered amidst the ruins of that city). Both types – and variants of these – appear to have co-existed, so the styles probably reflect local manufacturing practices rather than any deliberate change. Roman infantry swords tended to become longer in the 3rd century until they evolved into the spatha type – a much longer weapon of a kind long used by horsemen.

The battle rages beneath the walls of Kadesh in our refight of this famous battle between the Egyptians and the Hittites

CHARGE MOVES

A charge move is a move intended to bring a unit into contact with its enemy. Often a charging unit will make several moves one after the other, but only the **final move** into touch is a charge move as defined here. Watch out for this. When we say 'charge move' we do not mean all movement that proceeds from charge orders, only the actual move into contact.

A unit given a charge order must always move towards its target as quickly and as directly as it can, which is to say by the shortest possible route. This applies to **all** the moves made with the charge order, even though it is only the final move that is a charge move.

A charge does not necessarily represent a pell-mell dash upon the enemies' lines – though it might! A charge could equally well be a measured advance, or even a more drawn out process involving some initial skirmishing before opposing ranks close. We therefore employ the term charge because it is useful, dramatic and memorable rather than because it is a literal description of how a unit moves.

STATE YOUR INTENTION TO CHARGE

A player who wishes his unit to charge must be sure to say so when giving orders in the Command part of the turn. He should also indicate the target unit or units he intends to engage. A player who wishes a unit to charge using *initiative* must state his intention before moving. It is important to remember this because the enemy might be allowed to react and this can potentially affect the charger's own movement in some cases.

Unless a unit is specifically instructed to charge it will not do so, although note that such an instruction can sometimes result from a blundered order or a special rule (see page 30 for Blunders and A Selection of Useful Rules section on page 98 for instances of compulsory charges.)

BORN IN THE SADDLE

Speaking of the Avars and Turks – which he refers to collectively with other nomads as Scythians – The Byzantine Emperor Maurice says they, 'have been brought up on horseback, and owing to their lack of exercise they simply cannot walk about on their own feet.' Quite how this 'fact' came to be observed Maurice neglects to say – one can only imagine!

Before we proceed further, it is worth saying that a unit **can** be ordered to charge an enemy beyond its maximum reach as this saves excess measurement and gets troops moving in the right direction without any fuss. However, no advantage is ever allowed to a unit doing so. Any bonuses to command or free moves that otherwise apply to charging units are only taken into account where the enemy is within reach, i.e. where the charge is possible. This rule isn't intended to stop players taking a casual approach to such things, only to ensure that no unfair advantage is conferred, or embarrassment caused, when they do!

UNITS NOT ALLOWED TO CHARGE

In the following cases troops cannot be given an instruction to charge the enemy. Such units won't charge the enemy, whether by means of an order, on initiative, as a result of a blunder, or resulting from any other special rules or exceptions. They can't charge in these situations; it's as simple as that!

- **Units that are already engaged in combat.** Units that are already engaged in combat, whether fighting or supporting, cannot be given orders or use their initiative, and cannot charge in any circumstances even where the opportunity might present itself.

- **Disordered Units.** Units that are disordered cannot be given orders and cannot move on their initiative. Even where an exception applies permitting movement in some situations, disordered units cannot charge.

- **Shaken Units**. A unit that is shaken cannot charge. Shaken units are those that have suffered casualties equal to their Stamina value as described on page 48.

- **Column or Square.** Units that are in column or square formation cannot charge the enemy. Columns can be given an order to reform into a fighting formation and then charge, but cannot charge whilst they remain in a column. Squares cannot move other than to make a single formation change, and are therefore unable to change formation and charge in the same turn. See page 22.

- **Artillery.** Artillery units cannot charge in any circumstances.

- **Open Order.** Units in open order formation are not allowed to charge enemy infantry or cavalry unless these are also in open order. Other types of units can be charged in the usual way; for example, artillery, chariots, elephants and baggage. Troops in open order can also charge enemy occupying buildings. Troops capable of assuming other formations can be given an order to reform into a fighting formation and then charge.

- **Cavalry and Chariots against Pike Phalanx.** Cavalry and chariots are not allowed to charge home onto the front of a pike phalanx unless the pike phalanx is already *shaken* or *disordered*. See the rules for Pikes on page 103.

Note that we do not specifically forbid infantry from charging cavalry, although on the whole it is a rather reckless thing to do and likely to end in tears. Mounted troops attacked in this way are allowed to countercharge in most cases, which will usually spell disaster for an opposing infantry unit. See Countercharge on page 60.

MAKING THE CHARGE MOVE

Remember that the charge move is specifically the final move into contact, so in the case of a unit making three moves only the third move is a charge move as we define it. The rules described here apply specifically to this charge move. We shall also restrict ourselves to describing how formed units charge for the moment. Units in open order are treated a little differently and are described later (see page 59).

A unit can only make a charge move at an enemy unit it is **facing**. This means it must be able to see the target, and the target must lie directly in front of its centre-front or leader position as shown in the diagram below. For more about facing the enemy see Proximity of Enemy on page 34.

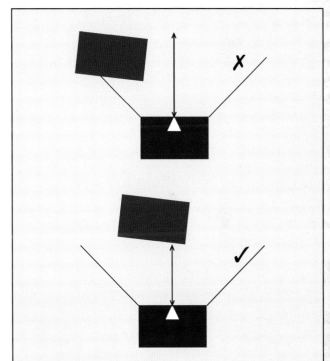

Chargers can only charge against units that lie in front of their leader position as shown by the example at the bottom. The example at the top cannot charge, as the enemy doesn't lie in front of the leader. In cases such as this a unit may have to reposition itself before it can make a charge. Note it doesn't matter that the target unit at the top is partly out of the charger's front quarter – only that it is not directly in front of the leader.

Change range is measured from the centre-front or leader model to the closest part of the enemy. If the target is within one move's distance of the leader then the whole unit is allowed to charge regardless of the distance any individual model may move. Some models will often end up moving further than their normal move allowance. This does not matter. Think of the unit quickening its pace as it approaches the enemy.

POSITION CHARGERS

In most cases opposing units will be facing each other and the charger will align against the front of the target in a straightforward manner. We'll consider situations where a unit charges against the flank or rear of an enemy in a moment. For now just imagine the charger is heading for the front of its target.

The charging unit must bring its own centre-front **and** as great a portion of both units' frontages into touch as possible. In most cases this will simply result in the units aligning against each other.

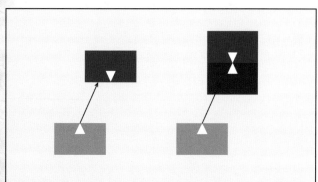

In most cases opposing units will be facing each other and charges take place in a straightforward manner like this. Note how the unit moves over to bring the greatest portion of both units into touch. This is why models often end up moving further than their standard move allowance when they charge.

Units that start their move off to one side of their target will usually align to the corresponding side of their enemy's formation as shown below. This gets the greatest portion of both units into touch in the most direct manner.

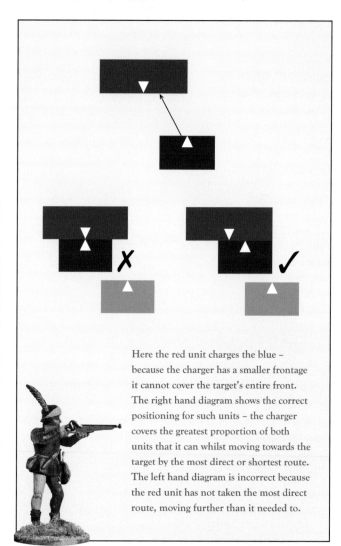

Here the red unit charges the blue – because the charger has a smaller frontage it cannot cover the target's entire front. The right hand diagram shows the correct positioning for such units – the charger covers the greatest proportion of both units that it can whilst moving towards the target by the most direct or shortest route. The left hand diagram is incorrect because the red unit has not taken the most direct route, moving further than it needed to.

CHARGES TO THE FLANKS AND REAR

So far we have dealt only with charges against the front of an enemy formation. Sometimes a charger may be able to move against the flanks or rear of the enemy, and we'll consider these situations here.

If a charging unit is positioned within its target's front quarter when the order is received then it must attempt to make its charge to the target's front. If the charger lies to a side quarter of the enemy when the order is received it charges to the side, and if to the rear it charges to the rear. Notice that it is the position of the charger **before** any moves are made that counts! Bear in mind this means it is not possible to order a unit to charge an enemy in the side if the charger lies to the enemy's front when the order is received. If given such an order, a unit will attempt to position itself to charge in its following turn – this being the most direct way of fulfilling the order. The distinction between front, side and rear quarters have already been explained and the diagram shown below will remind us.

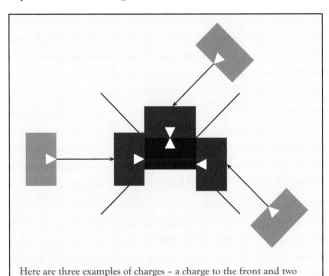

Here are three examples of charges – a charge to the front and two charges to the flanks of a unit. Notice how in both cases the flank charges move the shortest distance to bring the greatest portion of units into touch.

Often a charger will not lie wholly within any quarter of the target unit, but will straddle two quarters: for example, the front and side. In such cases the charger counts as in the quarter occupied by its front-centre or leader position. This should be easy enough to decide, but if in doubt players must defer to the umpire or roll a dice for it.

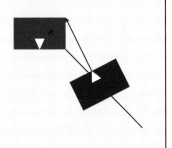

Red is positioned partly to the target's front and partly to its flank – because the centre-front or leader position lies to the flank this unit is allowed to make a flank charge. Watch out for charges like this against a unit's vulnerable flanks.

When charging into the flank of an enemy, or into any facing that is especially narrow, it is important to make sure the centre-front of the charger contacts the enemy unit. This is shown on the diagram below.

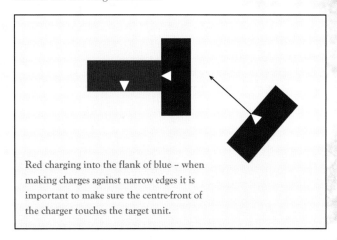

Red charging into the flank of blue – when making charges against narrow edges it is important to make sure the centre-front of the charger touches the target unit.

CAREFUL! YOU'LL HAVE SOMEBODY'S EYE OUT!

Livy writes of the near invulnerability of the Macedonian phalanx before going on to describe how the Romans valiantly overcome it – typical 'bigging up' the enemy to make your team look all the better if you ask me! He has this to say of the collapse of the Macedonian phalanx at the Battle of Pydna in 168BC.

'*The most manifest cause of the victory was the fact that there were many scattered engagements which first threw the wavering phalanx into disorder and then disrupted it completely. The strength of the phalanx is irresistible when it is close-packed and bristling with extended spears; but if by attacks at different points you force the troops to swing round their spears, unwieldly as they are by reason of their length and weight, they become entangled in a disorderly mass; and further, the noise of any commotion on the flank or rear throws them into confusion, and then the whole formation collapses.*'

Livy XLIV.41
Battle of Pydna and the defeat of Perseus

Bronze arrow heads c. 800BC Iran
(Perry Collection)

CHARGING TWO ON ONE

In most cases opposing units will have comparable frontages and combats are therefore fought one on one with other units supporting as described later. However, if opposing units have significantly different frontages, there can sometimes be room for two or more units to fight a single enemy. The following rules describe where this is normally allowed.

Where charging units move one after the other against the same enemy it is simply a matter of moving each unit in turn against whatever portion of the target unit is accessible to them. Where two or more units charge against the same enemy as a division order, units must still move one after the other for the sake of clarity. It is up to the player which unit he moves first. Depending on which unit the player moves first, this may or may not leave room for a second unit to charge and fight.

Where there are already friends fighting to the same facing edge, then another unit can charge **only** if there is clearly room for its centre front/leader to move into touch with the facing edge. The most common situation is where small units, or narrow based units such as elephants, are charging an enemy who is more widely based. A typical situation is shown below.

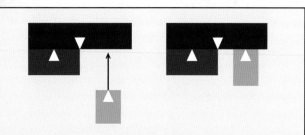

Red is a large unit and has been charged by a small blue unit from the left – because of red's large frontage there is room for the elephant to charge and fight – a typical two on one fight.

Where a target is already engaged, a second unit is allowed to complete a charge so long as its leader can see either the enemy unit or could see the enemy if it were not already engaged. The enemy unit must still lie directly in front of the leader, but the charger is allowed to draw a line of sight through friendly engaged units that are in the way. This just allows for the practicalities of moving units one after the other and makes provision for units to join combats that are underway where common sense demands they could.

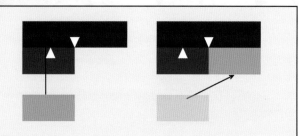

Here a unit charges against an enemy who is already engaged – it is allowed to charge even though the friends lie directly in front of the leader.

CHARGING ONE ON TWO

In some situations enemy units will be positioned in such a way that charging one will automatically bring another into touch. In these cases the obligation for a charger to bring as large a portion of its frontage into touch as possible extends to adjacent enemy units. The diagram below illustrates the principle.

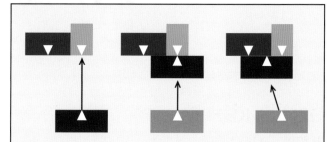

The red unit charges the blue elephant which is placed next to a small blue infantry unit – if the infantry were not there then red would charge directly ahead as shown in the middle – this being the most direct route. But, because the infantry will be contacted red must maximise contact against both units as shown on the right.

Adjacent units will fight if their centre-front position clearly contacts the charger or if the charger's centre-front contacts them. In such a case the unit is treated as having been charged, and it is allowed to react as if it had been the target of the charge in the first place (see Charge Responses below).

Units adjacent to the target of the charge will not fight if their centre-front or leader model position does not clearly touch the charger, and assuming the charger's leader position does not touch them. A unit that is not fighting may not react as if charged. The unit will probably be able to support in the engagement as described later.

Note that the obligation to cover an adjacent unit can result in the charger's centre-front touching a different unit to the intended target. This is fine so long as the original target is still fighting. Where the obligation to cover an adjacent target would otherwise result in the original target not fighting, don't move the charger beyond the point where the original target fights.

It is worth pointing out that we take a fairly lax attitude to the exact number of models in our units, and the widths of different units do therefore tend to vary within certain limits. Where this is the case it is important not to confer an unintended advantage when it comes to two-on-one engagements simply because of a unit's width. Sometimes a unit that is touching at its centre-front would not be so if it were a little wider. This is a case for judgement either by the players or umpire. As in all such cases we rely on the good sense of the participants to arrange things to their satisfaction.

CHARGING WITH OPEN ORDER UNITS

As we have already explained, troops in open order are not allowed to charge enemy infantry or cavalry unless these too are in open order or sheltering within buildings in the case of infantry. Units in open order are also not allowed to charge if doing so would bring an adjacent unit of a type they could not otherwise charge into the combat as a fighting unit.

Most charges by units in open order will therefore be against other units in open order or against buildings. The rules that follow explain how to move such units into combat. The same method is used whether open order units charge or are charged.

When a unit in open order charges, pick the model that is closest to a visible part of the enemy unit and measure the charge from that model. It doesn't matter which direction the model is facing as troops in open order can see all round. As open order units can sometimes be quite dispersed a charge may result in some models moving considerably further than others. We feel this is perfectly acceptable for troops unencumbered by a rigid formation and moving as individuals.

As with other charges, those in open order will charge to the enemy's front if they lie to their front quarter, to the flank if positioned to the side, and in the back if positioned to the rear. In practice, open order troops will usually charge other open order troops – so this distinction doesn't really apply.

When either charging or being charged, units in open order are brought into contact with their opponents in as satisfying a manner as possible. This is best achieved using the method shown below for an open order unit charging another; however, the same method also works if only one unit is in open order. Begin by moving the chargers up against the opposing models as shown in the diagram. Then bring enemy models forward to make as tight a line as possible. The normal rule that obliges open order troops to maintain a distance between the models is waived for the duration of hand-to-hand combat.

Combat between units in open order can get a bit messy. If other units are to become involved the players may be called upon to judge where a unit's flank lies, so it helps to think of the combat as taking place between two units in a rough line. A useful tip is to draw a line between the models on the extreme edges of the formation, ignoring those between, but common sense must prevail and we leave it to players to make whatever arrangement they feel best fits the circumstances.

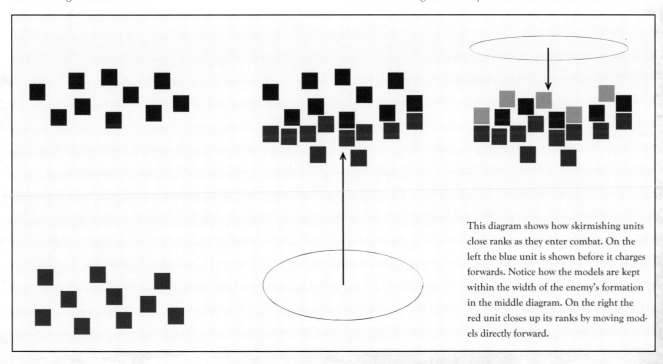

This diagram shows how skirmishing units close ranks as they enter combat. On the left the blue unit is shown before it charges forwards. Notice how the models are kept within the width of the enemy's formation in the middle diagram. On the right the red unit closes up its ranks by moving models directly forward.

CHARGE RESPONSES

Depending upon the situation, a unit that has been charged can opt to make **one** of the responses listed below. Only units that are not already engaged can respond in this way. Units that are already engaged will always 'stand'. The player whose unit has been charged must declare its response **before** his opponent makes his charge move. We assume units that would normally advance to meet their enemy do so, even though their response in the game is to *stand* and the models themselves are not moved. This is why we give all units a unique value for the first turn of hand-to-hand fighting (the *Clash* value).

- **Stand.** This is the default response and often the only option available. The unit remains where it is. In the case of a unit in open order it will close up its ranks as already described.

- **Closing Shots.** Troops with long range attacks can respond to a charge by shooting as described in the Ranged Attacks section page 40. Work out the result of closing shots once the chargers have moved into touch and before doing anything else. Units that elect to shoot at their enemy in this way are otherwise treated as standing.

- **Evade.** Only units in open order can attempt to evade a charge. Evading troops try to avoid combat by turning and running off – hopefully to regroup and return to the fight later. See Evade below.

- **Countercharge.** A cavalry or chariot unit that has been charged to its front can elect to countercharge assuming it would otherwise be allowed to charge the enemy concerned. This is explained under Countercharge below.

- **Turn to Face.** A cavalry or elephant unit that is charged to the flank or rear can respond by pivoting to face the enemy. This is explained under Turn to Face on page 61.

- **Parthian Shot.** Only a unit with the special Parthian Shot rule can choose this option, combining an evade move and closing shots into one manoeuvre. As this is an exception that applies only to specific troops it is covered in A Selection of Useful Rules on page 98.

EVADE

Only units in open order are allowed to try and evade from a charge. Units in open order have no formal facing, and will therefore always attempt to move directly away from the unit charging them. Units that are already *disordered* are not allowed to evade.

An evade interrupts the regular flow of play and takes place out of the normal turn sequence. The attempt is made once it has been established the charger can charge into contact, but before moving the charging unit.

A unit that evades successfully cannot evade again if charged by another enemy unit that turn. If charged a second time the unit is obliged to stand without making closing shots or any other response.

The evade move takes place exactly like a move given in the Command phase and requires an order in the usual way. In this case the order is 'evade' and, if the order is issued successfully, the unit is moved as far as possible one, two, or three moves into the quarter opposite the chargers. In the case of an evade order, if the test is failed the evaders can still move **once**, so evaders will always move one, two, or three moves depending upon their roll. If the evade order is given by the army's general the result can be re-rolled in the usual way (see page 80).

Once the evaders have moved, the chargers complete their move. Depending on how many moves the chargers have, they may be able to catch the evaders, or they may find the evaders have moved beyond range. In either case, the chargers must attempt to complete their order in the usual manner. If evaders have moved through other enemy to their rear, then the chargers can potentially charge these troops if their order has been framed in a suitable manner.

For example, if the order is simply 'charge the skirmishers' then the unit is obliged to do just that, and, if unable to complete their order because their target has evaded, the unit will not charge other enemies who happen to lie within reach. On the other hand, if the order is 'charge enemy to your front', or even 'charge the skirmishers, drive them away and charge the cavalry behind' the unit has a clear order to follow and will be able to charge a further target if evaders escape. For this reason it is important to frame orders carefully when charging troops who are likely to evade.

Evaders are automatically destroyed if their enemy catch them. The unit is removed from the table. The chargers are treated as having beaten their enemy in hand-to-hand fighting, and have the same options as described for victorious units. See Break Tests page 72.

If evaders are not caught, and assuming chargers do not redirect their charge to another unit indicated by their orders, then chargers are left high-and-dry and the normal sequence of play resumes. The evading unit is not otherwise penalised and can continue to move normally in the player's following turn.

It can happen that a unit attempting an evade rolls a blunder (double six) in which case we would suggest the unit rolls its blunder and acts accordingly. Even with a blunder there is a good chance of a unit moving away from the charger and out of reach.

COUNTERCHARGE

A cavalry or chariot unit that is charged to its front by another unit of any kind can respond with a countercharge. Units charged to the flank or rear cannot countercharge. Counterchargers must be of a type and status normally allowed to charge the enemy bearing down upon them. For example, units that are already *disordered* or *shaken* are not allowed to countercharge, and units in open order cannot countercharge formed units. Open order units can countercharge other open order units assuming they are otherwise able to do so.

A countercharge interrupts the regular flow of play and takes place out of the normal turn sequence. The move is made simultaneously with that of the charger and must be worked out before the charging unit moves.

A countercharge requires no order, and can be enacted automatically so long as the charger would otherwise either contact its target, or move to within one move's distance of the target's front. For example, if a charger is three moves from its target, then a countercharge is allowed if the charger rolls either two or three moves. Note that this means a countercharge is possible even in some situations where the charge would fail to contact their target.

Make the charger's and countercharger's moves simultaneously. Establish a point equidistant between and move both units so they contact at that position. Both the charger and countercharger are treated as having charged and both units receive all the combat bonuses as if charging, including any bonuses from weapons or special rules (see A Selction of Useful Rules on page 98).

If cavalry or chariots countercharge against infantry other than those in open order, then the infantry are automatically **disordered** and receive no 'to hit' bonus for charging. This does not apply if chargers are infantry in open order. Open order infantry can charge chariots or open order cavalry without becoming disordered. They are not allowed to charge formed cavalry so the situation will not arise.

If cavalry or chariots countercharge, then any other cavalry or chariots already positioned to support them in hand-to-hand combat can move with them and take part in the ensuing combat round. Just move the supporting units along with the counterchargers. See page 66 for more about the role of supporting units in combat.

TURN-TO-FACE

A formed cavalry or elephant unit that is charged to the flank or rear can respond by pivoting to face the enemy if it has room to do so, or simply turning about if charged in the rear. Units that are already *disordered* are not allowed to turn to face their enemy in this way.

A turn to face interrupts the regular flow of play and takes place out of the normal turn sequence. The move is made simultaneously with the move of the charger in a similar fashion to the countercharge.

No order is required for a unit to turn to face where it is allowed to do so. The turn happens automatically. If charged to its flank the unit is pivoted to confront the enemy head on if possible. If this is not possible it is pivoted sufficiently to bring the charge within its front quarter. The charger is then arranged against the front of the unit in the usual way.

Barbarian cavalry rampage through a Roman villa showing scant regard for the vegetable garden

FIGHTING

Regardless of which side's turn it is, every unit engaged in combat takes part every turn. All units that are fighting fight, and all units that are supporting contribute as supports. Because combat happens every turn, we often refer to combat in terms of 'rounds'. So, in Blue's turn fight a round of combat, in Red's turn fight a round of combat, then in Blue's turn another round of combat, and so on until the engagement is over.

During each round it is usual to work out one engagement in its entirety, then another, and so on until all engagements on the tabletop have been fought. So, if opposing cavalry are fighting each other on the western side of the table whilst two groups of skirmishers are engaged on the eastern side, it would be usual to pick one engagement (say the cavalry) and work that out completely, including any results and break tests, before turning to the skirmisher battle and resolving that in the same way. The player whose turn it is can decide the order in which to tackle engagements. Note that this can be quite an advantage as units victorious in one engagement can potentially move into or influence another.

ATTACKS

In reality units in hand-to-hand combat obviously strike at the same time; however, for the sake of our game it is convenient to work out all the attacks from one side, including any supporting attacks (see below), and then all the attacks from the other side. It doesn't strictly matter which side strikes first as all units fight with the status they had at the start of the combat round. We usually allow the player who charged or who is winning the fight to strike first, but this is by no means essential.

Hand-to-hand attacks are worked out in the same way described for ranged attacks. So, roll a dice for each attack and establish the number of hits inflicted on the enemy, the enemy makes morale saves if he has them, and any hits that are not saved are turned into casualties and recorded against the unit's Stamina value.

Two different combat attack values are used when fighting hand-to-hand combat: a unit's Clash value is used during its first round of each engagement, and a unit's Sustained value is used for subsequent rounds of the same engagement. In both cases the value indicates the number of dice rolled in the same way as for ranged attacks. Depending on the situation, we tend to refer to either of these values as the unit's *combat value*. Combat values for troops whose primary role is to fight hand-to-hand typically lie within the range of 6 to 9 for standard sized units.

If the unit is a tiny, small or large unit by the standards already discussed, then the indicated modifiers apply.

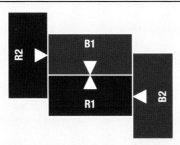

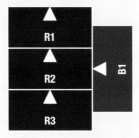

In this example Blue 1 has charged Red 1 to the front. In the following turn Blue 2 has charged Red 1 to the side. In the next turn Red 2 has charged Blue 1 in the side. All four units are interlinked by enemy units they are fighting – so this is a single combat engagement.

Fortunately most combat engagements are straightforward one-to-one affairs like the example shown here.

Blue 1 has charged Red 2 in the side – making incidental contact with Red 1 and 3 at the same time – all units are engaged.

Where a typical combat value is 6, units roll six dice if they are standard sized, eight if they are large, four if small and one dice if tiny. These adjustments are usually made to the basic stat line and are included in the example stats for appropriately sized units throughout this book.

We use these modifiers as a rule of thumb. They are not inviolable instructions handed from the heavens by Jove himself. Where a scenario or situation calls for finer tuning then players must make a sensible judgement.

Units in columns, squares, and occupying buildings can only attack in a very limited way. Their combat values are automatically reduced as shown on page 64. This applies whether they are fighting or supporting as described later (Supports page 66).

UNIT SIZE MODIFIERS FOR HAND-TO-HAND COMBAT	
Combat Value	Unit Size Modifiers
+2 Dice	**Large Unit.** The attackers are a large unit.
-2 Dice	**Small Unit.** The attackers are a small unit.
I Dice	**Tiny Unit.** Tiny units roll only one dice – their Combat Value is always 1.

What have the Romans done for us! Roads! Bridges! Boats! You can't stop progress can you – but these chaps are giving it a go

FORMATION MODIFIERS FOR HAND-TO-HAND COMBAT

Combat Value	Formation Modifiers
1 Dice	**Column.** Units in column have a combat value of one dice regardless of their size.
2 Dice per Face	**Square.** Units in square are limited to a maximum of two dice for any face up to their full combat value in total.
2 Dice per Face	**Buildings.** Units occupying buildings are limited to a maximum of two dice from any face up to their combat value in total – see the rules for buildings page 39.

To make your attacks roll the appropriate number of dice. Any dice scoring 4, 5 or 6 indicate that the attackers have inflicted a hit on their target. For example, six dice scoring 1, 3, 3, 4, 5 and 6 = 3 hits. In some situations it becomes easier or harder to score a hit. These situations are taken into account by adding or subtracting from the dice rolls as noted below. For example, if a unit is charging it is considered more effective and so +1 is added to the chance of scoring a hit – so dice rolls of 3, 4, 5 or 6 will hit.

Regardless of these modifiers a dice roll of a 1 is always a miss and a dice roll of a 6 is always a hit. There is no such thing as an automatic hit or miss. A unit normally fights to its front, but if attacked in the side or rear, or where it is attacked from several directions at once, then its own attacks are distributed as noted below. Where the player has a choice, it is necessary to declare where all the attacks will be made before rolling any dice – otherwise confusion will surely reign!

At least half of a unit's attacks must always be allocated to its front if it is engaged to the front. If engaged to the front by more than one unit then attacks must be divided as equally as possible amongst them. Whatever the situation, a unit cannot allocate more than half of its attacks against either flank. A unit can fight to the rear with all of its attacks assuming it is not also fighting to the front, and if fighting to the front and rear must allocate attacks as near as equally between them bearing in mind it cannot make fewer than half its attacks to the front.

'TO HIT' DICE ROLL MODIFIERS FOR HAND-TO-HAND COMBAT

Dice Score	Situation
+1	**Charging.** If the unit has charged or countercharged into combat the bonus applies in the first round of fighting. Charging units will therefore usually hit their enemy on the roll of a 3+ rather than a roll of 4+.
+1	**Winning.** If the unit fought and won the previous round of the same combat engagement then this bonus applies during the following round of fighting. As with chargers these units will usually score hits on a roll of 3+.
+1	**Uphill.** If the unit is uphill of its opponent and has neither charged/countercharged this turn nor moved following the previous round of the same engagement, then this bonus applies in the current round. If a unit moves following combat results the bonus is lost in the following round regardless of whether the unit won or lost the fight.
-1	**Shaken and/or disordered.** This applies if the attacking unit is either *shaken*, *disordered*, or both. These states are explained elsewhere and affect units in various deleterious ways.
-1	**Open Order.** This applies if the attacking unit is in open order formation. Such units prefer to skirmish rather than get stuck in and will generally require a 5+ to score hits rather than the usual 4+.
-1	**Flank/Rear.** This applies to all of a unit's attacks if it is engaged to either flank or to the rear, including to any attacks made to its front.

For example, a unit has 7 attacks and is attacked to the front and a flank. It could make 3 attacks against the flank as this is the most it can allocate to a flank, whilst it is obliged to make at least 4 attacks to its front as any fewer will be less than half.

MORALE SAVES

We have already discussed Morale saves at some length in the section on Ranged Attacks. Morale saves in hand-to-hand fighting are the same in all respects and you might wish to refer back to remind yourself how this works. See page 46. Modifiers to the Morale save are also the same as for ranged attacks, although there are also some additional modifiers, which take account of specific weaponry and strategies. These are covered as part of A Selection of Useful Rules on page 98.

In hand-to-hand combat the +1 bonus for *cover*, the +2 for *buildings*, and +3 for *fortifications* apply to any stationary unit that has been charged. These bonuses continue to apply from round to round until the unit loses a round of combat. Once the unit loses a round of combat, the enemy is assumed to have broken through any intervening cover, and the Morale save bonus is lost during further rounds.

For the avoidance of doubt, a unit that charges an enemy behind cover does not benefit from the cover itself even where a barrier physically separates both units. Only units that take up a position within cover receive the bonus. This should be obvious enough, but let us be clear and dispel any lurking confusion at this stage.

CASUALTIES

Once Morale saves have been taken, any hits that have not been saved are recorded as casualties on the unit. As with ranged combat, casualties inflicted in hand-to-hand-fighting represent men killed or wounded as well as other factors that we might expect to affect a unit's ability to fight such as exhaustion and loss of nerve. Casualties are recorded onto the unit using markers as already discussed in the section on Ranged Attacks page 40.

During a combat round it is important to keep a separate tally of the casualties inflicted on a unit in the current round. This can most easily be done by carefully keeping any fresh markers separate from casualties inflicted previously, or by means of a dice placed face up to indicate the number of casualties suffered that round. Players can use these or any other method to keep track of the casualties in the current round.

Once the combat has been worked out, the result established and break tests taken, all casualties suffered in excess of a unit's Stamina value are removed. These excess casualties are either redistributed amongst supporting units as described later, or discarded altogether. Once a unit is *shaken* – i.e. casualties have reached its Stamina value – casualties must still be recorded for purposes of determining winners, establishing if units are shattered and for taking break tests as described later.

ONE HUMP OR TWO?

Our ancestors were always open to all manner of unorthodox tricks and ruses that might give them an advantage in a fight. One famous example took place during the Battle of Thymbra between the Persians and Lydians in 547BC. The Lydians under their King Croesus ruled a powerful empire in western Anatolia, and they were especially famous for the quality and ferocity of their cavalry. To counter this threat the Persians arranged their camels – probably baggage animals – in front of their troops, reasoning that the unfamiliar smell of these strange creatures would spook the Lydian horses. In the battle this is exactly what happened and Croesus was defeated and his capital Sardis captured.

"In war, events of importance are the result of trivial causes."

Julius Caesar

CLOSE RANKS

Shield-carrying heavy infantry units fighting in a battle line formation are allowed to close their ranks during any round of hand-to-hand combat, except for the initial round if the unit has either charged or countercharged. This represents the unit drawing into the kind of dense 'synaspismos' formation associated with Hoplite warfare and with the 'shieldwall' of Dark Age infantry. Only heavy infantry units equipped with shields are allowed to do this, and it is a useful way of reducing the number of casualties likely to be inflicted by both sides that round.

If a player wishes a unit to close ranks he must say so before either side strikes blows. Once a unit has closed ranks it fights with a –1 'to hit' penalty when making its own attacks, but adds a +1 bonus when making its morale saves. So, a unit that would normally hit on 4+ and save on 4+ will instead hit on 5+ and save on 3+.

Closing ranks only takes effect for a single round – so if a player wishes his troops to close ranks throughout the combat he must announce that he is doing so at the start of each round.

SUPPORTS

Supports are units positioned either alongside or behind fighting units in such a way that they can be imagined contributing to the combat either with missiles, by relieving fighting troops, or by striking blows themselves.

Units in open order, artillery and baggage units fighting in hand-to-hand combat **cannot** be supported by other units of any kind. In these cases the fighting units are either too dispersed or represent too few combatants to benefit from supporting friends. Units fighting from buildings cannot normally be supported either, although they can be supported by other units in the same building where the building is large enough to hold them. Units in square or testudo formation also cannot be supported by other troops because of their closed and, in the case of the square, multi-directional formations. Units in wedge formation can only be supported by friends enclosed within the wedge. Units that cannot be supported in hand-to-hand combat are listed below.

- Units in open order
- Artillery
- Wagons and baggage
- Cavalry cannot be supported by elephants

- Units in buildings except from troops within the same building
- Units in squares
- Units in testudo
- Units in wedge, except by enclosed friends
- Scythed chariots

Practically all units are allowed to support apart from baggage units, which are understandably reluctant to get involved in combat at all if they can help it. Heavy and medium artillery is unable to support only because it lacks the necessary short ranged combat value with which to do so. Note that light artillery is allowed to support and has the requisite short range value needed. In addition elephants are not allowed to support cavalry – see Elephants page 99.

Except as noted below, a unit can be moved into support during normal movement in the Command part of the turn. In cases where a group of units is ordered to charge the same enemy, units unable to complete their charge will always try and support where they can. Such units are trying to fulfil their orders in the best way possible. Supporting units are considered to be engaged in combat, and may find themselves fighting in subsequent rounds if more enemy pile into the engagement.

In the following situations units cannot deliberately join an engagement to support a fighting unit whether by means of an order, initiative move, free move or whatever. Such units can sometimes find themselves in a position to support as a result of other units' movement, for example an enemy charge against a neighbouring unit, and they are allowed to support in these situations.

Disordered Units. Disordered units are not allowed to move in the Command part of the turn in most cases, and where allowed to do so are generally obliged to retreat. In any case, even where allowed a move, disordered units cannot use it to join an engagement as a support.

Engaged Units. Units that are already engaged in combat are already fighting or supporting and can't move other than as dictated by the results of combat.

Shaken Units. A unit that is already *shaken* cannot move to join an engagement as a support. Shaken units are those that have suffered casualties equal to their Stamina value as described on pages 48.

Column, Square or Wedge. A unit that is in a *column*, *square* or *wedge* cannot move to join an engagement as a support. A column or wedge can be given an order to reform into an appropriate combat formation and then join as a support. A square is unable to change formation and move in the same turn, so it can only support if changing formation alone puts it into a supporting position.

Heavy and Medium Artillery. Heavy and medium artillery cannot join an engagement as a support. Even if they find themselves in a supporting position as a result of other movement they will not support – they lack the short ranged attacks with which to do so in any case.

Elephants supporting cavalry. Elephants are not allowed to move into support of cavalry, or to support cavalry where they find themselves in position to do so.

Scythed Chariots. Scythed chariots are something of an exceptional weapon and are covered by their own rules on page 104. Scythed chariots cannot support in hand-to-hand combat.

Note that a testudo joining an engagement either by charging or by moving into a supporting position automatically changes to a battle line. See the rules for the Testudo on page 105.

POSITION SUPPORTING UNITS

Units supporting from a flank must be positioned beside the fighting unit and aligned with its front. Alternatively, the supporting unit can be hinged at the front of the fighting unit and inclined towards the enemy along the lines shown. Either way, a fighting unit can only ever be supported by one unit to each flank and never by two.

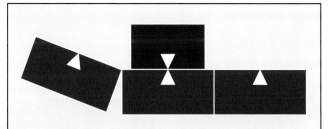

Basic positions for supporting units to the flank. Note that units do not have to be touching the enemy to support, it is their position relative to the fighting unit that counts

When arranging supports in this manner we have never found it necessary to insist on absolute precision, and we happily allow units to align into support as shown so long as at least part of the unit can reach the fighting unit's front. Thus we allow for the practicalities of play and avoid the game becoming overly enslaved to Euclid.

Units supporting from the rear are positioned behind and touching the fighting unit. At least part of the supporting unit must lie directly behind the mid-point of the fighting unit. Generally speaking only one unit can support from the rear. The exception is the *Pigs head* formation described in A Selection of Useful Rules on page 98.

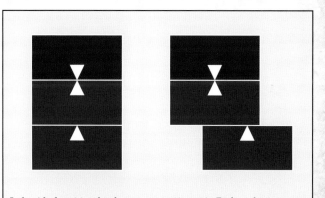

Left – ideal position for the rear supporting unit. Right – this is acceptable as the middle of the fighting unit is covered.

In many situations a unit moving into support will touch the enemy as shown below. The unit is still supporting so long as its centre-front does not touch the enemy unit, and the enemy's centre-front does not touch it.

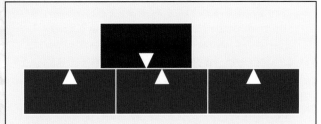

All three blue units have charged. The units either side cannot fight because their centre-front is not engaged. In both cases they move into support. We show them moving to the flanks, assuming they have the movement to reach

If a unit moves into an engagement as a support and its centre-front or leader position touches the enemy, or the leader position of the enemy touches it, then the unit joins the engagement as a fighting unit and **not** as a support. This does sometimes allow a unit to join a combat as a fighting unit where it could not otherwise charge, but note that the unit is **not** 'charging' and doesn't get 'To Hit' bonuses or any bonuses due to special rules when charging.

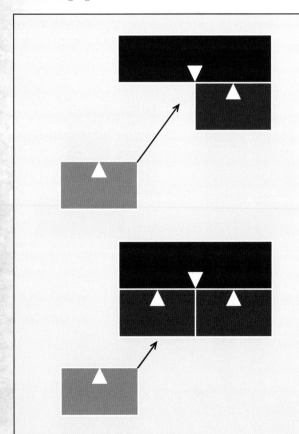

This unit cannot charge the enemy because the target does not lie in front of its leader, but it can move into support. As it does so its centre-front comes into touch with the enemy, so instead of supporting the unit will fight instead. This tends to happen more commonly with units that have very narrow frontages such as elephants.

Hittite and Canaanite chariots prepare to spring their ambush from the wooded banks of the Orontes river

It is conceivable to have a situation where a supporting unit can potentially support two fighting friends. In such cases divide the unit's attacks between both units in proportion to the degree of contact – in so far as is reasonable.

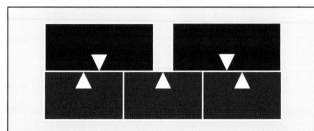

In this engagement the middle blue unit is supporting both friends. In this case it would be appropriate to simply divide the unit's support as equally as possible.

For avoidance of doubt, only one unit is allowed to support from each flank and the maximum number of units that can support a single fighting unit is three (one from each flank and one from the rear). In the rare position where two or more units are positioned so that they could both support the same flank, the one that is most directly facing the enemy will do so.

OPEN ORDER UNITS AS SUPPORTS

Units in open order cannot be supported, but they can support fighting units and this is often their primary role once battle is joined. Such units are arranged loosely to the fighting unit's flank or rear with at least one model touching the supported unit's flank or rear edge to show that the unit is supporting.

As supporting open order units are not fighting they do not close up their ranks as described for fighting units, but they are obliged to do so if brought into the engagement as a fighting unit at any point, e.g. as a result of an enemy charge during a subsequent turn. Open order units make quite good supports but are best kept away from the risk of actual fighting if possible!

SUPPORT ATTACKS

Supporting units make their attacks in a comparable way to fighting units. These attacks are always struck against the same enemy as the attacks of the unit they are supporting. If their friend is fighting more than one enemy, then flank supports strike against the closer target, and rear support attacks are divided in the same proportion as the fighting unit's own attacks in so far as possible.

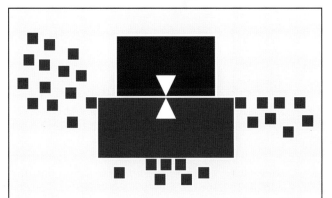

Basic positions for open order supporting units to the flank and rear. Compare with the equivalent positions for formed up units page 67. Note that the supporting units have to be touching the unit they are supporting as this makes their position clear.

MARIUS' MULES

It was the Roman general Marius who decided that, from henceforth, rather than compromise the mobility of the Roman legions with such nonsense as baggage trains and hordes of servants, the Roman legionaries would carry their own kit as they marched. With 60 pounds to carry per man the legionaries became known as Marius' Mules! Amongst this considerable weight is included a dolabra which is the Roman version of an entrenching tool – this would have seen far more use that the legionaries' arms and armour. Rations were carried for several days and included the Roman equivalent to hard tack which was called buccellatum. Some kind of water flask was essential too, and not forgetting the ubiquitous mess-tin cum cooking pot the patera. Heavier items including the legionaries' tents and millstones used to grind their corn rations were carried by real mules – usually one per contubernium of eight men.

The number of supporting attacks is the Short Range value for the unit – i.e. the value normally used for short-ranged attacks and skirmishing. This value is adjusted by formation modifiers in the same way as for units making short ranged attacks in the Ranged Attacks part of the turn (see page 44).

Roll the dice to score hits. No dice bonus 'to hit' is applied to supporting units for either charging or for winning the previous round. Other hand-to-hand combat dice modifiers apply as normal, for example if the unit is disordered or shaken. For this reason it is often necessary to roll supporting attacks separately from fighting attacks as a different roll may be required to score hits.

Hits scored by supporting units are treated exactly as any other hits. Morale saves are taken, and any hits that fail to save are converted to casualties. As a fighting unit can take casualties from enemy it is fighting **and** from three supporting units, it is entirely possible to suffer a great many casualties during large combats.

French High Command of the Hundred Years war

INCIDENTAL CONTACTS

It can happen that a unit which cannot be supported (artillery or skirmishers for example) has friends arranged alongside in what would otherwise be a supporting position. As shown here.

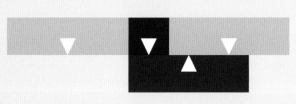

The artillery unit in the centre is flanked by infantry units on either side. Even though they are positioned to offer support these infantry are unable to do so as artillery cannot be supported.

A charge made against the artillery will inevitably touch both flanking units. Where possible the charger must move in such a way as to bring one or other of the flanking units into combat, for example as shown below.

In this case the charger has chosen to 'maximise frontage' against the unit on the right allowing it to fight in the combat. Note that the artillery unit is still fighting – as its own centre-front leader position is touching the enemy.

There will be occasions when, because of the constraints of other units or terrain, it will not be possible to bring these flanking units into the combat engagement. In these cases a unit may find it is touching an enemy but not engaged in combat. Units that are touching but neither fighting nor supporting do not take part in the engagement, but they still have a useful role to play in holding back enemy who might otherwise advance forward after combat. The example below shows such a situation.

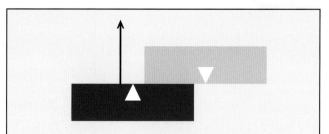

Now the artillery unit has been defeated and destroyed – leaving the charger in contact with the flanking unit even though they are not engaged in combat. The units are left 'hanging'.

See Combat Results and Incidental Contacts page 79 for rules about how to resolve these situations following combat.

COMBAT RESULTS

Combat results are worked out for each engagement as soon as all units taking part have fought, including any supports.

To work out which side wins, add up the number of casualties inflicted by each side during that round. Do not include any casualties inflicted by closing or traversing shots prior to the round of combat itself. The side that has inflicted the most casualties is victorious and the other side has been defeated. If both sides suffer the same number of casualties then there is no clear winner or loser and the result is a draw.

The fighting unit that has been defeated may be destroyed outright. Such units are described as **shattered**. Otherwise it is obliged to take a **break test** to determine whether it breaks and is destroyed, if it gives ground, or if it holds its ground undaunted.

REALLOCATING CASUALTIES

As soon as you have worked out which side has won make a note of the difference in the number of casualties scored by each side that round. For example, if one side scores 4 casualties on the enemy who scores 7 casualties in return, then the enemy have won the combat by 3. This value affects the result of the subsequent break test so it is important to establish this first before doing anything else.

Once you have worked out which side has won and by how much, identify any fighting units that are **shattered** and remove them immediately. Shattered units are those that have lost the combat and sustained a total of at least double their Stamina value number of casualties. Such units are destroyed without recourse to a break test. Note that only fighting units that are defeated can be shattered, not units that win or draw a combat.

Once you have removed shattered units, take any excess casualties inflicted on fighting units from both sides and redistribute them amongst their supporting units. Don't forget to redistribute excess casualties from shattered units; these casualties must still be redistributed amongst the shattered unit's supports. Excess casualties are those in excess of the unit's Stamina value, so a unit with a Stamina of 6 and which has a total of 8 casualties has 2 excess. Excess casualties are distributed amongst each fighting unit's supports as equally as possible, starting with supporting units that are touching the enemy; otherwise the owning player can choose which units will suffer odd casualties. If a defeated unit has no supports any excess casualties are simply removed. Where a supporting unit already has its maximum number of casualties, any additional casualties accrued to it are also removed. Supporting units cannot be shattered as a result of this redistribution of casualties. The most number of casualties a unit can have once reallocation is complete is its Stamina value.

BREAK TESTS

Once an engagement has been fought, results worked out and any casualties reallocated to supports as necessary, the side that has been defeated must take a **break test** for each surviving unit that is fighting the enemy. This won't be necessary if a unit has been *shattered*, as shattered units are destroyed automatically as already explained. The rules for break tests are given in the following section on page 72.

Note that a separate break test is taken for each fighting unit in the engagement, so it is possible for one unit to hold its ground whilst another breaks, for example. Only fighting units test initially. Supporting units don't automatically need to take a break test when their side loses a combat. Supports only have to test if the unit they are supporting is *shattered* or if the unit they are supporting *breaks* as a result of its own break test

In the case of a draw, fighting units from either side must take a break test if they are already shaken. This can result in opposing units both giving ground or even breaking and being destroyed in some cases. Supporting units are not required to test in a drawn combat, even if they are shaken, but will have to test subsequently if the unit they were supporting breaks in the same way as for defeated units.

END OF COMBAT

Once a fight has been resolved units are often left in place facing each other, in which case the combat engagement continues into the following turn. Few engagements will be resolved in one round of fighting, especially between equally matched close fighting infantry.

Sometimes the losing side will give ground, moving away from the enemy, in which case the victors have a choice of whether to follow them up and continue the engagement. This is covered in the section on Break Tests, along with the rules for moves resulting from combat.

BREAK TESTS

A break test is taken to determine how a unit reacts in perilous circumstances. Most commonly, tests are required when defeated in hand-to-hand fighting. Troops will also be called upon to take a break test if they are shaken by ranged attacks, and in other situations as noted below. A unit that fails a break test by a sufficient margin is removed from the game; its warriors turn tail and flee, dispersing beyond recall or falling beneath the blades of their enemies. This is often how units are defeated and destroyed in our game, so it is an important part of play as can readily be imagined. Break tests don't always result in a unit's destruction. Sometimes units will be obliged to retreat, they might become disordered, or they could simply hold their ground.

There are two different *break test tables*. One is used for ranged combat and the other for hand-to-hand combat. Tests are required in the following situations as described in the relevant sections of the rules.

Test in the Ranged Attacks part of the turn
- If a unit is *shaken* by ranged attacks.
- If a unit that is already *shaken* suffers casualties from ranged attacks.
- On the roll of a 6 'to hit' by ranged attacks requiring better than 6 to hit.
- On two rolls of 6 'to hit' by ranged attacks requiring 6 to hit.

A test is also required on account of ranged attacks in other parts of the turn
- If a unit is shaken by closing and/or traversing shots.
- On the roll of a 6 'to hit' against units where closing shots/traversing shots require better than 6 to hit.
- On two rolls of 6 'to hit' against units where closing shots/traversing shots require 6 to hit.

Test in the Hand-to-Hand Combat part of the turn
- If a fighting unit is defeated in hand-to-hand combat.
- If a fighting unit that is shaken draws a hand-to-hand combat.
- If a unit is supporting a fighting unit that breaks or is shattered.

Tests can also be taken on either table at the discretion of the umpire or the agreement of the players as seems reasonable at the time. Thus we can take account of otherwise extraordinary events should we wish, such as the proximity of stampeding elephants, the occurrence of earthquakes, the occasional solar eclipse and so on. Think of this as divine intervention on the part of the umpire.

TEST CATEGORIES

There are three different categories for troop types shown on the break tables. These are:

Infantry – this category covers all infantry except for skirmishers, and it also includes artillery crew.

Cavalry – this covers mounted troops of all kinds namely cavalry, camels, chariots and elephants.

Skirmishers – which covers infantry skirmishers. It also includes baggage, and – where necessary – civilians.

TESTS FROM RANGED ATTACKS

Only one test is taken during any part of the turn. So if an enemy makes ranged attacks by two, three or more units against the same target only one test is required. Even where several 6's are rolled, or where 6's are combined with a unit becoming shaken, only one test is needed. It is necessary to wait until all ranged attacks against a unit are complete, as casualties inflicted in excess of the target's Stamina value will affect the result.

To take the test, roll two dice and add the scores together to get a result between 2 and 12. If the unit is shaken when the test is taken and has also suffered casualties in excess of its Stamina value, then **deduct the number of excess casualties** from the result. For example, a unit with Stamina of 6 and 8 casualties is shaken with an excess of 2; therefore subtract 2 from the dice roll.

BREAK TESTS FROM RANGED ATTACKS

10+	Infantry	Hold your ground without penalty
	Cavalry	Hold your ground without penalty
	Skirmishers	Hold your ground without penalty
9	Infantry	Hold your ground without penalty
	Cavalry	Hold your ground without penalty
	Skirmishers	Retreat in good order
8	Infantry	Hold your ground without penalty
	Cavalry	Hold your ground without penalty
	Skirmishers	Retreat disordered
7	Infantry	Hold your ground without penalty
	Cavalry	Retreat in good order
	Skirmishers	Retreat disordered
6	Infantry	Hold your ground disordered *or* Retreat in good order
	Cavalry	Retreat disordered
	Skirmishers	Retreat disordered
5	Infantry	Hold your ground disordered *or* Retreat in good order
	Cavalry	Retreat disordered
	Skirmishers	Break if shaken *otherwise* Retreat disordered
4	Infantry	Retreat disordered
	Cavalry	Break if shaken *otherwise* Retreat disordered
	Skirmishers	Break if the unit has suffered any casualties *otherwise* Retreat disordered
3	Infantry	Break if shaken *otherwise* Retreat disordered
	Cavalry	Break if shaken *otherwise* Retreat disordered
	Skirmishers	Break
2 or less	Infantry	Break if unit has suffered any casualties *otherwise* Retreat disordered
	Cavalry	Break if unit has suffered any casualties *otherwise* Retreat disordered
	Skirmishers	Break

RANGED ATTACK TEST RESULTS

Hold your ground without penalty. The unit has passed the test, remains where it is, and suffers no penalties. If the unit is testing on account of closing or traversing shots during a charge, then this result does not stop it charging home successfully.

Retreat in good order. The unit makes one move in so far as it can away from the enemy. Move the unit into the quarter opposite the enemy: for example, if attackers lie to the front the unit moves to its rear quarter, whilst continuing to face its opponents. If the unit is unable to comply because there are friends, enemies, combat engagements or terrain that prevent it doing so, then the unit complies as far as it can and becomes disordered. If the unit is testing on account of closing or traversing shots, then it retreats away from the engagement without fighting.

Retreat disordered. This is the same result as *Retreat in good order* except that the unit becomes disordered at the end of its move regardless of circumstances.

Hold your ground disordered. The unit stays where it is and becomes disordered. If the unit is testing on account of closing or traversing shots during a charge, then the unit charges home successfully and fights close combat disordered.

Break if shaken. If the unit is shaken it breaks and is removed from the table as destroyed.

Break if the unit has suffered any casualties. If the unit has already suffered any casualties it breaks and is removed from the table as destroyed.

Break. Break! The unit is removed from the table as destroyed.

DISORDER

Disorder often results from a break test, or from a test for moving through or out of the way of other units.

Disorder also occurs automatically in some situations, notably where formed infantry are countercharged by cavalry or chariots, and where the movement of retreating units is blocked or compromised as noted under Retreats on page 75.

Disorder represents a unit losing its cohesion either due to panic or, more likely, to its ranks becoming disorganised or thrown into disarray. A disordered unit suffers various penalties, the most significant of which is that it is not allowed to receive orders or use its initiative in the Command part of the turn. See Disordered Units and Orders on page 32.

Note that disordered units can still move during the Ranged Attacks and Hand-to-Hand Combat parts of the turn, and are often obliged to do so due to break test results.

Units cannot recover from disorder whilst they remain engaged in combat, whether they are fighting or supports. Otherwise, units usually recover from disorder at the end of their own turn. Once the player's turn is otherwise finished he removes all outstanding disorder markers from units not engaged in combat and his turn is then complete. Some special rules do affect a unit's ability to recover from disorder for better or worse. See A Selection of Useful Rules page 98.

Disorder can also result from special rules in some cases. For example, cavalry charging the front of infantry armed with long spears risk becoming disordered (see page 101). As these rules are both optional and mutable there is little point in listing them all, so refer to A Selection of Useful Rules for more details.

Players should bear in mind that where a game is run by an umpire it is entirely feasible to allow for discretionary tests for disorder where he feels it appropriate to do so. Like the thunderbolts of Jove such proclamations should fall upon the players as judgements from heaven! We leave such matters to the participants to arrange to their liking, and as seems the most appropriate for the game played.

RETREATS

It is worth saying a little more about how retreats work as units are often obliged to retreat in the face of enemy shooting. Wherever possible, a retreating unit makes a single move away from the closest enemy that attacked it. However, if the players or umpire agree that the balance of threat lies in another direction, the unit retreats away from that instead. The retreating unit makes one move into the quarter opposite to the closest attacker/greatest threat, in the same way as a move made in the Command part of the turn. If the retreating unit is already facing an enemy unit within 12" then it must continue to face the same enemy (see the Proximity rule page 34).

If a unit cannot move exactly into the quarter opposite the closest attacker/greatest threat, then it must attempt to do so in so far as it can. If a friendly unit blocks its path it will move through it, and will make two or three moves where necessary to clear the position of other unit/s. If presented with terrain it cannot enter, enemy units, units from either side engaged in combat, or other insoluble impediments to movement, the retreating unit will move as far as it can. A retreating unit that is obliged to make additional moves to clear the position of friends is automatically disordered once it has done so. Units moved through risk becoming disordered in the usual way (see page 35). A retreating unit that cannot make its full move because of impenetrable terrain or enemy units is also disordered once it has moved as far as it can.

TESTS FROM HAND-TO-HAND COMBAT

Tests for hand-to-hand combat are a little more complex than those for ranged attacks comprising tests for units that are fighting following defeat or a draw, and tests for units supporting friends who break or become shattered.

Fighting units must test if they are defeated in combat. Such units will have been beaten by a difference of one, two, three or more casualties as described in the section on hand-to-hand combat results (page 70). This difference is deducted from the unit's test score, so the greater the difference in casualties the worse the outcome. Note that there is no additional penalty for shaken units that have taken excess casualties as there is for ranged attacks. In break tests for hand-to-hand fighting it is only the **difference in casualties** that matters.

Test for the unit by rolling two dice and adding the scores to get a result between 2 and 12. Then deduct the difference in casualties inflicted by both sides during the combat. For example, if the winning side inflicts 5 casualties and the loser inflicts 2 the difference is 3, so deduct 3 from the dice total. Refer to the chart below for the result.

Units that are fighting must also test if the combat is a draw and the unit is shaken. As it is possible for both sides to be shaken it is also possible that both will have to test. It doesn't matter which side tests first in such a case.

If a unit breaks or is shattered, then all units supporting it must take a break test. Only one test is required for a unit during any turn, even where it is supporting two friends who break – the unit's first test result will stand for both. Deduct

BREAK TESTS FROM HAND-TO-HAND FIGHTING		
10 or more	Infantry	Hold your ground without penalty
	Cavalry	Hold your ground without penalty
	Skirmishers	Hold your ground without penalty
9	Infantry	Hold your ground without penalty
	Cavalry	Give ground in good order, together with supports
	Skirmishers	Give ground disordered
8	Infantry	Hold your ground without penalty
	Cavalry	Give ground in good order together with supports
	Skirmishers	Break if shaken *otherwise* Give ground disordered
7	Infantry	Give ground in good order, together with supports
	Cavalry	Give ground disordered, together with supports
	Skirmishers	Break
6	Infantry	Give ground in good order, together with supports
	Cavalry	Give ground disordered, together with supports
	Skirmishers	Break
5	Infantry	Give ground disordered, together with supports
	Cavalry	Break if shaken *otherwise* Give ground, together with supports – all disordered
	Skirmishers	Break
4	Infantry	Break if shaken *otherwise* Give ground, together with supports – all disordered
	Cavalry	Break if shaken *otherwise* Give ground, together with supports – all disordered
	Skirmishers	Break
3	Infantry	Break if shaken *otherwise* Give ground, together with supports – all disordered
	Cavalry	Break
	Skirmishers	Break
2 or less	Infantry	Break
	Cavalry	Break
	Skirmishers	Break

THE MURDEROUS GLADIUS!

The gladius was a proficient weapon in the hands of a determined warrior whether used to stab or cut at the enemy. The Romans placed great store in training soldiers to use these swords to deadly effect, with emphasis on the stabbing blow. This is what Vegetius has to say on the matter – he was writing in the 4th century AD but referring to traditional Roman fighting methods.

'A stroke with the edges, though made with ever so much force, seldom kills, ... On the contrary, a stab, though it penetrates but two inches, is generally fatal. ... the body is covered while a thrust is given, and the adversary receives the point before he sees the sword. This was the method of fighting principally used by the Romans...'

Vegetius De Re Militari

When the Romans expanded eastwards they came into conflict with the Macedonians, whose troops were equipped as phalangites with long pikes and light swords. Livy describes how the Greeks were horrified by the ghastly wounds inflicted by the heavy-bladed Roman gladius.

'Accordingly, those who, being always accustomed to fight with Greeks and Illyrians, had only seen wounds made with javelins and arrows, seldom even by lances, came to behold bodies dismembered by the Spanish sword, some with their arms lopped off, with the shoulder or the neck entirely cut through, heads severed from the trunk, and the bowels laid open, with other frightful exhibitions of wounds: they therefore perceived, with horror, against what weapons and what men they were to fight. Even the king himself was seized with apprehensions, having never yet engaged the Romans in a regular battle.'

Livy XXXI 34

the difference in casualties suffered during the combat from the dice roll as before. Refer to the table on page 75 and read off the result for the troop type under test.

HAND-TO-HAND COMBAT TEST RESULTS

Hold your ground without penalty. The unit has passed the test, remains where it is, and suffers no penalties. Thank Jove! However, note the exception for fighting against troops who enjoy an uphill advantage.

Give ground in good order, together with supports. The unit moves 6" directly away from the enemy it is fighting. Any supporting units also move back up to 6" whilst remaining in supporting positions in so far as they can. See *Give Ground* below for more about these moves.

Give ground disordered, together with supports. This is the same as described above for 'Give ground in good order, together with supports' except that the unit also becomes disordered. Note that only the fighting unit is disordered, supporting units retain good order assuming they had it to start with.

Give ground, together with supports – all disordered. This is the same as described above for 'Give ground in good order, together with supports' except that the unit and all of its supports are disordered.

Break if shaken. If the unit is shaken it breaks and is removed from the table as destroyed. Supporting units must then each take a separate break test.

Break. Break! The unit is removed from the table as destroyed. Supporting units must then each take a separate break test.

GIVE GROUND

A unit giving ground is moved 6" directly away from the enemy unit it is fighting. In most cases this will be directly backwards. It doesn't matter how fast the unit normally moves, all units give ground 6". The exceptions are artillery and baggage units, which do not give ground but are destroyed instead (see below).

If a unit is fighting to its own flank or rear it gives ground in the opposite direction. Just slide the unit along in whatever direction is required without altering the unit's formation or facing. If fighting to the front and a flank at the same time, then consider the weight of attacks from each foe

Unwelcome visitors trouble a lakeside beauty spot – settlements like this were a feature of the European Bronze Age

and move the unit at what seems a reasonable compromise angle. If a unit is fighting enemy in opposite directions – front and rear for example – then it can't give ground and is destroyed.

Supporting units must also give ground when the unit they are supporting does so. They are moved up to 6" and must try to remain in the same relative position so they can continue to support in the next round of combat.

If a defeated fighting unit is unable to give ground because of intervening enemy, engaged troops, friends who do not move out of the way, or impassable terrain then it breaks and is destroyed. If supporting units are unable to give ground for the same reasons, they will attempt to do so to the best of their ability but are otherwise not penalised. Supporting units that are unable to maintain a supporting position are allowed to 'drop out' of the engagement if that is their only option.

Friendly non-disordered and non-engaged units in the path of troops giving ground can move out of the way by up to one normal move. Disordered units and units engaged in combat cannot move out of the way. The unit giving ground automatically becomes disordered if it is not already disordered, and every unit moved to make room also becomes disordered on a dice roll of 1, 2 or 3. If friends are not able, or are unwilling, to move to make room for a fighting unit that is giving ground then the fighting unit is broken and destroyed just as if surrounded by enemy. This will trigger further break tests for supports as if the unit had been destroyed in combat.

THE UPHILL ADVANTAGE

A fighting unit that is uphill of its enemy, and which has not charged/countercharged this turn, nor moved following the previous round of the same engagement, receives a +1 'to hit' to account for its uphill advantage. This bonus is included in the 'To Hit' dice roll modifiers for Hand-to-Hand Combat on page 64. Basically – the bonus applies so long as the unit is uphill of its enemy and so long as it remains stationary. The bonus is lost if the unit is defeated and gives ground, or if the unit is victorious and follows up its enemy. Whilst a unit benefits from the bonus it is said to have an uphill advantage.

If troops are engaged against enemy with an uphill advantage then any Hand-to-Hand Combat break test result of 'Hold your ground' is treated as 'Give ground in good order together with supports.' The best result that such troops can get is therefore to give ground. Bear in mind that if their enemy gives ground and a unit with the uphill advantage follows up, then it will have moved and therefore loses the uphill advantage during the following round.

Note that the bonus for uphill advantage and the bonus for charging/winning the previous round are mutually exclusive. If a unit with the uphill advantage wins the engagement its enemy will always give ground and either the combat ends or the victors follow-up. They gain the bonus for winning the combat but lose the uphill advantage. However, so long as they remain uphill it is possible for a unit to regain the uphill advantage in subsequent rounds if combat is drawn or if a defeated unit holds its ground.

ARTILLERY AND BAGGAGE GIVING GROUND

Artillery and baggage units that are obliged to give ground in combat are destroyed instead. This applies to units that are fighting and to supporting units that are obliged to give ground together with fighting units. This takes into account the immobility of such units and avoids the unwelcome sight of siege engines pushing to-and- fro in combat. We humanely assume crews abandon their machines to the enemy and flee for their lives.

SUPPORTING UNITS

Following combat, supporting units will do whatever the unit they are supporting does in principle. So, if a fighting unit gives ground, supports must also give ground whilst continuing to support where possible. If a victorious fighting unit moves forward to maintain contact with retreating enemy, then supports must also press forward and continue to support where they can. Victorious supports will always attempt to continue to support where they can, and if doing so brings them into a fighting position then this is allowed. If a fighting unit breaks then its supporting units do not automatically break as well, each must take a break test and abide by the result.

Where a unit is dividing support between fighting units to either flank, then it follows the first unit tested and ignores the second unit. On the whole this is considered the most practical way of dealing with such a situation. The umpire or players may consider it appropriate to follow one unit rather than another in some circumstances; this is up to those concerned.

MOVES BY VICTORIOUS UNITS

If neither side moves or breaks following combat, units remain in place and continue to fight in the following round. It is quite likely that other units may join the engagement over the following turn, and this can happen over several turns causing a fight to swing one way and then the other.

If all of the enemy in contact with a victorious fighting unit **give ground** or are **destroyed** then the victors are allowed to make a move. They do not have to do so. They can remain where they are if preferred. If they do move then the victors are bound by the proximity rule assuming there are enemy within 12" to their front. See page 34.

A move can take a unit forward to maintain contact with the enemy who has given ground, thereby continuing the combat into the following round. When following up in this way move the victors so they contact with as much frontage as possible in the same fashion as a charge – see Position Chargers on page 56.

Units that press forward to maintain contact with their enemy count the +1 'to hit' bonus for winning the combat in the next round of fighting. Note that a victorious unit can do this even if disordered, as disorder does not affect moves resulting from break tests or hand-to-hand fighting (see Disorder page 74).

A victorious unit can move in any other way normally allowed, but note that if facing their enemy during the combat the proximity rule will dictate they remain facing the same enemy as they move. This allows a unit to reposition itself to some extent whilst withdrawing from hand-to-hand combat, and it permits the unit to fall back if desired.

SWEEPING ADVANCE

If all the enemy fighting a victorious unit are destroyed, and no other enemies remain in contact to their front, the victors may be allowed to make a sweeping advance as an alternative to a single ordinary move as explained above. A unit can only make a sweeping advance if it is neither shaken nor disordered. However, a unit making a sweeping advance must roll a dice once it has done so, and becomes disordered on a roll of 4, 5 or 6.

When making a sweeping advance the proximity rule is likely to apply. This will constrain the move somewhat. A sweeping advance is up to two normal moves into the unit's front quarter. If a suitable target presents itself a sweeping advance can be used to charge against another enemy, in which case it is a sweeping charge. Declare the charge before moving the unit as you would for a charge order in the Command part of the turn. Often a target will be a unit previously offering rear or side support to a destroyed fighting unit.

A sweeping charge can result in a unit rejoining the same engagement, in which case the combat continues in the following round and the unit making the sweeping advance counts as charging in that round. This is the most common situation, where a victorious unit plunges straight into an enemy previously supporting the unit that has been destroyed.

A sweeping charge can also potentially enable a unit to charge into a previously unengaged unit, for example a fresh enemy positioned a little distance behind the enemy that has been destroyed. In this case the charge initiates a new engagement and this is worked out immediately. This means that the unit making the sweeping advance will fight twice during the round. Resolve the combat right away before dealing with any other fighting. If the victorious charging unit is fortunate enough to destroy this second enemy then it may not make a further sweeping advance. Only one sweeping advance is allowed in any round.

A sweeping charge can also potentially enable a unit to charge into another engagement that either has or hasn't already been fought. If the engagement has already been fought then the charger joins the engagement and fights in the following round and counts as charging in that round. If the engagement has not already been fought then the charger joins the engagement and fights this round, and counts as charging.

Because a sweeping charge is a charge, enemy units are allowed to make a response in the same way as when charged in the Command part of the turn. Similarly, units with a long ranged attack may be entitled to make closing shots, whilst adjacent units are allowed to make traversing

shots where they can. Note that these shots can potentially lead to a break test.

The sweeping charge can be a decisive moment in a combat, as it allows a victorious unit to fold into the flank of a long battle line and potentially 'roll up' several units one after the other. This tactic can be countered by a second line of troops – or careful placement of reserves – so watch out for it and try not to be caught out.

COMBAT RESULTS AND INCIDENTAL CONTACTS

It can happen that a unit is positioned alongside a fighting unit and touching the enemy, but is unable to support because the fighting unit is of a type that cannot be supported (such as skirmishers). Such units are described as incidental contacts.

Units positioned as incidental contacts will block further moves by enemy after combat is complete. For example, a victorious enemy will be unable to follow up a unit giving ground because it cannot move through the incidental contact.

In situations such as that shown below, where the combat engagement ends but units are left in incidental contact, then units that were engaged must move 6" back just like units giving ground. They have to do this even if they won or drew the combat.

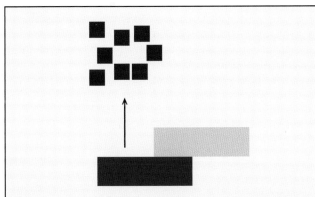

This skirmisher unit has lost the combat and given ground – leaving the enemy in contact with the flanking unit even though it is not engaged in combat. The victorious unit cannot follow up back into touch with the skirmishers because the flanking unit is blocking its move.

There will be occasions when units are blocked to a trivial degree, or where a block results purely from inconsequential differences in frontage, and in such cases we would defer to the umpire's judgement rather than be pernickety about things. The idea behind blocks is simply to stop players taking advantage of small, weak and vulnerable units to break through an otherwise solid battle line.

Note that is also possible for comparable situations to occur because units have been placed in supporting positions that are of a type not actually allowed to support: notably baggage and medium or heavy artillery units. It seems wrong that incidental contacts of these kinds should block an enemy's follow-up, so we usually consider such units to

be destroyed if they would otherwise stop a victorious enemy making a follow-up or sweeping advance. A scenario, circumstance or umpire may suggest otherwise – but as a general rule it is best to remove such units as casualties.

UNITS IN OPEN ORDER

If a unit in open order has closed up its ranks to fight in combat, then it automatically disperses into open order again if it is no longer fighting once the engagement is complete. This prevents open order units being left in a 'closed up' fighting position once they are no longer engaged. The player rearranges the models into open order around the centre of the unit as best as can be managed.

SQUARES

Units in square formation ignore all break test results of 'Retreat or give ground'. They treat all such results as 'Hold your ground' instead. This does not affect results of Disorder, so a unit that rolls a result of 'Gives ground disordered' will 'Hold your ground disordered' instead. This makes squares especially resilient as a result of Break is needed to destroy them.

UNITS IN BUILDINGS

Units in buildings are treated the same way as units in squares and ignore all break test results of 'Retreat' or 'Gives ground'. They treat all such results as 'Hold your ground' instead. As with squares this does not affect results of Disorder, so a unit that rolls a result of 'Give ground disordered' will 'Hold your ground disordered' instead.

OCCUPYING BUILDINGS

Where a combat takes place for possession of a fortified position, building or something along those lines, the victors can always move into the position and occupy it once the enemy have been broken and destroyed. This is just the equivalent to taking a move after combat. The unit moves into the building and is positioned within it. If a victor does this then supporting units are under no obligation to maintain support and can make a single move forward or back instead.

COMMANDERS

In ancient times men with aspirations to rule were obliged to lead from the front – and all too frequently they died there too! Politics was a serious business in those days. This wasn't just true of the chieftains and officers in charge of individual bands of warriors – even the highest in the land were looked upon to do their part. The loyalty of the army was often intensely personal, and the death of the overall commander could result in troops abandoning the battle or suing for peace. Naturally, we shall demand that our leaders live up to the expectations of their troops and peers – be quite sure that our model commanders and generals will be seeing their fair share of action.

COMMANDER MODELS

As discussed already each commander is represented by a suitably sized base bearing the great man plus supernumeraries and/or scenic elements as deemed appropriate. We do not feel the need to specify dimensions for bases when it comes to commanders: we only require that they be a convenient size and shape for purposes of play. Measurements are always taken from the commander's head – or centre of the base if preferred – so the size of the base isn't critical to the game.

Commanders can be on foot or mounted – as deemed most realistic for the force they lead – and they can ride elephants or chariots if their actual counterparts did so. Elephants and chariots were a mark of status in some armies, and we would obviously ask our commanders to come up to scratch as regards their personal transport. We will consider suitable rules for individuals so mounted later; for now we shall simply say that it makes no difference how a commander is mounted when it comes to issuing orders. Commanders can issue orders just as well whether on foot, astride a horse, stood in a chariot, atop an elephant, riding a donkey or taking a bath.

Players will need a commander model to lead each separate division in the army. Ideally, players should have a few reserve commanders ready and waiting to take their place should the originals be killed. Where commanders ride chariots or elephants it is a good idea to have a few reserve commander models on foot or riding horses.

RESERVE COMMANDERS

Commanders often get killed in action, and when this happens we assume the most senior of the deceased's subordinates immediately takes over. The slain commander model is removed and a reserve commander is placed within 12" of any unit in the same division. He can be placed with a unit if you wish, even a unit that is already fighting a combat. We assume the reserve commander was previously one of the commander's close companions and subsumed within his base; or perhaps he was one of a network of subordinates not otherwise represented in the game. Either way, the dead commander is removed as a casualty and the reserve commander takes his place at the head of his division.

Reserve commanders have a leadership rating **one less** than their predecessor. So, if the original commander has the average rating of 8, then his replacement has a rating of 7.

If a reserve commander is slain then the next in line takes over in the same way, and so on. Fear not – there is no shortage of budding officer material amongst our armies. The only problem is that each replacement has a leadership rating one less than his predecessor, to a minimum value of 5. We sometimes find it convenient to set the minimum value higher than this – at 6 or even 7 – especially where an army might reasonably be assumed to have a number of capable officers and an organised structure. This is up to the participants.

If a commander rides an elephant or chariot then we require that his replacement should be on foot or mounted on a horse. This isn't an absolute necessity by any means; but we find the sight of elephants and chariots popping onto the battlefield a little too discomposing for our tastes!

THE GENERAL

The player must nominate one of his commanders to be the general. The general is the overall leader of the army, but otherwise takes the role of an ordinary commander and leads one of the divisions. The general usually has the same leadership rating as his fellows – although we sometimes favour him with a value one higher where merited. To start with we'd recommend a leadership rating of 8 throughout until players have a good grasp of how the rules work.

The general is also entitled to a special re-roll bonus. This allows the player to re-roll any order test result rolled by the general. It does not matter whether the result is passed or failed or even if a blunder is scored, the player is allowed to re-roll the general's dice once in the Command part of each of his turns. When the dice are re-rolled in this way the re-rolled score stands even if the result is worse than the original score or if it is a blunder. Should the general fall casualty then his re-roll is lost as well, his successor lacking the great man's talents.

The use of the general's re-roll is considered entirely optional and players who prefer to do without can certainly do so. It is possible to conjure other special abilities to reflect the individual skills and foibles of generals – but such things are inevitably bound to specific scenarios and are best left to umpires to devise according to need.

FOLLOW ME!

Commanders are allowed to join a unit from their own division and lead it personally. This is called a follow me! order. It is a good idea to forego the use of these orders until you have a good idea of how the game works, as they introduce additional complexity and detail into the command system.

If a commander is within 12" of a unit from his own division then he can join it and lead it personally by issuing a follow me! order. Once a commander has given a follow me! order then, regardless of whether he is successful or otherwise, he cannot give any more orders that turn. Attempting a follow me! order always ends a commander's orders for the turn. As with any order a commander can only give a follow me! order to a unit from his own division.

To issue a follow me! order the commander nominates the unit he intends to lead, declares that he wants the unit to follow me! and makes the usual test to see if the order is obeyed. If the order is issued successfully the commander is immediately placed with the unit, and the unit, together with the commander, can make up to three moves.

There is no need to declare what the unit is doing before the order is issued, the unit simply makes three moves as the player wishes. The unit can change formation and/or charge as part of its move even though no previous declaration has been made. The player should still state what he is doing before he moves for the sake of clarity and also because the enemy may be allowed a response such as an evade, countercharge or closing shots in some cases.

Once the unit has moved the commander remains with it. He has joined the unit and cannot move further that turn. Note that the follow me! order only lasts for a single turn just like any other order, and if the same commander wishes the same unit to follow him in the subsequent turn a new follow me! order must be given.

If a commander fails to give his follow me! order then the unit receives no order and will be unable to move. Bear in mind that units entitled to a free move will not be able to move at all if they fail a follow me! order because they have no instructions to follow. See Free Moves page 31.

RALLY!

Rally! Is another kind of special order and it is given in a similar way to the follow me! order. A rally! order allows a unit to recover its stamina, reducing the number of casualty markers it has suffered. As with the follow me! order we recommend that players ignore the Rally! order until they have a good grasp of the game mechanics.

If a commander is within 12" of a unit from his division that has suffered two or more casualties then he can issue a rally! order. Once a commander has given a rally! order then, regardless of whether he is successful or otherwise, he cannot give any more orders that turn. Attempting a rally! order always ends a commander's orders for the turn. As with any other order a commander can only give a rally! order to a unit from his own division.

To issue a rally! order the commander nominates the unit he wishes to rally and makes the usual test to see if the order is obeyed. If the order is successful the commander is placed with the unit and one casualty marker is removed from the unit's total.

Once a unit has rallied the commander remains with it. He has joined the unit and cannot move further that turn.

If a commander fails to give his rally! order then the unit receives no orders and will be unable to move.

JOINING HAND-TO-HAND COMBAT

A commander who has not already joined a unit can join any unit in his division if it is fighting hand-to-hand combat within 12". He can do so at any time prior to the combat being worked out and even during the opposing player's turn. Note that he can only join a unit in this way if it is **fighting** and not a unit that is merely supporting, although he can join a supporting unit in his own turn by moving in the normal way if the player wishes.

Once a commander joins a unit that is engaged in combat he is obliged to remain with it whilst the unit is engaged. If the unit is *broken or shattered* (i.e. destroyed) then the commander may be wounded or slain as noted below.

Shoddy workmanship Marcus! This milefort along Hadrian's Wall is supposed to stand for two thousand years you know!

RISK TO COMMANDERS

If a commander is moved over by an enemy unit, then he must immediately join a friendly unit within one move's distance. If he is unable to do so he is captured and removed from the battle, counting as a casualty. Note that only units of troops can capture an enemy commander by moving over him and not enemy commanders. Opposing commanders can move over or through each other without penalty. As

commanders can move up to 24" at a time this isn't likely to happen too often.

If a commander has joined a unit that is *broken* or *shattered* then roll a dice to determine his fate. On a score of 1 or 2 the Commander is slain outright, on a roll of a 4 or 5 he is wounded as described below, on a roll of 5 or 6 he is unharmed. Whether wounded or unharmed he can make an immediate move to join a unit from his division, and if unable to do so is captured by the enemy and considered a casualty.

Commanders also risk being slain or wounded if they fight hand-to-hand combat or if they are with units that are shaken by ranged attack as described below.

RISK FROM RANGED ATTACKS

If a commander has joined a unit he risks being wounded or killed if that unit is *shaken* by ranged attacks, or if it is already *shaken* and suffers further casualties from ranged attacks. Where this is the case, the opposing player rolls two dice once all ranged attacks have been worked out and the commander is hit on a roll of 12. To determine his fate roll a dice, on a score of 1, 2 or 3 the Commander is slain outright, on a roll of a 4, 5 or 6 he is wounded as described on page 83.

RISK FROM HAND-TO-HAND COMBAT

If a commander is with a fighting unit then he risks being wounded or slain regardless of whether the unit wins or loses the combat. The chance of the commander being slain depends upon how ferociously he throws himself forward at the head of his troops. We represent this by the number of attacks he adds to the unit as described under Fighting Values of Commanders below.

Once both sides have fought and before taking a break test for the loser, the opposing player rolls two dice to determine if he has hit his opponent's commander. On the roll of 12 the commander is hit. The opposing side adds +1 to his unit's result score in combat just as if he had inflicted an extra casualty.

If the commander has added more than one attack to his unit in the combat round then the chance of being hit is increased. Add +1 to the risk dice roll for each extra attack used. So, if a commander fights with two attacks he is hit on a roll of 11 or 12, if he fights with three attacks he is hit on a roll of 10, 11 or 12 and so on.

Once a commander is hit roll a dice to see what has happened to him, on a score of 1, 2 or 3 the commander is slain outright, on a roll of a 4, 5 or 6 he is wounded as described below. Note that he still counts +1 to the other side's combat result regardless of whether he is killed or wounded.

FIGHTING VALUES OF COMMANDERS

Commanders have a number of attacks reflecting their personal valour and their ability to inspire the efforts of their men. Generals usually have three attacks and other commanders two. Any or all of a commander's attacks can be added to the total number of attacks made by a fighting unit he has joined and are treated as struck by the unit with any associated bonuses or penalties to the dice rolls. The commander's attacks simply boost those of the unit he has joined.

Reserve commanders have a maximum fighting value of 1, thus the loss of a division's commander will reduce its fighting power as well as its leadership. Indeed, any commanders can be set a lower or higher maximum value if it is felt appropriate to do so. The likes of Alexander the Great might justly scoff at a mere 3 attacks. If he isn't worth 4, 5 or even 6 I don't know who is! Of course, the greater the number of attacks used in a fight the greater the risk of the commander being wounded or slain.

Regardless of what fighting value you care to assign to a commander, he is never allowed to enhance a unit's attacks by more than double. So, a unit with only one attack can only benefit by one further attack from a commander, for example.

A commander can only join a unit from his own division, so in normal situations it is only possible for a single commander to join a unit. However, just to be doubly sure, we should emphasise that only one commander can fight with a unit at any time.

THE GENERAL AS COMMANDER-IN-CHIEF

An alternative way of fielding generals is to have a commander for each division and a separate general model as a commander-in-chief. This can be a useful way of representing the general's role, especially in very large games where it allows the general to sit back and leave the work to his subordinates.

The commander-in-chief can only give orders to troops by moving into touch with another commander and taking over his division. This allows the commander-in-chief to move from one division to another, spreading his special talents where needed. He can only join with one commander at once, so he will only be able to take over a single division in any turn. The commander he has joined is unable to issue orders whilst accompanied by the commander-in-chief.

A commander-in-chief can only join a unit in company with the commander he has joined, in which case the player can use the higher of the two's fighting value. Where commanders risk being slain or wounded in this situation, then randomise between them to find out which is affected.

WOUNDED COMMANDERS

Once a commander is wounded then he can no longer fight in hand-to-hand combat. If he is with a unit that is already fighting hand-to-hand combat he must remain with it, but can no longer make his attacks. He can still issue orders, move and otherwise act as normal.

VICTORY AND DEFEAT

This section of the rules is about how to recognise the moment when the battle is done and one army has defeated the other. Generally speaking, our preferred approach is for the umpire to set objectives for each side before the game. This will vary according to the nature of the game being played: escape an ambush by breaking through a blocking force and reaching the opposing table edge, assault and capture a fortress, attack and burn a settlement and drive away cattle... these kinds of scenarios require the players to set objectives before the game begins. Often we will agree targets for outright victory and degrees of success, depending upon the number of objectives taken from, or denied to, the foe. The examples of battles included in this book will give a good idea of the sort of thing intended.

In many battles the opposing armies will have no special objective other than to defeat their enemy. The following rules have been devised to provide a tangible objective based on destroying enemy units. We use these rules for games which otherwise have no specific objectives, and we also use them in other games as a way of ending a battle whether objectives have been met or not. The rules are offered as

guidelines and are not meant to be immutable by any means, but form a useful starting point and can easily be adapted to suit particular circumstances as required.

DEFEAT

An army is deemed defeated once **more than half** of its divisions are broken as defined below. At this point all the army's remaining divisions are also judged to have been broken. Often this is the signal for the battle to end – the losing army is assumed to quit the fight, leaving the field to the victor. If a scenario suggests it is worth fighting on then players can always agree to do so, and this is left to the participants to decide at the time.

This simple rule does assume the army has at least three divisions. Should you be playing a small game where this is not the case you might agree to call a halt once one division is broken. We'd recommend that armies have at least three divisions though. If playing a very large game you might want to set the point of defeat at half the number of divisions rather than more than half, if only to make the game playable over a shorter period.

BROKEN DIVISIONS

If a division has lost a substantial part of its fighting strength then its remaining units will attempt to quit the field. We refer to such divisions as **broken divisions**.

A division is deemed broken if at the start of the player's turn **more than half** of its units are destroyed or have left the table whilst shaken (such units are unable to return and are therefore as good as destroyed).

A division is also deemed broken if at the end of the player's Command part of the turn **all** of the division's remaining units are shaken. This is intended to give the player a chance to rally units in the Command part of the turn and avoid breaking the division.

Where divisions contain a mix of troops it is often necessary to ignore some units when it comes to making these calculations. Elite units of heavy infantry are not likely to show much concern just because a few skirmishers have perished or run away into the wild blue yonder. Skirmishers, light artillery, and tiny units are generally ignored unless they make up the majority types in the division.

For example, in a division of four heavy infantry units, a light artillery unit and two skirmishers, only the heavy infantry units count. This division is broken once three heavy infantry units are destroyed, or if all the remaining heavy infantry units are shaken.

We also sometimes ignore light infantry or light cavalry belonging to divisions chiefly comprising heavier troops, but this can be decided on a case by case basis before the battle as best suits the army's historical counterpart. The same goes for divisions that combine poor quality levies or similar lack-lustre troops with good quality units, the levies might be ignored or a number of units counted as one for purposes of calculating broken divisions.

Once a division is broken all units that are currently shaken or which become shaken from that point on are not allowed to rally. This is why commanders get a chance to rally units in the Command part of the player's turn before establishing whether a division is broken due to all of its units being shaken.

Once a division is broken all of its units are obliged to quit the field as explained below. Units from broken divisions are allowed to make a special **retire** move.

RETIRE

Broken divisions must attempt to leave the battlefield as expediently as is practical.

Once a division is broken the only orders it can be given must facilitate its escape by whatever route or exit is most appropriate. In most cases, where armies advance from one table edge or other, troops will retire from the same table edge. Any initiative moves the unit makes must take it away from the battlefield and danger in so far as possible.

Units from broken divisions are allowed to make a single free move if they fail their order, and can make a single free move even if they are not issued an order and are unable to use their initiative. This move must follow the same general lines give for orders and initiative moves. They can make a free move even if disordered – this being a general exception to the rule that prevents disordered troops from moving. This means units from broken divisions can always move once – assuming they are not engaged in combat or otherwise rendered immobile in some fashion.

Medium and heavy artillery pieces belonging to broken divisions are abandoned by their crews. They are treated as destroyed and removed.

Units from broken divisions cannot charge the enemy, though they can countercharge if normally able to do so. Bear in mind shaken units won't be able to countercharge in any case. Units from broken divisions engaged in hand-to-hand combat will always choose to end the combat by holding their ground or falling back if victorious.

There is nothing to stop units from broken divisions making ranged attacks or from fighting if engaged in hand-to-hand combat. On the whole though, once a division is broken its remaining troops are a spent force and no longer present a significant threat to the enemy.

TROOP TYPES

Troops are divided into infantry, cavalry, chariots, elephants, artillery and baggage – although this last really represents non-combatant elements of the army rather than troops as such. In addition we break down the main categories into more specific types represented by typical fighting qualities. These give us the basic troop types that constitute our armies. The values given here are not fixed or absolute – and we will often have cause to vary them – but they are a good starting point.

HEAVY INFANTRY							
Type	Combat				Morale Save	Stamina	Special
	Clash	Sustained	Short Range	Long Range			
Heavy Infantry	7	7	3	0	4+	6	

These are the game values for typical close fighting, heavily armed and armoured infantry equipped with swords, shields and some kind of javelin or spear that can be thrust or thrown. These are your Roman Legionaries and Viking Hirdmen – they have high values for hand-to-hand combat and a good morale save. Heavy infantry also benefit in that they are harder to score hits against with ranged attacks representing their close, shielded formation (see the 'to hit' modifiers for ranged attacks).

MEDIUM INFANTRY							
Type	Combat				Morale Save	Stamina	Special
	Clash	Sustained	Short Range	Long Range			
Medium Infantry	6	6	3	0	5+	6	

These are the values for close fighting but more lightly armed or poorly trained troops and close fighting barbarians. They are armed with javelins or spears that can be thrust or thrown, or may include a mix of arms in some cases. These are the base values for most close-fighting barbarian units and for most infantry of the Biblical era.

"The Spartans do not enquire how many the enemy are but where they are."

King Agis II of Sparta

> "In peace sons bury fathers, but war violates the order of nature, and fathers bury sons."
>
> Herodotus

LIGHT INFANTRY							
Type	Combat				Morale Save	Stamina	Special
	Clash	Sustained	Short Range	Long Range			
Light Infantry	5	5	3	0	6+	6	

These are the values for troops who would typically fight in a looser order than the 'heavies', but who are still expected to fight hand-to-hand when the occasion demands. They typically carry javelins and light shields, but wear little if any armour beyond a helmet. Peltasts are the classic example of this troop type. Unlike heavier kinds of infantry, light infantry can form into open order without restriction and can combine a formation change to or from open order with a single move.

SKIRMISHERS							
Type	Combat				Morale Save	Stamina	Special
	Clash	Sustained	Short Range	Long Range			
Skirmishers as standard sized unit	5	4	3	0	0	6	
Skirmishers as small unit	3	2	2	0	0	4	

These are the values for a unit of purely skirmishing infantry typically armed with javelins. Skirmishers are limited to open order and column. They cannot form a battle line or other formations. They are highly mobile troops and can combine a formation change between column and open order with a single move. In addition, no distance penalties are applied to skirmishers when issuing orders. Skirmishers wear no armour and might carry a small shield or none as reflected in their lack of Morale save. They would not usually expect to engage in close combat except, perhaps, with others of their kind. They are usually fielded as small units and so we have shown the values for both standard and small units for convenience.

CATAPHRACT CAVALRY							
Type	Combat				Morale Save	Stamina	Special
	Clash	Sustained	Short Range	Long Range			
Cataphract Cavalry	9	6	3/0	0	4+	6	

These are the most heavily armoured of all cavalry comprising riders often clad from head to toe in iron or bronze armour and horses wearing armour that protects their front quarters and often their entire bodies. Parthian and Sassanid Persian Cataphracts are the most well known cavalry of this kind. They are typically armed with long lances or a very long spear held in both hands (the kontos). Cataphracts fought in much closer formations than other cavalry sacrificing mobility for protection. Our units move more slowly than other cavalry to reflect this. In addition they have a short range value of 3 when supporting in combat, but 0 attacks for ranged combat – lacking weapons they can throw and being insufficiently mobile to skirmish ahead of their main formation. However, thanks to their exceptionally heavy armour, enemies making ranged attacks suffer a –1 to hit penalty against Cataphracts (see the 'to hit' modifiers for shooting attacks).

HEAVY CAVALRY							
Type	Combat				Morale Save	Stamina	Special
	Clash	Sustained	Short Range	Long Range			
Heavy Cavalry	9	6	3	0	4+	6	

These are heavy armoured cavalry riding big and occasionally partially armoured horses. They are typically armed with spears, lances, or the two handed kontos and often carry missile weapons in addition. They are supremely dangerous upon contact with a high clash value and they have a hefty morale save. Generally speaking we give them a Short Range value of 3 regardless of armament to reflect their mobility - i.e. sending individual squadrons ahead to chase off light troops or harass dense formations. However, this can be reduced for ranged attacks in the same way as Cataphracts where it is felt appropriate - most specifically in the case of cavalry armed with lances or kontos. Note that cataphracts and heavy cavalry have the same values, but cataphracts have the advantage of being much more resistant to missile fire to reflect the effect of their near-complete armour.

MEDIUM CAVALRY							
Type	Combat				Morale Save	Stamina	Special
	Clash	Sustained	Short Range	Long Range			
Medium Cavalry	8	5	3	0	5+	6	

These are close fighting cavalry and likely to be armoured and heavily armed, making up all cavalry types not otherwise classified as cataphract, heavy or light. Probably armed with spears, but could carry javelins instead or in addition.

LIGHT CAVALRY

Type	Combat				Morale Save	Stamina	Special
	Clash	Sustained	Short Range	Long Range			
Light Cavalry as standard sized unit	7	5	3	0 (3*)	6+	6	
Light Cavalry as small unit	5	3	2	0 (2*)	6+	4	

*if bow armed

These are lightly armed, fast moving cavalry mounted on nimble ponies or small horses. They rely heavily upon missile fire and most carry javelins or both bows and javelins. They are highly mobile troops and when in open order they move at the fastest rate of all cavalry (12"). In open order they incur no distance modifiers when given orders. Unlike heavier kinds of cavalry, light cavalry can form into open order without restriction and can combine a formation change to or from open order with a single move. They are usually fielded as small units, so we have shown the values for both standard sized and small units.

HORSE ARCHERS

Type	Combat				Morale Save	Stamina	Special
	Clash	Sustained	Short Range	Long Range			
Horse Archers as standard sized unit	6	4	3	3	6+	6	
Horse Archers as small unit	4	2	2	2	6+	4	

These are the values for a unit of horse archers. These are the lightest kind of cavalry, carrying no weapons aside from a bow and possible a light side arm. Like infantry skirmishers they are only permitted to form open order and column formations. Like light cavalry they can combine a formation change to or from open order with a single move. Not all cavalry who carry bows are categorized as horse archers. The type more accurately describes Scythian and Parthian cavalry whose role is to shoot and run, avoiding contact with the enemy where possible.

"I am not afraid of an army of lions led by a sheep: I am afraid of an army of sheep led by a lion."

Alexander the Great

LIGHT CHARIOTS							
Type	Combat				Morale Save	Stamina	Special
	Clash	Sustained	Short Range	Long Range			
Light Chariots	6	6	3	0 (3*)	4+	6	
						*if bow armed	

These are the values for chariots of the Egyptian and Hittite type pulled by two horses. They make good supporting units and have sufficient hitting power in hand-to-hand fighting to disperse contemporary infantry. Light chariots can combine a formation change to or from open order with a single move, which makes them very manoeuvrable in the same way as light cavalry. This is the usual kind of chariot to be found in late Bronze Age armies of the Near East from Mitanni through to Egypt. The riders are armed with bows, javelins and light spears. Primarily spear-armed, or more heavily built chariots can be given higher Clash value – typically 8 – to reflect this.

A further type of chariot is drawn by four horses but still fights in a highly mobile way unlike heavy chariots described below. Examples of these can be found in the early armies of the Carthaginians, as well as in the forces of their Berber neighbours the Libyans. Indian armies also included a variety of chariot types of different sizes, with different numbers of crewmen, and with more or fewer draught animals.

The distinction between light chariots and heavy chariots is the way they fight, as heavy chariots are slow, retain a solid formation at all times, and rely upon the shock of impact to scatter their enemies. They are like small fortresses, creaking forward and crammed with spearmen and archers. Light chariots, on the other hand, are far more mobile regardless of the number of horse or crew, although for obvious reasons they will tend to have fewer crewmen and be more lightly built than heavy chariots.

We usually give these four-horse chariot types a better clash value than the standard type – typically 8 – but otherwise treat them as the same as two-horse chariots. Because of the width of the models it is necessary to reduce the number of chariots in a unit in the same way as for heavy chariots.

HEAVY CHARIOTS							
Type	Combat				Morale Save	Stamina	Special
	Clash	Sustained	Short Range	Long Range			
Heavy Chariots	9	5	3	0 (3*)	3+	6	
						*if bow armed	

These are the values for heavy chariots of the later Assyrian and Persian type pulled by four horses. They move at infantry speed and are well protected with armoured crew bearing shields and the chariots themselves are sturdy and high-sided. They can be used offensively, but will be quickly overwhelmed if they do not dispose of their enemy in the first round of combat. For this reason we give them a reduced sustained value compared to a standard light chariot.

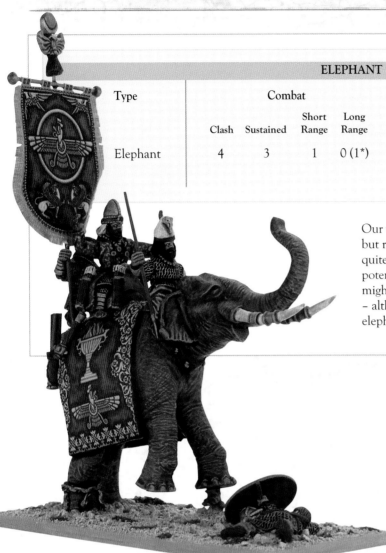

ELEPHANT

Type	Combat				Morale Save	Stamina	Special
	Clash	Sustained	Short Range	Long Range			
Elephant	4	3	1	0 (1*)	4+	6	Elephant

*if bow armed

Our values for elephants may look a little on the low side – but remember a unit of elephants is one model – so it is quite possible for a unit to end up fighting two or potentially three elephants all at once. Such an elephant might have a howdah and crew armed with javelins or bows – although howdahs were not always used and some elephants may have had no crew at all!

"Si vis pacem, para bellum (If you seek peace, prepare for war!)."

Vegetius

LIGHT ARTILLERY

Type	Combat				Morale Save	Stamina	Special
	Clash	Sustained	Short Range	Long Range			
Light Artillery	1	1	2	2	0	3	

This defines a small bolt throwing engine along the lines of a Roman scorpion. These weapons have a range of 24" and enemies struck by their missiles suffer a –1 morale save penalty.

"There is nothing impossible to him who will try."

Alexander the Great

MEDIUM ARTILLERY							
Type	Combat				Morale Save	Stamina	Special
	Clash	Sustained	Short Range	Long Range			
Medium Artillery	1	1	0	3	0	3	

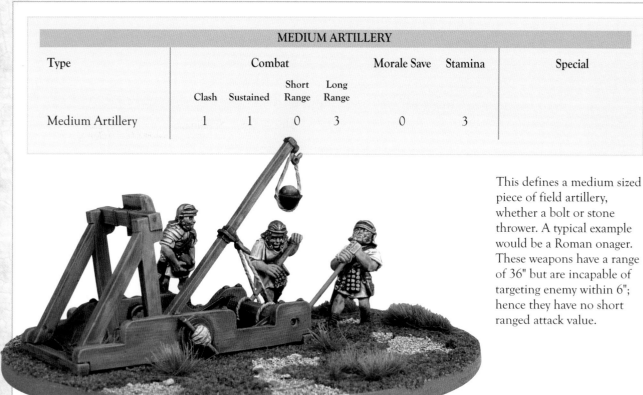

This defines a medium sized piece of field artillery, whether a bolt or stone thrower. A typical example would be a Roman onager. These weapons have a range of 36" but are incapable of targeting enemy within 6"; hence they have no short ranged attack value.

HEAVY ARTILLERY							
Type	Combat				Morale Save	Stamina	Special
	Clash	Sustained	Short Range	Long Range			
Heavy Artillery	1	1	0	3	0	3	

Heavy artillery represents larger stone throwing engines that would be used during sieges or assaults upon fortifications – they are not field weapons as such, but we feel no need to confine ourselves to battles of that kind. Heavy artillery has the same combat values as medium artillery, but a longer range at 48".

WAGONS AND BAGGAGE							
Type	Combat				Morale Save	Stamina	Special
	Clash	Sustained	Short Range	Long Range			
Wagons and Baggage	3	1	0/1	0	0	6	

These are the kind of values we'd give baggage units, although it is rare for them to get anywhere near the fighting in most situations. They have some capacity to put up a fight – but will quickly despair in a prolonged combat. We give them some ability to make short ranged attacks, but note that they cannot support in combat, so their short ranged attack is restricted to shooting.

OTHER COMMON TROOPS

The troop types given are used as the basis for working out all other values. This includes types that are very common in some armies such as archers, pike-armed phalanx, and massed barbarian warbands. The values for these common examples are as follows.

LIGHT INFANTRY ARCHERS							
Type	Combat				Morale Save	Stamina	Special
	Clash	Sustained	Short Range	Long Range			
Light Infantry Archers as standard sized unit	4	4	3	3	0 (6+ if armoured)	6	
Light Infantry Archers as small unit	3	3	2	2	0 (6+ if armoured)	4	

These are the values we'd normally give to units armed with long ranged missile weapons be they bows, slings, or crossbows – they are basically light infantry with reduced hand-to-hand fighting values and morale save, and ranged fighting values that reflect their armament. Armoured or professional archers qualify for the increased morale save value. These troops are *light infantry* type, so they can adopt an open order formation as they move as for other light infantry.

MEDIUM INFANTRY ARCHERS							
Type	Combat				Morale Save	Stamina	Special
	Clash	Sustained	Short Range	Long Range			
Medium Infantry Archers	5	5	3	3	5+	6	

These are the values for formed bodies of archers in most armies that have them, including Biblical armies such as Egyptians and later Near Eastern armies such as Persians. Basically they are medium infantry with reduced hand-to-hand combat values and long ranged attacks in addition. Often the same troops can be arguably fielded as light or medium – the principle difference being the ability of the light troops to break into open order, although the mediums are more resilient fighters overall.

MEDIUM INFANTRY SPEARS AND BOW							
Type	Combat				Morale Save	Stamina	Special
	Clash	Sustained	Short Range	Long Range			
Medium Infantry Spear and Bow	6	6	3	3	5+	6	

These are the values for Persian infantry carrying both spears and bows – *Sparabara* – and they are basically medium infantry types with the addition of a ranged attack. We would tend to use the same values as the basis for units with mixed weapons: shielded spear-armed troops at the front and archers in the rear ranks. These are considered 'medium' types in temperament and general tactical method, they may have armour and could even be elite or otherwise very able troops.

MEDIUM INFANTRY WARBAND							
Type	Combat				Morale Save	Stamina	Special
	Clash	Sustained	Short Range	Long Range			
Medium Infantry Warband	7, 8 or 9	6	2	0	5+	6	

These are the values we'd use for barbarian warbands such as Britons, Gauls and early Germans. They have good – or even very good – fighting abilities in the first round of combat, but tail off markedly after that. The actual clash value tends to vary a bit depending upon how aggressive we want to make these troops, but we tend to stick to 9 in games against Romans. They have reduced short ranged attacks to represent a generally poor degree of coordination. Warbands fight in dense blocks 4 deep – the warband formation.

HEAVY INFANTRY PIKE PHALANX							
Type	Combat				Morale Save	Stamina	Special
	Clash	Sustained	Short Range	Long Range			
Heavy Infantry Pike Phalanx	7	7	3/0	0	4+	6	Phalanx

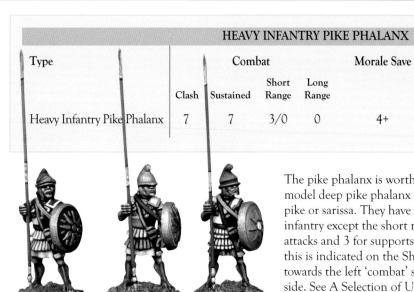

The pike phalanx is worthy of special note as it combines the four model deep pike phalanx formation with a unique weapon, the pike or sarissa. They have the same basic values as other heavy infantry except the short ranged attacks value is split: 0 for ranged attacks and 3 for supports in hand-to-hand combat. As you can see this is indicated on the Short Range stat as 3 slash 0 – with the 3 towards the left 'combat' side and the 0 towards the right 'range' side. See A Selection of Useful Rules for rules governing pikes and phalanx formations (page 103).

HEAVY INFANTRY LONG SPEAR PHALANX							
Type	Combat				Morale Save	Stamina	Special
	Clash	Sustained	Short Range	Long Range			
Heavy Infantry with long spear	7	7	3/0	0	4+	6	Phalanx

Heavy infantry armed with long spears also have the split Short Range value as described for pikemen, unless they are also armed with missiles such as javelins or darts, or if their formations include troops who would typically fight ahead of the main formation to chase away lighter troops or harass more heavily armed enemy. Where this is the case it can also be a good idea to give such units a reduced number of ranged attacks for example 3/1 or 3/2. The phalanx rule can be applied or not, depending on the degree of discipline and training represented. Note that units can be given different values for the phalanx rule as described on page 102. Rules for long spears are given on page 101. Greek Hoplites are the prime example of these troops.

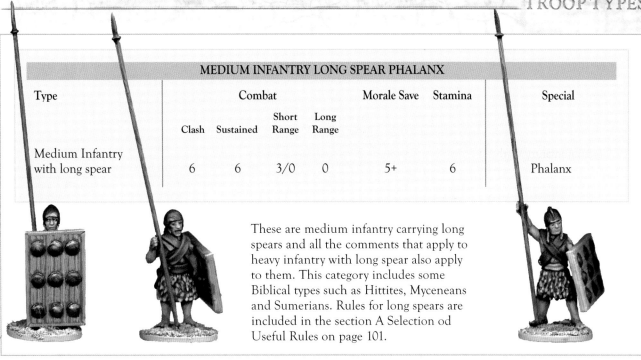

MEDIUM INFANTRY LONG SPEAR PHALANX

Type	Combat				Morale Save	Stamina	Special
	Clash	Sustained	Short Range	Long Range			
Medium Infantry with long spear	6	6	3/0	0	5+	6	Phalanx

These are medium infantry carrying long spears and all the comments that apply to heavy infantry with long spear also apply to them. This category includes some Biblical types such as Hittites, Myceneans and Sumerians. Rules for long spears are included in the section A Selection od Useful Rules on page 101.

HEAVY INFANTRY WITH TWO-HANDED AXES, ETC

Type	Combat				Morale Save	Stamina	Special
	Clash	Sustained	Short Range	Long Range			
Heavy Infantry with double-handed weapons	8	7	2/0	0	4+	6	

These are the game values for close fighting, heavily armoured infantry equipped with axes, swords, clubs and all comparable very heavy cutting and crushing weapons wielded in two hands. Such troops generally have a boosted Clash value and reduced Short range value. They have a split Short Range value in the same way as most other troops carrying dedicated close combat weapons. E.g. they would have a value of 0 for ranged attacks, but 2 for support in hand-to-hand fighting. Rules for double-handed weapons are included in the section A Selection od Useful Rules on page 98.

MEDIUM INFANTRY WITH TWO-HANDED AXES, ETC

Type	Combat				Morale Save	Stamina	Special
	Clash	Sustained	Short Range	Long Range			
Medium Infantry with double-handed weapons	7	6	2/0	0	5+	6	

These are medium infantry carrying two-handed weapons and all the comments that apply to heavy infantry so equipped also apply to them. This category includes some Biblical types such as Egyptians and Hittite Guard. See page 98 for rules covering double-handed weapons.

SKIRMISHERS WITH LONG RANGE WEAPONS							
Type	Combat				Morale Save	Stamina	Special
	Clash	Sustained	Short Range	Long Range			
Skirmishers with ranged weapons as standard sized unit	4	4	3	3	0	6	
Skirmishers with ranged weapons as small unit	2	2	2	2	0	4	

These are the values for a unit of purely skirmishing infantry armed with long-ranged weapons such as slings or bows. The difference between these troops and javelin-armed skirmishers is that they have the appropriate long ranged attacks and lose a clash attack to reflect their preference for shooting over close-quarter fighting. Special rules can be applied to long range weapons, as noted in the section A Selection of Useful Rules on page 98.

BRITISH CHARIOTS							
Type	Combat				Morale Save	Stamina	Special
	Clash	Sustained	Short Range	Long Range			
British Chariots	6	5	4	0	4+	6	

Because many of our games feature Romans and Britons we make regular use of the British Light Chariot. This is a variant of the light chariot type and a good example of how the values can be readily tweaked to emphasise one aspect of the type's ability or de-emphasise another. In this case we take our cue from Caesar who describes the Britons either skirmishing by hurling weapons on the move, or dismounting to fight briefly before returning to their chariots and making good their escape. So, we increase our short ranged attack value to 4 – which makes our chariots very effective indeed when it comes to short ranged attacks and supporting hand-to-hand combat. But we reduce the sustained combat value to reflect a reluctance to get trapped in prolonged combats. The result is a type that is excellent for preliminary skirmishing and for fighting alongside warbands as supports.

"The God of War hates those who hesitate."

Euripides

PERSIAN SCYTHED CHARIOT							
Type	Combat				Morale Save	Stamina	Special
	Clash	Sustained	Short Range	Long Range			
Persian Scythed Chariots as small units	7	0	0	0	3+	4	

These are the values used for the rather unusual Persian and later Seleucid scythed chariots driven directly at the enemy in the hope of scattering his ranks and sowing disorder. As such they were very much one-hit weapons festooned with projecting spear-points and blades. We give them a solitary clash value. Special rules apply to scythed chariots and limit them to a single round of combat, after which they are destroyed whether successful or not (see page 104). The values are given as a small unit of heavy chariots as this is the size at which we'd suggest fielding them, i.e. normally 1 model. Note that it will often be necessary to mount these chariots on bases that are wider even than a standard heavy chariot due to all the projecting 'spiky bits'.

"The art of war is, at the final count, the art of keeping one's freedom of action."

Xenophon

ADJUSTING THE BASIC TYPES

Obviously some troops are better or worse than others even of the same type. This can be reflected by special rules in some cases, but sometimes it is more effective to simply boost a combat value by +1 or, in the case or poorer troops, reduce it by –1. We would not suggest boosting or reducing values beyond this range. Morale saves are best left as they are on the whole, except with Biblical armies where it is useful to have medium infantry with a 4+ save as an intermediary type, for example armoured Assyrians and Babylonians. Similarly, although it is certainly possible to adjust stamina value up or down by 1, we tend not to do so because it is then necessary to remember which units have differing values when it comes to establishing whether troops are shaken.

Often troops will combine long ranged attacks from bows with an otherwise standard type. For example, Persian heavy cavalry with spears and bows are such a type, as are the mixed Spear and Bow medium infantry given above. In such cases the general method is to combine the standard type with the usual ranged attack value for a unit, which is 3. In some cases we would then adjust the clash and/or sustained values, down by 1 if we felt the troops were more likely to shoot than get stuck in. Conversely, where more likely to get stuck in we might reduce the long ranged attack value down by 1. A good example would be Sarmatian cataphracts who were notorious for charging at the first opportunity, despite the fact they carried bows! We do not always do this – it is a matter of judgement – the medium *Sparabara* infantry armed with spears and bows given as an example have retained their basic fighting values to reflect their status as front-rank fighting troops. Nor do we see the need to be entirely consistent. Sometimes the circumstances of the battle will suggest a minor modification to a value. The standard size adjustments for small, large and tiny units are given in the rules and are repeated here for convenience.

SIZE ADJUSTMENT TABLE							
Type	Combat				Morale Save	Stamina	Special
	Clash	Sustained	Short Range	Long Range			
Standard	Basic	Basic	Basic	Basic	Basic	6	
Large	+2	+2	+1	+1	Basic	8	
Small	-2	-2	-1	-1	Basic	4	
Tiny	1	1	1	1	Basic	1	

A SELECTION OF USEFUL RULES

Up to this point we have discussed the basic rules for the conduct of battle. In this section of the book we shall consider some of the occasional and alternative rules employed to give our warriors particular and differing qualities. These rules might reflect our troops' training or discipline, their armament or tactical skills, and their cultural or personal inclinations. We have also given rules to represent specific weapons, including the pilum, sarissa, lance, long spear and kontos, as these are all cases that beg for unique treatment for one reason or another. Some of our rules are more involved and cover unusual troop types or formations that otherwise have no place amongst the preceding sections: for example, elephants, scythed chariots, and the wedge formation.

All of the rules presented here are intended as examples, being modifications and additions that we have developed during and for our own games. They are not a definitive 'tool set' and can be changed, added to, and developed as players wish. We freely confess that the emphasis has been on our own armies as shown throughout this book and featured in the battle reports. Players who have collected a particular army will doubtless acquire a fair amount of expert knowledge of the forces, battles and tactics of their chosen subject, and must therefore feel free to create rules to reflect such qualities as they feel appropriate. Indeed, we rather assume that players will want to do so, as a great deal of the enjoyment of wargaming comes from developing one's own rules of play to reflect personal research and preferences.

All of these modifications are intended to allow us to better represent particular troops or circumstances, either in general or in particular battles. Our objective is to endow our model warriors with something of the character associated with their historical counterparts. We see no need to be consistent in the way these rules are applied. What is suitable for one battle may not be suitable for another, even where the same troops are involved.

BRAVE
- *Shaken units rally without an order*

If the unit is shaken (i.e. it has taken its full quota of casualties) it can attempt to rally at the end of the Command part of the turn if it is more than 12" from any enemy. It does not matter if the unit has moved or not that turn, either because it has been given an order or if it has used its initiative.

Roll a dice. On the score of 4, 5 or 6 the unit recovers 1 casualty –remove 1 casualty from the unit.

This rule is too fiddly for larger games as it allows units to 'come back' to the fight, potentially prolonging the battle unduly. It is very useful in smaller actions where a few brave warriors are ambushed or surrounded by hordes of enemy. The dice score required to rally successfully could be varied, but seems to work nicely enough as a 50/50 roll.

CROSSBOWS
- *Enemy Morale capped at 5+*
- *No closing/traversing shots*

In most circumstances there is no need to differentiate between ordinary bows and crossbows, as the crossbow used by such early peoples as the Romans and Picts was a relatively weak affair offering no significant advantages over other bows. More powerful crossbows are represented by the following minor modifications.

Enemy Morale saves are capped at 5+ when hit by crossbows. This means the roll 'to save' can never be better than 5+.

Crossbows are not allowed to make closing shots or traversing shots. This is because, although powerful, crossbows are slow to load compared to ordinary bows.

DOUBLE-HANDED INFANTRY ARMS
- *Enemy Morale capped at 5+*

Infantry with double handed weapons of all kinds, be they clubs, swords or axes such as the Danish axe carried by the English, huscarls at Hastings, are generally given their own stats as described in the section on Troop Types (page 95). Such weapons required considerable expertise to use effectively. Their weight gave them great hitting power, especially against armoured troops who were otherwise safe from the blows of ordinary weapons. Balanced against this they are heavy and cumbersome to fight with, limiting the role of troops so equipped.

Enemy Morale saves are capped at 5+ when fighting against troops equipped with double-handed weapons. This means the roll 'to save' can never be better than 5+.

This is a rule that makes double-handed weapons worth having in battles against heavily armoured opponents. Against more lightly equipped enemy their lack of ranged ability is a disadvantage – see Troop Types for stats for troops carrying double-handed weapons.

DRILLED
- *Free move on a failed order*
- *Move through or out of the way of friends without risk of disorder*

In this case we have combined two abilities into a single rule – although there is no reason why one can't be applied without the other should you so wish. We found it convenient to consider the two together as it seemed a better representation of professional, drilled troops, and also easier to remember.

Drilled units make one free move if they fail their order, unless a blunder is rolled in which case this takes precedence. If a division order encompasses units that are drilled and units that are not, then only the drilled units are entitled to this free move.

Drilled units do not risk becoming disordered when moving through other drilled units where both are in a battle line formation. Drilled units do not risk disorder when moving out of the way of other drilled units that are giving ground in hand-to-hand combat and where both are in battle line formation.

The 'drilled' rule is used to represent the most disciplined and professional troops such as Roman legionaries, Greek mercenaries and Macedonian phalangites (although note that phalangites in a 4-deep pike phalanx won't benefit from the rule for moving through or out of the way of friends as they are not in a battle line). Whether you choose to categorise troops as drilled is up to you. It is not obligatory to do so. It's a useful rule for emphasising the cool-headedness of professional units, especially compared to barbarians, hurriedly mobilised militia or weary garrison troops.

EAGER
• *Free move on charge order*

Units given an order to charge an enemy within charge range always make one move even if they fail their order, assuming they don't blunder. If a blunder is rolled the result is always taken as 6 on the blunder result table – Uncontrolled Advance! If a division order encompasses units that are eager and units that are not, then only the *eager* units are entitled to the free move.

This rule is used to represent troops who are headstrong, rash or impetuous – eager for battle and difficult to hold back once the enemy are close by. Barbarian warbands are usually given this rule – though it could equally apply to religiously or idealistically motivated troops, vengeful mobs, or any troops whose eagerness to get to grips makes them difficult to restrain.

ELEPHANTS
• *Defeated enemy re-roll 1 dice for Break Tests*
• *Open order opponents +1 to hit*
• *Elephants giving ground stampede on D6 roll of 1.*
• *Free move along road or as part of marching column*
• *Elephants cannot support cavalry.*
• *Cavalry charging elephants lose charge bonus and risk disorder.*

If a unit is fighting against an enemy elephant in hand-to-hand combat and is obliged to take a break test, the opposing side can ask the unit to re-roll whichever of its two break test dice scores highest. For example, if the player rolls 3 and 4 for a total of 7 his opponent can ask him to re-roll the 4. The re-rolled score stands regardless of the result, even if a better score is rolled the second time around. Note that this rule only applies where the elephant is fighting and not where it is merely supporting.

If infantry in open order are fighting an elephant in hand-to-hand combat they do not suffer the usual –1 'to hit' for being in open order, and instead they receive a +1 to hit the elephant. Elephants were especially vulnerable to troops

fighting in open order, who were able to avoid the creature's attacks and work their way around and beneath them. Note that this rule only applies to units that are fighting elephants and not to units that are merely supporting.

Elephants are not permitted to support cavalry in combat, or to move into support of cavalry who are fighting. The presence of pachydermic perils being far too disconcerting for the horses.

A cavalry unit charging against elephants loses its charge bonus as follows. Roll a dice once the cavalry has charged. On the roll of a 1, 2 or 3 the cavalry are disordered.

If an elephant gives ground in hand-to-hand fighting, roll a dice once it has moved. This applies whether it is fighting or supporting. On the score of 1 the elephant has panicked and immediately turns to face its rear and stampedes out of the fight a distance equal to the total of 3 dice (i.e. 3D6 inches). It will stampede straight through any units in the way, diverting only to avoid terrain or buildings it cannot move through. If an elephant would otherwise end its move on top of a unit it moves whatever additional distance is required to move all the way through. Any units stampeded through must take a break test as if struck by shooting. Once an elephant has stampeded it is removed from the table as a casualty.

Because elephants are fielded as units of one model it feels odd to talk in terms of 'formations'. None the less, for the sake of our game elephants are treated as being in a battle line and cannot adopt other formations, not even to move through terrain that is otherwise impassable. However, if positioned along a track or taking their place as part of a marching column, they are allowed to count as if in column and receive a free move. This is just so that they can keep up with other marching troops. Note that this is purely a concession to practicality and the elephant retains its battle line formation and is not otherwise treated as being in column.

ELITE
• *Recover from disorder on roll of 4+*

At the start of the Command part of the turn, before any units are moved or orders given, the player rolls a dice for each elite unit that is currently disordered and which is not already engaged in hand-to-hand combat. If the dice scores 4, 5 or 6 the unit re-orders its ranks and the disorder marker is removed immediately. If successful, the unit can then be given an order or it can use its initiative to move in the normal way.

This is a very useful rule and one we trot out quite often to represent the most cool-headed and disciplined troops, especially when outnumbered or facing barbarian hordes. On occasions we extend the rule to lesser units by allowing them to recover from disorder on the roll of 5 or 6, or sometimes 6. Such differences can be noted as Elite 4+, Elite 5+ and Elite 6+ as required.

FANATIC

- *Morale save +1 until shaken*

Fanatic troops have a Morale value bonus of +1 regardless of type – they are so intoxicated by drugs or fervour that they ignore all but the most fatal wounds and fight with utter disregard for their own safety. This effect lasts until the unit is *shaken*. Once the unit is shaken it loses its special Morale save bonus and reverts to whatever Morale value it would normally have for its type. The bonus is set at +1 as we found +2 simply too effective, but it remains an option should the occasion demand the appearance of virtual demi-gods.

Fanatic troops are often given other wild and dangerous qualities such as tough or wild fighters, frenzied charge and eager. Norse Berserkers and Celtic Fanatics spring to mind when considering troops of this kind.

FEIGNED FLIGHT

- *Can move out of combat*

A unit with the feigned flight ability can be given orders to move, or can use its initiative to move, when it is engaged in combat. This enables the unit to move out of combat during the command part of its turn.

This ability allows a unit to break contact with an enemy. It is usually given to light infantry or light cavalry units and used as part of a deliberate ploy to draw enemy out of position.

FRENZIED CHARGE

- *Must charge with 3 Moves Allowed*

If there are visible enemy within charge reach and which the unit can potentially charge, then the unit **must** be given a charge order. The player has no choice in the matter. If issued a successful charge order the unit always moves up to three moves regardless of the result. If the order to charge is failed the unit still makes one free move. In addition, the unit must use its initiative to charge where it can do so, and can make up to three moves to reach the enemy when it does. Note that shaken or disordered units are not allowed to charge and so are not affected. Units have to be able to charge to be affected by the Frenzied Charge rule.

This rule is usually reserved for fanatical, out of control, or frenzied troops who just can't hold back! There can be circumstances where the obligation to charge doesn't quite work – for example assaulting fortifications – so exceptions must be made as the situation demands.

FRESHLY RAISED

- *Check Unit in First Round of Combat*

The unit's capabilities are uncertain and its behaviour in battle cannot be entirely predicted. This is taken into account in the first round of hand-to-hand fighting. Roll a dice at the start of the combat.

	FRESHLY RAISED TABLE	
1	Terror	The unit is momentarily overcome with terror – for this round only all attacks need 6s to hit and the unit becomes disordered if it is not already so.
2-3	Panic	The unit is momentarily overcome by panic – for this round only all attacks need 6s to hit.
4-5	Determined	The troops do their duty – no effect.
6	Inspired!	The unit fights with unexpected fervour – the unit gets an extra bonus attack this round.

The result applies only for the first round fought during the game – thereafter the unit fights normally. This is an entertaining rule that introduces a little uncertainty into the performance of troops as yet untested by combat.

KONTOS

- *Counteracts enemy charge bonus.*
- *Counteracts long spear armed infantry disorder test*

The kontos is a very long spear held in both hands by mounted troops, typically by cataphract cavalry. The long reach afforded by the kontos enables a rider to jab away at an enemy whilst keeping a safe distance, and also enables him to get the first strike during any initial clash. These very long spears were carried by such foes of the Romans as the Parthians and Sarmatians, and later on by the Romans themselves.

If a unit of charging or countercharing cavalry is armed with the kontos, then any enemy charging or countercharging them to their front lose their +1 'to hit' bonus for charging unless they are also cavalry armed with kontos or infantry pikemen. This represents the longer reached weapons striking ahead of their opponent.

If a unit of kontos armed cavalry charges the front of an infantry unit armed with long spears, then the cavalry are exempt from the usual test for disorder when cavalry charge long spears. The cavalry will still lose their own charge bonus for 'charging long spears' as explained in the *long spear* rule.

Kontos armed cavalry usually lose their short range attack unless they also carry missile weapons.

The kontos rule is enough to make a difference compared to spear armed cavalry who will typically lose their charge bonus when they go head-to-head with kontos-armed opponents. Although pikemen are also judged exempt from this penalty, their own weapons being longer than the kontos, the opportunities for pike-armed infantry to charge stationary cavalry to the front will be rare. If countercharged they lose their charge bonus in any case. However it can happen!

LANCE

- *-1 Morale on charge/countercharge*

The couched lance is associated with mounted medieval knights equipped with stirrups and is a characteristic weapon of the Middle Ages.

When a lance armed cavalry unit charges or countercharges, the enemy suffer a –1 penalty to their morale save in the first round of combat. Where two lance-armed cavalry units charge and countercharge this penalty will apply to both.

We apply this rule to lance armed medieval cavalry giving them a natural advantage on the charge. It might arguably be used for any cavalry armed with long spears, but we generally reserve it for medieval knights.

LEVY

- *Must roll 4+ to recover disorder at end of turn*

Units that are designated as levy do not automatically recover from disorder at the end of their turn. They must roll a dice and only recover successfully on the roll of a 4, 5 or 6.

The levy rule is a way of representing ill-disciplined or poorly trained troops. It is a severe penalty, as such troops may be unable to move from one turn to the next. The score required can be changed to make levy recover more or less easily should we wish; for example levy 2+ recover on a score of 2 or more, levy 5+ on the score of 5 or 6. We sometimes combine a levy 2+ with the freshly raised or militia rules to represent poorly trained or disaffected troops.

LONG SPEARS

- *Charging cavalry/chariots disordered on roll of 1, 2 or 3 (except kontos)*
- *Chargers lose charge bonus (except other long spears and pikes)*

The long spear was the characteristic weapon of Greek hoplites and a fairly common armament for many warriors of the ancient world. In the hands of closely ordered troops it could be used to form a wall of spear points with the weapons of warriors in the second and third ranks projecting forward of the front of the formation. Such a barrier presents a formidable obstacle to less densely packed troops and especially to cavalry whose horses would be unwilling to move against a mass of spear points.

Cavalry and chariots charging or counter-charging onto the front of an infantry battle line armed with long spears must test for disorder once they have done so. Roll a D6. On a score of 1,

2 or 3 the chargers are disordered. Kontos armed cavalry are exempt from this rule due to the length of their own weapons as explained above under *kontos*.

All enemy who are not themselves infantry armed with long spear or pikes lose their 'to hit' bonus for charging or counter-charging against the front of an infantry battle line armed with long spears.

Note that the long spear rule only comes into play when the troops are deployed into a battle line. Units deployed in open order or column formation get no benefit, for example, as these formations don't allow the warriors to wield their weapons as a dense 'hedge' of spears.

We apply this rule to heavy infantry units armed with long spears – but not necessarily to medium or light infantry on the basis that they lack either the training, closeness of formation or determination to maintain an unbroken wall of spear points. It makes infantry so armed quite solid, though not invulnerable, in the face of cavalry. It would be possible to change the chance of disordering cavalry either up or down, but we have always stuck to a 50/50 roll and rather enjoy the resulting sense of trepidation.

MARAUDERS

- *Ignore distance penalty for command*

Marauders ignore the distance penalty that is normally applied when giving orders to units more than 12" from their commander. Note that units in open order formation are already exempt from this penalty anyway. The rule is properly applied only where units wouldn't otherwise benefit.

This rule just extends the exemption for distance modifiers that normally apply to units in open order. We often give it to light cavalry to give them a roving role regardless of their formation.

MARKSMEN

- *Re-roll one missed shot*

The unit can re-roll a single failed ranged attack each time it 'shoots' in the ranged combat part of the turn, or from closing or traversing shots.

This rule is used to single out the abilities of expert missile men be they archers, slingers, artillerymen or whatever.

MILITIA

- *No move on equal command roll*

Units that are designated militia will fail a command on a dice roll equal to the score required to give the order. For example, if the roll normally required is 8 then a roll of 5 is three moves as normal, a roll of 6 is two moves as normal, a roll of 7 is one move as normal, and a roll of 8 is fail where normally it would be one move. Where a division consists of militia and other units, then only the militia will fail their order on an equal dice roll – other units move once as normal.

Greek chaps about to get up close and personal – hoplites carry long spears and can have the phalanx rule

The militia rule is a useful way of representing ill-disciplined or poorly trained troops, citizen militias, and perhaps levies of not overly enthusiastic subject peoples. It is a fairly simple rule and easy to apply without imposing too harsh a handicap on a player.

PARTHIAN SHOT
• *Can evade and make closing shots.*

The unit can both evade from an enemy charge and make closing shots as it does so. Parthian shots are worked out slightly differently from normal closing shots as units normally evade **before** the enemy make their charge move whilst normal closing shots are worked out **after** the enemy has charged.

Work out the Parthian shot as follows. If the chargers are already within a single move of their target then work out closing shots immediately. If the chargers are further away, then they make the necessary one or two moves to put them within a single charge move of their target before working out closing shots. In either case, the closing shots are worked out with the enemy within a single charge move of their target.

Work out the closing shots in the usual way, mark any casualties, and apply any break tests that result. The usual –1 'to hit' penalty for closing shots applies.

Once the unit has shot it evades in the standard way, and does so even if the chargers are unable to complete their charge because they are forced to hold their ground or retreat following a break test. Where a break test is required chargers will always fail to complete their charge. The best result they can get is to hold their ground.

This ability is usually given to nomadic or eastern horse archers such as the Scythians and Parthians after whom it is

named. The Parthians were famed for their ability to shoot behind as they rode away from their enemy. Note that only troops in open order can evade and this rule is not intended to override that.

PHALANX
• *Hand-to-hand combat defeats by up to 2 are treated as a draw.*

The term phalanx properly describes a formation of Greek hoplites or pike-armed phalangites. In antiquity it was sometimes used to indicate any body of close fighting infantry. We created the following rule specifically to better represent the push, shove and sudden collapse of hoplite warfare, but it could be applied to any body of troops that you wanted to make especially resilient in the first rounds of hand-to-hand fighting.

Troops designated as phalanx treat any hand-to-hand combat defeat by up to a predetermined number of casualties as a draw. We generally set this level as 2, though there is no reason not to allocate different levels to represent troops who are more or less resistant. Units can even be assigned different values in the same battle if you wish – so long as you can remember which is which of course! We recommend sticking to 2, at least to begin with. So, a unit losing a combat by 5 casualties to 3, for example, would treat the result as a draw and would not have to take a break test. The same unit losing by 5 casualties to 2 would be defeated by 3 and would therefore have to take a break test with a minus 3 penalty to the result. Note that once a unit is shaken (i.e. once it has suffered casualties equal to its Stamina value – usually 6) it will be obliged to take a break test following a draw in any case. Where a phalanx unit is obliged to test on a draw because it is shaken the full difference in casualties counts: for example, a phalanx unit losing a combat by 6 to 4 must take a test deducting 2.

PIG'S HEAD FORMATION

- *Fighting unit supported by two from rear*

It is no easy matter to reconstruct what the late Roman writer Vegetius meant by the enigmatically named Pig's Head formation or what exactly its role was when it came down to fighting. It might also be referred to as a 'wedge', but seems to have been a different kind of thing to the wedges referred to by Caesar in his Gallic Wars. We take the view that the Pig's Head describes a body of troops supported from behind by a great mass who contribute to the fighting by throwing missiles over the heads of those in front. Thus it is a way of concentrating fighting power across the width of a unit. Perhaps it is a style of fighting that entered the Roman army along with the Germans who increasingly filled its ranks in the later Empire. Whatever the case, this is how we choose to interpret the Pig's Head in our game.

The Pig's Head was probably a common formation of later Roman and Germanic units, and of warriors such as Saxons and Danes during the centuries following the fall of Rome. However, it may have been more widespread and is perhaps a natural formation for relatively small armies of infantry with no obvious need to extend their lines.

The Pig's Head consists of three separate units of infantry arranged with one unit in front and two behind as shown here.

When arranged in his fashion in hand-to-hand combat the unit at the front cannot be supported from either flank, but both the units behind count as supporting.

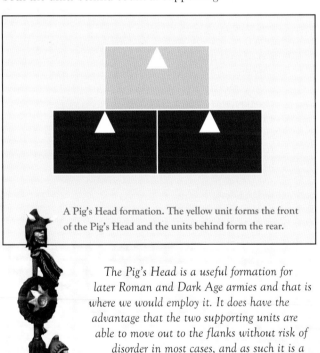

A Pig's Head formation. The yellow unit forms the front of the Pig's Head and the units behind form the rear.

The Pig's Head is a useful formation for later Roman and Dark Age armies and that is where we would employ it. It does have the advantage that the two supporting units are able to move out to the flanks without risk of disorder in most cases, and as such it is a flexible formation whose reduced width makes it possible to manoeuvre more easily across a crowded field. It is also a good formation for forces that have a mix of well-armoured first-class troops (at the front) and poorer fighters you would prefer to keep out of the front line (at the back).

PIKES

- *Cavalry/Chariots cannot charge pikes unless disordered or scythed chariot*
- *Cavalry/Chariots charging disordered pike must test for disorder*
- *Chargers lose charge bonus (except Pikes)*
- *Phalanx*

Pikes – properly the Macedonian sarissa – are hefty spears in the region of fourteen to twenty feet in length. They are the characteristic weapons of the armies of Alexander the Great and his Successors. Troops so armed made up the dominant military arm until the rise of the Roman legions. Pikemen fight in a very close, deep formation – the pike phalanx – and for this reason are generally known as phalangites. The array of multiple spear points projecting beyond the unit's front is almost impossible for cavalry to approach

Cavalry and chariots are not allowed to charge or countercharge the front of a unit of pike-armed infantry in phalanx or square formation unless the pike-armed unit is already *shaken* or *disordered*. The exception to this is the scythed chariot, which is allowed to charge/countercharge, and may be obliged to do so, as explained in the rules for *scythed chariots*.

Cavalry and chariots that do charge home onto the front of a pike-armed infantry unit must test for disorder as they do so, in the same way as described for long spears. Note that cavalry armed with the kontos are not an exception in this case; they must test just like other troops, as the pike is longer even than the kontos.

All enemy that charge or countercharge to the front of a pike-armed infantry phalanx or square, apart from another pike phalanx, lose their +1 'to hit' charge bonus. This applies regardless of whether the phalanx is disordered, or shaken, or otherwise.

Pike-armed troops always have the Phalanx rule in addition. If fielded together with long-spear phalanxes, pike phalanxes always have a level at least one greater, because they represent deeper formations with longer weapons.

PILUM

- *Enemy –1 Morale save in first round*

The pilum is associated with Roman infantry. It is a heavy javelin with a long, thin iron shank, a small tip, and usually an additional lead weight to boost its penetrating power. Although the pilum was probably the most sophisticated weapon of this kind it was not necessarily the first or only one. A heavy javelin made of iron called a soliferrum was used by the Spanish and Celtiberians in their wars against the Romans (and one imagines with each other). From the third century the Romans themselves continued to employ cruder weighted javelins and darts. These went by various names including the spiculum and plumbata. Once again, similar weapons were used by contemporary barbarians, all characterised by a relatively long, thin shank, small head, and being carried in sufficient number to facilitate throwing. Examples include the German angon and the bebra cited by Vegetius.

If a unit is armed with pila or the equivalent, then any enemy the unit is fighting to its front suffers a –1 Morale save penalty against hits inflicted by the unit in the first round of each and every hand-to-hand engagement. This penalty applies regardless of whether the unit charges or is charged, and note that it applies in the first round of every combat engagement and not just the first combat engagement of the battle. We assume the legionaries are carrying sufficient pila to remain effective throughout the battle. Also, remember the penalty to the enemy's Morale only applies where the pilum armed unit is fighting to its front and not where it is merely supporting the combat or fighting to its sides or rear.

For example, a Roman cohort charges a Gallic warband and attacks with 7 dice scoring 4 hits – the Gauls have a Morale Save of 5+ but this is reduced to 6+ because they are fighting pila in the first round. Four dice are rolled scoring 1, 4, 5 and 6 equals 1 save.

SCYTHED CHARIOTS

- *Frenzied charge – must charge with 3 moves allowed*
- *Drilled heavy infantry can open ranks on roll of 4, 5 or 6*
- *Defeated enemy become disordered*
- *Scythed chariots are removed after one round*
- *Cannot support/be supported*

By scythed chariots we do not intend ordinary chariots romantically kitted-out with sharpened wheel-spinners in the fashion of Ben Hur, but heavy armoured chariots armed with projecting spears and scythes used to deliberately break apart enemy formations. Chariots of this kind had a single crewman whose only hope lay in bailing out at the last moment, his rather unenviable mission being to drive the chariot at full pelt directly towards the enemy lines. To achieve this it would probably have been necessary to work the team up into a state of blind terror, as no horse would willingly throw itself upon a body of formed men. As such these are one-shot weapons. Disciplined troops would typically respond by opening gaps in their lines which the terrified horses would naturally bolt through.

Scythed chariots are heavy chariots and also have the *frenzied charge* rule that obliges them to charge where they can.

If scythed chariots charge unengaged drilled heavy infantry to the front, then the enemy will automatically try and open up his ranks to channel the chariots harmlessly to their rear. Once the chariots have charged roll a dice, on the score of 4, 5 or 6 the infantry have succeeded in diverting most of the chariots through their lines – the chariots are removed immediately and inflicts no damage. On the roll of a 1, 2 or 3 most of the chariots crash into the infantry and combat is worked out in the usual way.

Scythed chariots only ever fight one round of hand-to-hand combat after which they are removed as destroyed. Work out the combat in the usual way. If the enemy are defeated they automatically become *disordered* prior to taking their break test. Whether defeated or victorious the scythed chariots are removed once the result of the combat is established without making any further moves.

Scythed chariots are the only chariots that are allowed to charge a pike phalanx. They still lose the usual 'to hit' bonus for charging though.

Scythed chariots cannot support other friendly units in combat and cannot be supported either.

SLINGS
- *Enemy Morale -1 at short range*

Slingshots were impossible to see in flight and dealt horrendous wounds, often battering through arms or shields. To represent this we reduce the enemy's Morale save at ranges of 6" or less (short ranged attacks).

Enemy Morale saves are reduced by 1 from hits at short range (6" or less). Where a significant proportion of shooters are at a different range, it may be necessary to roll two batches of dice – with only those attacks made at short range incurring the Morale save penalty.

STEADY
- *Ignore first '6' for break tests each turn*

Steady units ignore the first '6' rolled against them for purposes of taking break tests from ranged attacks each turn. The '6' is still resolved as a hit and will cause a casualty if not saved. The rule applies during the ranged attacks part of each enemy turn, and also when shot at from closing and/or traversing shots.

This represent units that are 'steady under fire' in part because of training or experience, and in part due to armour and large shields. It is a useful bonus for games where close fighting troops are advancing upon hordes of bowmen; for example, the Greek hoplites at Marathon. Our feeling is that such chaps are not likely to be put off by the first flurry of arrows. It is usually applied to heavy infantry units, although it could be extended to any troops where appropriate.

STUBBORN
- *Re-roll failed Morale save*

A unit that is stubborn is allowed to re-roll a single failed Morale save each time the unit suffers casualties – but only once during any part of the turn. This means they can re-roll one failed save when they are shot at by the enemy in his turn, and they can re-roll one failed save during any hand-to-hand combat round – including against casualties suffered by closing or traversing shots as they charge. If the re-roll is successful the casualty is not inflicted, the unit's stubbornness has won out.

We sometimes place a further limit on stubborn troops, permitting a re-roll only so long as the unit has suffered 0, 1, 2 or 3 casualties maximum, depending upon how 'stubborn' we want our units to be. Stubborn troops can be very frustrating because – with luck – they can hang on practically forever! As such the full rule is best reserved for games featuring the few against the many, perhaps where a small force must hold out whilst reinforcements arrive. In larger games it is more

"Remember upon the conduct of each depends the fate of all."

Alexander the Great

practical to field stubborn troops with a casualty limit, for example 'Stubborn 3' where the rule ceases to apply once the unit has 4 or more casualties. 'Stubborn 0', where the rule applies so long as the unit has no casualties already, should not be dismissed lightly. For well armoured troops it is almost comparable to an extra half point of stamina.

SUB-UNIT

• *Unit and sub-unit must remain within 1 move's distance.*

The unit has an attached body of troops of a different type, or differently armed, forming a sub-unit. For example a Republican Roman century consists of heavy or medium infantry with a sub-unit of light infantry.

The sub-unit must remain within 1 move's distance of its unit where possible, and where this is no longer the case the sub-unit must endeavour to come within a move where possible. This will override any orders it is given.

The sub-unit rule is imposed upon troops that fought in these mixed formations of which the Republican Roman Legions are the most well known, but some Spanish and German armies reputedly fought with cavalry supported by infantry, and light infantry were reportedly trained to operate alongside cavalry in the Peloponnesian War. Such matters might best be left to the players to arrange for themselves where historical precedent suggests it – but we have included the rule, as it is a straightforward way of representing such formations without too much fuss.

TESTUDO FORMATION

• *Free move*
• *+2 Morale saves from ranged attacks*
• *Counts 'front' all round to ranged attacks*
• *Make no ranged attacks*
• *Adopt battle line if engaged.*

The Roman testudo – tortoise – is a close order formation of interlocked shields designed to protect legionaries as they advance under missile fire. Because we play a lot of games with Romans we have developed our testudo rules to serve, and present them here as part of our selection of special, unusual and useful rules. We have also incorporated the various penalties and bonuses into the main body of the rules, as that seemed the easiest and most convenient thing to do.

To form a testudo the unit is arranged in so far as possible into a square shape with all the models facing forward. If you have a specific model to represent the testudo then remove the unit and replace it with the testudo model. The model should have a total frontage of about half that of a standard battle line, something as shown below.

A unit in testudo formation has a free move and therefore always moves at least once when given an order, unless a blunder is rolled. If the unit suffers a blunder its formation limits its movement to forwards only (i.e. a result of a 5 or 6) see page 30.

A unit in testudo formation has a Morale save bonus of +2 from ranged attacks (see page 46). In addition all faces of the formation count as the unit's front to enemies making ranged attacks against it, and will therefore suffer the –1 'to hit' penalty for shooting at the front of a heavy infantry formation.

A unit in testudo formation makes no attacks in the ranged attacks part of the turn. The testudo is essentially a formation for movement, an armoured column, and not prepared for missile combat.

A testudo that becomes engaged in combat automatically changes to a battle line as it does so, troops spreading out into a fighting formation. So, if a testudo charges into combat it automatically changes to a battle line formation at the same time. If a testudo moves into an engagement as a support it also changes into battle line. Similarly, if the testudo is

Roman players will find it useful to have a Testudo model to substitute for their units when the Testudo formation is used in battle.

charged it automatically responds by changing into a battle line formation facing the enemy as soon as it becomes engaged. This formation change happens automatically in both cases and no account is made of it as a move.

Note that because troops in testudo formation spread out on contact with the enemy it is necessary to leave sufficient space to enable them to do so. Where there is insufficient room for the unit to deploy in this way it still counts as a battle line and fights as such. In this case the unit must be rearranged into a battle line at the first opportunity, even where giving ground or making a move following combat. This rather flexible ruling is intended to allow a testudo to make assaults along narrow roads or ramps and into breaches, as are common in many siege situations. In cases where a testudo is unable to form a satisfactory battle line because of restricted width, we would tend to reduce the combat value of the unit in proportion to the frontage achieved, deferring to the merciful umpire's good sense as in all such matters.

TOUGH FIGHTERS

- *Re-roll one missed combat attack*

The unit can re-roll a single failed hand-to-hand combat attack each round of hand-to-hand fighting.

This rule is a good way of representing especially competent fighters, veterans and professional mercenary troops. It is a considerable bonus and not one to be spread too widely – save it for the best troops where some predictability might be expected.

VALIANT

- *Break test re-roll once per battle*

The unit can re-roll its first break test result of 'break' during the game. This only applies once during the whole game.

This is a very useful bonus that can keep a unit in the game for at least another turn. We usually apply it to professional and highly disciplined troops – the best of the Hellenistic phalangites, Greek mercenaries and Roman legions.

WAVERING

- *Take a break test when you take a casualty*

The unit must take a break test whenever it takes a casualty. If the unit takes one or more casualties from shooting it must take a break test even where no 6s are scored. If the unit suffers one or more casualties in hand-to-hand combat it must take a break test, regardless of whether it wins or loses the combat.

This is a harsh penalty to apply to any unit. We have only used it for angry mobs and rioting drunkards! It could also be applied to scratch units of any kind, but remember such units will not last long, unless they are very lucky indeed.

WEDGE FORMATION

- *Free move*
- *Counts 'front' all round to attacks*
- *Counts 'front' all round for own ranged attacks*
- *+1 Morale saves against all attacks*
- *Cannot support/be supported except by enclosed friend*
- *Can make own attacks all round*
- *Enemy giving ground to front are burst through*
- *Wedge can make three moves when enemy break or are burst through*

When different ancient authors refer to the 'wedge' formation they may not always mean the same thing and probably don't! A shallow 'V' shape is a natural formation for advancing cavalry, for example, as it allows the riders to see and follow their standards and leaders, but it is likely that a 'wedge' so formed would level up as battle lines clashed. However, when Caesar describes surrounded legionaries forming a wedge and cutting their way through a Gallic army he is undoubtedly describing a formation of densely packed troops in what we might typically think of as a wedge or arrowhead shape. Modern re-enactors have re-created this formation for public display, and the result is quite convincing even if comprising only a few dozen legionaries rather than hundreds. In any case, we have taken this interpretation as the model for our 'wedge'. It is a formation designed for breaking through and moving beyond enemy lines – a 'breakout and escape' formation.

A unit can make a wedge formation by arranging itself into a wedge shape along the following lines. In practice we limit this formation to Romans and to games that suggest its use, and would imagine that players will want to take a similar approach. It is not envisaged that armies form up in wedge formations as a matter of habit, but of dire necessity only!

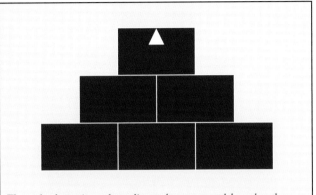

The wedge formation – depending on how your models are based some compromise may be required, but this isn't overly important. Just arrange the models in a wedge shape so far as you can.

A unit in wedge formation has a free move in the same way as a unit in testudo: if the unit's order is failed it can still make one move. If the unit suffers a blunder its formation limits its movement to forwards only (a result of 5 or 6) see page 30.

A unit in wedge formation still has a front, rear and two sides, but treats all as 'fronts' for fighting purposes. A unit in wedge does not suffer the 'to hit' penalty for fighting to its sides or rear, and all of its facings are considered fronts for other fighting purposes. For example, enemy shooting at a heavy infantry wedge will suffer the –1 to hit penalty for shooting at the front of heavy infantry even when shooting at the sides or rear. The wedge can direct its own ranged attacks from any facing.

A unit in wedge formation has a Morale save bonus of +1 for both ranged and hand-to-hand combat.

In combat a unit in wedge formation is allowed to make any or all of its attacks to its front, sides or rear, it is not limited in the number of attacks it can make to its side as units normally are.

A wedge **cannot** be supported unless it includes another unit within its formation as explained below. If it includes other units one of these can support. A wedge **cannot** support other units in hand-to-hand combat.

Once hand-to-hand combat is over take any break tests as normal. If the wedge is forced to give ground and is unable to do so because it is surrounded then it is destroyed, as any unit would be in that situation. If the enemy are forced to give ground then those at the sides and rear do so as normal, moving directly back. If the unit at the front of the wedge is forced to give ground then it is 'burst through' together with any supporting unit behind. Units that are burst through and any other engaged units must be moved out of the path of

the wedge in as practical a manner as possible and are then disordered if they were not disordered already. If necessary the units that are burst through can be arranged into a rough mass to make room, in which case they count as having been forced into open order, losing their formation as they are swept aside by the wedge.

If a wedge either bursts through an enemy formation, or if its frontal opponents break, the wedge can make up to **three** moves forward, and can make a sweeping advance or charge where an enemy presents itelf. See Sweeping Advance on page 78.

Note that we oblige our victorious wedge to move **forward**, and we would prefer this to be as straight ahead as possible. In any case, where it is necessary for a wedge to deviate from straight ahead to avoid terrain, make for a bridge, follow a path, avoid or charge enemy, etc, it must always move to its own front quarter as it lies during the combat engagement. This doesn't prevent the wedge pivoting at the end of its burst through move to align itself for a change in direction in its following turn, but it does mean the wedge must head in the direction it is pointing.

Caesar refers to baggage and light troops taking shelter within a wedge, and we shall allow this too. It is practical to limit such additional units to a single fighting unit and a single baggage unit, and to place a few token models amongst the wedge whilst temporarily removing the remainder of the units in question. This just stops the wedge becoming huge! The fighting unit can support the wedge in combat. Note that it doesn't matter if models from the enclosed units actually appear on the outside of the wedge, as this is sometimes unavoidable depending on how the models are based, they are still treated as being inside the wedge, whose boundaries are formed by the main unit.

WILD FIGHTERS

• *Re-roll missed combat attacks in the first round of the game*

The unit can re-roll failed hand-to-hand combat attacks in the first round of hand-to-hand combat during the game. The maximum number of attacks the unit can re-roll may be 1, 2 or 3, set before the game. For example 'Wild Fighters 1' are allowed just a single re-roll. Alternatively, the number can be randomised 1, 2 or 3 before the re-rolls are taken. No matter how many re-rolls are permitted, they only apply in the unit's first round of hand-to-hand combat in the entire game – so try to make the most of them.

Wild fighters are typically tribal troops who attack in an aggressive and barely controlled way, but who quickly tire and lose enthusiasm if their enemy do not break at once. We routinely apply this rule to Celtic and early German warbands. It can be applied to any enthusiastic but untrained warriors, armed mobs and tribal troops as required.

SUMMARY OF USEFUL RULES

Brave	Shaken units rally without an order.
Crossbows	Enemy Morale capped at 5+. No closing/traversing shots.
Double-handed Infantry arms	Enemy Morale capped at 5+.
Drilled	Free move on failed order. Move through friends without risk of disorder.
Eager	Free move on charge order.
Elephant	Defeated enemy re-roll 1 dice for break tests. Open order opponents +1 to hit. Elephants giving ground Stampede on D6 roll of a 1. Free move along road or as part of marching column. Elephants cannot support cavalry. Cavalry charging elephants lose charge bonus and risk becoming disordered.
Elite 4+	Recover from disorder on roll of 4+
Fanatic	Morale save +1 until Shaken.
Feigned Flight	Can move out of combat.
Frenzied Charge	Must charge with 3 moves allowed.
Freshly Raised	Check unit in first round of combat.
Kontos	Counteracts enemy charge bonus. Counteracts Long Spear armed infantry disorder test.
Lance	-1 morale on charge/countercharge.
Levy	Must roll 4+ to recover disorder at end of turn.
Long Spears	Charging Cavalry/Chariots disordered on roll of 1, 2 or 3. All chargers lose charge bonus (except other Long Spears and Pikes).
Marauders	Ignore distance penalty for command.
Marksmen	Re-roll one missed shot.
Parthian Shot	Can evade and make closing shots.
Phalanx	Hand-to-hand combat defeats by up to 2 are treated as a draw.
Pig's Head Formation	Fighting unit supported by two from rear.

Pikes	Cavalry/Chariots cannot charge Pikes unless disordered or Scythed Chariot. Cavalry/Chariots charging disordered Pikes must test for disorder. Chargers lose charge bonus (except Pikes). Phalanx.
Pilum	Enemy –1 Morale save in first round.
Scythed Chariots	Frenzied Charge – must charge with 3 moves allowed. Drilled Heavy Infantry can open ranks on roll of 4, 5 or 6. Defeated enemy become disordered. Scythed Chariots are removed after one round. Cannot support/be supported.
Sling	Enemy -1 Morale at short range
Steady	Ignore first '6' for break tests each turn.
Stubborn	Re-roll failed Morale save.
Sub-Unit	Unit and sub-unit must remain with 1 move's distance.
Testudo Formation	Free move. +2 Morale saves from Ranged Attacks. Counts 'front' all round to Ranged Attacks. Make no Ranged Attacks. Adopt battle line if engaged.
Tough Fighters	Re-roll one missed combat attack.
Valiant	Break test re-roll once per battle.
Wavering	Take a break test when you take a casualty.
Wedge Formation	Free move. Counts 'front' all round to all attacks. Counts 'front' all round for own ranged attacks. +1 Morale saves against all attacks. Cannot support/be supported except by enclosed friend. Can make own attacks all round. Enemy giving ground to front are burst through. Wedge can make three moves after enemy break/burst through.
Wild Fighters	Re-roll missed combat attacks in the first round of the game.

Pillaging Goths threaten to set fire to the homes of these proud citizens of the Roman Empire

Look smart there Marcus! Roman troops prepare to move from their encampment

THE CHARIOT ERA

The glittering civilisation of the Nile continues to fascinate people today just as it did during the age of great discoveries in the nineteenth century. Few could fail to recognise such images as the golden funerary mask of Tutankhamun, the temples of Karnak and – of course – the Pyramids of Egypt themselves. Many of the wars of the Pharaohs were fought for control of Palestine, Lebanon and Syria (an area often referred to as the Levant), and so enter into Biblical history. Indeed, those who choose to wargame the battles of this era often refer to it as the Biblical Period unless they prefer the more sober and rather academic sounding title of the Late Bronze Age. It is a period that corresponds with the Egyptian New Kingdom – the 18th, 19th and 20th dynasties. Needless to say, none of this would have made much sense to Thutmosis III or Rameses II – two of Egypt's greatest warrior Pharaohs.

Although organised warfare did not begin with the chariot, it is with the introduction of the chariot and the development of powerful bows that we will make a start. Both reflect a growth in technology – for, although we tend to think of chariots as primitive weapons of war, their construction and maintenance was a complicated and expensive business. The manufacture of spoked wheels, of shaped wooden components, and the specialist bronze fixings that go into making a chariot were all cutting-edge stuff in the second millennium BC. Both chariots and the war-winning composite bow were introduced into Egypt by conquerors – the Hyksos – whose exact identity remains something of a mystery (though it is worth pointing out a number of their rulers have Canaanite names). Following the expulsion of the Hyksos, Egypt emerged as a politically centralised and ambitious nation under a new dynasty of warrior Pharaohs – the age of the New Kingdom had begun.

The Egyptian New Kingdom spans the years from the 1550's to 1077BC and includes the many campaigns of Thuthmosis III (1479-1425). Thuthmosis led Egyptian armies through the Levant over the Euphrates and against Mitanni. During his reign the Egyptians defeated the Canaanites at the Battle of Megiddo (1457) the first ever battle recorded in any detail. Following a period of internal and religious dissention under the monotheistic Pharaoh Akhenaten, the eighteenth dynasty died out and was replaced by rulers who were bent on restoring an empire that had been eroded by years of internal strife at home and peace with neighbours. Amongst these Pharaohs we will recognise Seti I, who set about recapturing the cities of Kadesh and Amurru, and his more famous son Rameses II (1279-1213). Rameses fought the Hittites at the Battle of Kadesh (1275) possibly the largest chariot battle of all time. Rameses claimed the victory, but wars against the Hittites continued for twenty years and were concluded with the first recorded peace treaty (1258). The twentieth dynasty offers only Rameses III (1186-1155) as a candidate for greatness – his battles against the Sea Peoples are recorded upon the walls of his mortuary temple and show the Pharaoh defeating his enemies in a series of land and sea battles (1178). Rameses preserved Egypt from invasion at a time when most of the eastern Mediterranean was falling to wild and foreign armies. Sadly, his successors were unable to maintain control and Egypt gradually slid into anarchy. The New Kingdom came to an end with Egypt divided into numerous factions with a new dynasty ruling much of Lower Egypt from Tanis and the High Priests of Amun ruling Upper Egypt from Thebes.

Warfare in Mesopotamia has a history at least as old as in Egypt, but by far the most popular subject for wargames are the wars of the Assyrians, specifically of the empire of the early Iron Age, approximately from the 8th to 7th centuries BC, when Assyria was at its height. During these few hundred years the Assyrians developed a centrally organised state and a well provisioned and disciplined army, which was feared throughout the Near East. Many of the Assyrians' battles were sieges – which sometimes lasted for years. Sargon II conquered the Kingdom of Israel and carried off its population into captivity before turning his attentions northwards, against Armenia and Syria, and eastwards, against the Medes. He also suppressed one of many revolts by the Babylonians and their Elamite allies. Sargon died fighting the Cimmerians, a tribe of horse-nomads who lived between the Black and Caspian Seas.

Under Esarhaddon and his son Ashurbanipal the Assyrians extended their empire as far as Egypt – but theirs was never a realm at peace. As well as constant wars against the Medes, Armenians and Cimmerians the Assyrians were faced with periodic rebellions by their Egyptian and Babylonian vassels. It was all too much, and within a generation after Ashurbanipal's death the empire was toppled by its many enemies. Medes, Cimmerians and Scythians overran much of the Near East – joining forces with Assyria's old enemy the Babylonians to attack and destroy Nineveh in 612BC.

Chariots are the all-important part of Bronze Age armies, not least in the force of the Egyptian Pharoah Rameses. Egyptian chariots are light, manoeuvrable missile platforms.

Much of what we know of the forces of Egypt's opponents comes from Egyptian representations of battles and from the descriptions of Egyptian documents. So we much accept a certain inherent bias as well as a fair amount of supposition on behalf of the Egyptians themselves.

We are all familiar with the armies of the Hittites, Egyptians, Assyrians and other forces of the Near East. Meanwhile in Western and Northern Europe, kingdoms rose and fell without the benefit of historical or monumental records. These are warriors typical of the place and time.

By the time of the Assyrian empire cavalry had entered the ranks of armies and supplanted many of the roles previously performed by chariots. Horses and horsemanship progressed rapidly under the influence of nomadic tribes, and soon chariots were reduced to a more specialised role. Assyrian chariots were far larger and heavier than those used in previous centuries – and grew heavier over time – acquiring three and then four horses to pull them and a heavily armed crew of up to four infantry. Gone were the mobile missile-armed vehicles of the Pharaohs – these heavy chariots were designed to rumble forward and scatter enemy formations.

Horsemen took over the role of scouts, pursuit of the enemy, and rapid moving bowmen.

The most powerful weapon amongst the foot troops remained the bow, but the Assyrians' heavy armour and large shield was a sure sign of things to come in the ensuing age of classical warfare. Even so, Assyrian formations combined spear and bow armed troops – even cavalry units were divided in this way – so that the Assyrian armies mixed something of the battle-winning bow fire of earlier forces and the solidity of later heavy infantry.

THE BATTLE OF KADESH 1274BC

The Battle of Kadesh is one of the great conflicts of the age of chariot warfare and also one of the first battles to be described and recorded for posterity. Because Kadesh is so well known – or rather because it is one of the few Bronze Age battles of which anything is known at all – it has long been a popular subject for wargames re-enactment. Michael and Alan Perry were sufficiently inspired by this tale of Rameses' campaign in Syria that they not only designed an entire range of Egyptian and Hittite models to represent the rival armies, they also hand-built the scene of the battle in miniature, complete with the walls of Kadesh and the banks of the Orontes. Needless to say, the battle of Kadesh, and variants thereof, have raged across this tabletop numerous times over the years, with honours pretty much divided between the Egyptians and Hittites. The participants in our game were therefore looking forward to seeing how the Hail Caesar rules dealt with the peculiarities and challenges of this familiar battle.

Kadesh was the key battle during the early part of Rameses' campaign against the Hittites. Over the preceding years the Hittites had extended their rule over lands previously subject to Egyptian control. Kadesh was a large, powerful fortified city and also the main Hittite fortress along the border. The pharaoh was determined to re-establish Egyptian dominion in Syria, and the city of Kadesh was to be his target. Rameses led his army northwards through the Orontes valley. His forces probably amounted to about 20,000 troops in all including 2,000 chariots. The Egyptian army was formed of four divisions called Amun, Ra, Ptah, and Seth. The pharaoh himself led the Amun division at the front, followed by Ra, Ptah and Seth at the end of the column.

As the Egyptian army marched, it first crossed the Orontes at a ford, and then headed through a wooded part of the valley, before crossing a tributary that flowed past Kadesh itself. It is

Rameses and Amun make camp beneath the walls of Kadesh. The Royal Guard deploy to protect the pharaoh

likely that the Egyptians had no idea the Hittite army was nearby. This explains why Rameses allowed his four divisions to become strung out over twelve miles or so of road. As Amun was making camp within sight of the walls of Kadesh, Ra was still marching to join them, whilst Ptah was traversing the woodland some miles behind. Seth was yet to cross the Orontes twelve miles to the south.

As the Amun division was making camp, with its chariot horses unharnessed and picketed, the entire Hittite army suddenly appeared from behind Kadesh where it had been hiding. The Hittite chariots crossed the Orontes at a ford just south of the city, and smashed into the flank of Ra division whilst it was still on the march. Ra was scattered and at a stroke the Hittites had successfully divided the remaining Egyptian forces in two. The Pharaoh and Amun were isolated in their camp to the north, and Ptah was still struggling through the wooded valley. Seth was still many miles distance and was to take no part in the ensuing battle.

The Hittite chariotry pursued the fleeing remnants of Ra into the camp causing untold confusion and mayhem. Rameses bravely gathered his troops and fought his way out of the camp. The Egyptians began to rally for a counter-attack. Fortunately for the Pharaoh, the Hittite attack was starting to falter. Many of their chariots had been lost in the fighting. Worse still from the point of view of Muwatallis the Hittite king, rather than following up the attack on Amun his troops stopped to loot the Egyptian camp. This gave Rameses the chance he needed to re-organise his scattered army. Rameses counter-attacked, forcing Muwatallis to commit more chariots to the fight. However, the Egyptians had the best of it, driving the Hittites back towards Kadesh and the river.

It was at this moment that Ptah division appeared on the scene, advancing upon the Hittite chariotry in a two-pronged attack together with the elite Na'arun chariotry. Now the Hittites found themselves caught by surprise. Their chariots turned in disarray and headed back over the river. Many crews supposedly abandoned their chariots before attempting to swim the Orontes. Upon the far bank of the river the remaining Hittite infantry stood immobile and uncommitted. Some of the charioteers were slain by Egyptian arrows as they crowded about the ford, others were drowned in the river itself.

Both sides were brazen enough to claim the victory. Casualties had certainly been high amongst both armies. Afterwards, Rameses soon abandoned his attempt upon Kadesh and withdrew. The Hittite king had lost many of his chariots. The two empires were to fight on for years to come, without either side ever decisively overcoming the other. Fifteen years following the battle of Kadesh, the Egyptians and the Hittites signed a peace treaty recognising their respective spheres of influence. The text of this treaty survives both in Egyptian and Hittite versions and it is the earliest such treaty ever recorded.

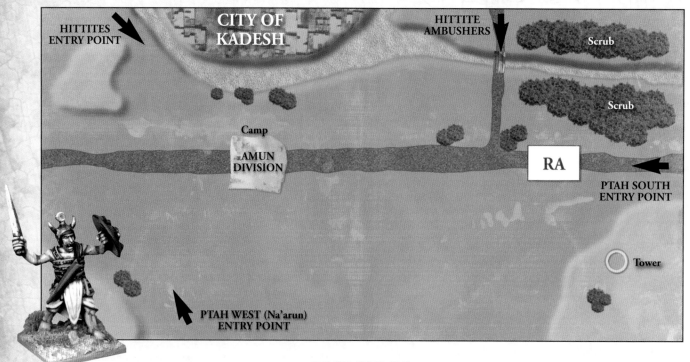

THE SIDES

The Hittite Command is organised into five divisions. Every division commander had a Leadership rating of 8. Muwatallis commands number five 'Chariot' division and has the general's re-roll ability.

The Egyptian command was organised in four divisions: Amun, Ra, Ptah South, and Ptah West. Every division commander had a Leadership rating of 8. Rameses commands Amun and has the general's re-roll ability.

ONE – AMBUSHERS
- 4 units of Hittite Chariots

TWO – HITTITE INFANTRY
- 4 units of Hittite Spearmen
- 1 small unit of Skirmishers with javelins

THREE – ALLIED INFANTRY
- 4 units of Spearmen
- 1 small unit of Skirmishers with bows

FOUR – ALLIED INFANTRY
- 2 units of Spearmen
- 2 units of Archers
- 1 small unit of Skirmishers with javelins

FIVE – CHARIOTS
- 3 units of Hittite/Allied Chariots

AMUN
- 3 units of Egyptian Chariots
- 1 unit of Royal Guard Infantry
- I tiny unit of Cavalry Scouts

RA
- 2 units of Egyptian Spearmen
- 1 unit of Sherden
- I small unit of bow-armed Skirmishers

PTAH SOUTH
- 3 units of Egyptian Spearmen
- 1 unit of Egyptian Archers

PTAH WEST (NA'ARUN)
- 3 units of Egyptian Chariots

Type	Combat				Morale Save	Stamina	Special
	Clash	Sustained	Short Range	Long Range			
Egyptian Spearmen (Medium Infantry)	6	6	3	0	5+	6	
Egyptian Guard Infantry (Medium Infantry)	7	7	3	0	5+	6	Elite
Egyptian Bowmen (Medium Infantry Archers)	5	5	3	3	5+	6	
Sherden Infantry (Medium Infantry)	7	7	3	0	5+	6	Elite
Sherden bow-armed Skirmishers (small)	2	2	2	2	0	4	
Egyptian Chariot (Light Chariot)	6	6	3	3	4+	6	Elite
Hittite/Allied Spearmen (Medium Infantry)	6	6	3	0	5+	6	
Hittite/Allied Skirmishers with javelins (small)	3	2	2	0	0	4	
Allied Bowmen (Medium Infantry Archers)	5	5	3	3	5+	6	
Bow-armed Skirmishers (small)	2	2	2	2	0	4	
Hittite/Allied Chariots	7	7	3	0	4+	6	

FORCE STATISTICS

HOW IT WAS FOUGHT

The table was arranged as shown on the map with the walls of Kadesh and Egyptian camp at one end of the table and Ra division in column of march at the other. Rameses and Amun division were arranged within and around the camp. Our umpire explained to the Egyptian players that the infantry of Ptah would be allowed to enter the table behind Ra on a dice roll from turn two onwards, a roll of 6 being required at the start of turn two, a 5 on turn three, and a 4 on subsequent turns. At the same time the chariotry of Ptah would arrive in the west opposite the Egyptian camp. Unknown to the Egyptians, the umpire had allowed the Hittites to arrange their forces on either side of Kadesh, rather than all on the southern side as the historical battle. This would certainly give Rameses something to think about! None of the Hittite forces were deployed on the table at the start of the game. The chariots that would mount the ambush in the south were hidden amongst the low scrub by the banks of the river. The remaining Hittites prepared to march onto the table at the signal of the Hittite commander.

The game began with the Hittite chariots emerging from the river bank and speeding rapidly towards Ra. The Hittites were allowed a minimum one move measured from the river on the first turn. Fortunately for the troops of Ra division, one move was all the Hittite commander could manage, leaving his chariots careering across the intervening scrubland towards the Egyptians' flank. In their turn the Egyptians were informed that, because they had been caught by surprise, their usual automatic move for troops moving in column would be suspended and their Leadership rating reduced to a pitiful 6 for the first turn (as opposed to 8). Wails and lamentations from the Egyptian commanders were followed by a dice roll of 5 allowing Ra to successfully reorder its ranks into a fighting formation facing the Hittite chariots. At the other end of the table Rameses troops were judged to be busy encamping requiring an order to regroup ready to fight from the following turn. With divine aid the brave pharaoh roused his warriors with a successful dice roll.

Perhaps it was the sight of mighty Ra that caused the Hittite chariotry to hesitate. Maybe some of those Hittite allies were less enthusiastic than their commander might have liked. Either way the dice dictated that the Hittite ambush would falter. The Hittite chariots failed to move.

Hittite chariots lie in wait whilst hapless Egyptians march towards Kadesh

Ra in trouble! The Egyptians put up a stiff fight

The Egyptians rearranged Ra into a better fighting line with the support of some skirmishing archers. Seeing the danger, and ever eager to give his foes a good smiting, Rameses gathered the forces of Amun and advanced to the aid of Ra.

With Rameses still a good way off and no sign of Ptah, the Hittite chariots attempted to mount their charge upon the troops of Ra. The chariots rolled forward to within short missile range but failed to contact. The next turn would do it though, and the Egyptians responded by hurling missiles and shooting arrows at the Hittites, sending their ranks into disarray. Thanks to a round of excellent dice rolling and poor missile break tests from the Hittites, the chariot division was forced out of formation with one unit disordered. To make matters worse Rameses with three chariot units was now approaching from the North.

Seizing their moment, the three Hittite chariot units that were still in good order fell upon the troops of Ra using their initiative moves to do so. One of the chariots had positioned itself for a flanking attack and things looked pretty bad for Ra. So it was to prove, with the flanked unit broken and destroyed in a single turn and the remaining units badly mauled. The wily Hittite commander was not going to take unnecessary risks though, so he withdrew the flanking chariot unit from the fight and prepared to face the wrath of Rameses.

As the battle between the Hittite chariots and Ra division raged in the southern part of the table the Hittite commanders launched their second surprise: advancing onto the table from the north of Kadesh. This caught Rameses on the hop as he had already pretty much abandoned his camp to lead his chariots to the rescue of Ra. Only a unit of infantry remained behind to protect the camp. Now, with the Egyptian chariots drawn away, it looked as if the camp would be overrun.

Leaving the fate of his camp in the hands of the gods (and the Royal Guard), Rameses ordered his chariots to the attack. Three Egyptian chariot units thundered into the lone Hittite chariot unit that stood in their path. The Hittites responded with a determined countercharge and the two forces met beneath the walls of Kadesh itself. It would be the first chariot clash of the game and the Egyptians were feeling pretty confident. So, confident in fact, that Rameses, observing from a nearby rise, saw little need to commit his divine person to the fray.

Rameses confidence appeared to be justified. Things certainly seemed to be going the Egyptians' way. The first infantry unit of Ptah marched onto the southern edge of the board, and three units of chariots did likewise in the west. In the ensuring hand-to-hand fighting the remaining troops of Ra managed to defeat the Hittite chariots arrayed against them, driving the enemy back in disorder. It was a gallant and some might say lucky bit of fighting by Ra, and largely down to the grim determination (and successful saving throws) of the elite Sherden. With the Hittite ambush convincingly rebuffed, Rameses turned confidently to his chariots. Now at this stage it is worth pointing out that we

allowed for the supposedly 'lighter' Egyptian chariots to have better shooting ability than the Hittites, whilst the Hittites were given a slightly more favourable hand-to-hand combat value to represent their heavier chariot. None-the-less the Egyptians had the advantage of two supporting units giving them the upper hand. Rameses confidence quickly ebbed as fortune suddenly deserted him. What was a clear advantage quickly turned to abject defeat. How he wished he'd been there amongst his troops, calling down the wrath of the gods and adding his own three dice to the fight. Alas it was not to be. Not only were the Egyptian chariots soundly defeated, but they failed their break test and were destroyed. As a result the supporting units also had to test, and one also broke and was removed immediately, whilst the single remaining unit retreated back towards the Egyptian camp. It was a spectacularly poor show from Rameses' troops. How much better it would have been to have brought the chariotry of Egypt to within bow range of the Hittites and peppered the foe with arrows, rather than entering into a close combat where the Hittites had the advantage.

In their turn the Hittites advanced from the north of Kadesh. Their forces divided into two groups: one heading towards the fighting with Ra and the other heading towards the Egyptian camp and chariots of Ptah. The camp was still held by infantry from Amun division but things were looking distinctly shaky for the Egyptians. In the centre the victorious Hittite chariot unit retreated back towards Kadesh. Having suffered five casualties, the Hittite player was keen to get the badly mauled unit out of missile range of Ra's remaining bow-armed skirmishers. In the south the Hittite chariots found themselves pressed by the remnants of

Where did they come from! The Hittites engage the chariots of the Na'arun (Ptah West division)

Ra's infantry as well as the infantry of Ptah who were now making their way onto the battlefield.

In the following turn the Hittites and Egyptians converged to the north of Kadesh. The Egyptians tried to take advantage of their long ranged missile fire to disrupt the Hittites. Infantry defending the camp took every opportunity to pelt the Hittites with missiles as they swept past. The Egyptian plan seemed to be working, with several of the Hittite chariots and infantry forced into a disordered retreat. Meanwhile in the south, the Hittite chariots had once again clashed with the remnants of Ra. The Egyptians were pushed back onto high ground where Ra and Ptah arranged their troops into a defensive line. A unit of Ra was broken, which also broke the division. The remaining units of Ra were shaken whilst their enemies were either shaken or almost so. Neither side felt able to press the attack and the Hittites retreated back towards the scrub adjoining the riverbank.

With the game reaching its tenth turn and two of the Egyptian divisions broken, both sides agreed to call it a day. The Egyptians had lost Amun division – the survivors of which were huddled in their camp. Ra was also broken with the remnants of Ra's infantry clustered around the high ground west of the road to Kadesh. On the plus side the chariots of Ptah had successfully stayed the Hittite advance

upon the camp. Ra had held out against the odds and pretty much put the opposing Hittite division out of action. The umpire decreed that the road was open for the surviving Egyptians to withdraw, leaving Rameses to escape and return to Egypt. He would have plenty of time to come up with a suitably glorious account of his 'victory' on the way.

All the players agreed it had been an edge-of-the seat game that could easily have gone either way. The Hittite players decision to put the bulk of their forces north of Kadesh obviously made a big difference compared to the actual events. This left the ambushing force to the south not really big enough to flatten Ra in one fell swoop. There was some discussion whether the Hittites should have been allowed to spring their ambush closer to Ra, but in end all agreed that both sides had had their chance. Rameses admitted that launching Amun's chariots straight into the lone Hittite chariot unit had been a huge tactical mistake that stemmed from overconfidence. Charging the enemy had simply allowed the Hittites a chance they would never have had if the Egyptians had stood off and shot. Even if the Hittites had subsequently charged, the Egyptian chariots could have inflicted devastating damage with closing shots or counterchanged themselves. After the defeat of Amun's chariots the Egyptians were forced into a holding action. It was to the Egyptian players' credit that they managed this with reasonable success. On the other side of the Orontes the

The encampment surrounded by swirling chariotry – in the background Egyptian bowmen give chase

The Hittite hordes pour onto the battlefield from the East

Hittites were quick to claim the victory, with the hated Egyptians driven from the gates of Kadesh and their own forces still in pretty good shape. Nevertheless, the initial ambush had been slow to get going, and the infantry of Ra had denied the Hittites control of the road south. In the north the Hittite forces had swarmed around the Egyptian camp, but never succeeded in mounting an attack upon it. Overall, it was agreed that Rameses did somewhat less well than his historical counterpart, whilst the Hittites had succeeded in preserving their chariotry and had therefore improved upon history.

NOTES ON COMPOSITION AND STATISTICS
We have taken a fairly broad brush to the various contingents that made up both sides, treating all the Egyptian and Hittites infantry, and their respective allies as medium infantry types without differentiating between them. The Egyptian Royal Guard and Sherden are treated as better quality medium infantry with high close combat values. These troops are also considered to be elite, enabling them to potentially shrug off the effect of disorder. The Sherden were placed with Ra to give the division some backbone. We also wanted to reflect the supposed difference between the lighter, missile-oriented Egyptian chariots and the heavier, combat-oriented Hittite chariots. For this reason we gave the Egyptian chariots an extended missile range and made them elite to reflect both added manoeuvrability and high status. The Hittites receive a higher that usual combat value to represent the heavier style of chariot but forego the longer missile range and elite status.

THE CLASSICAL AGE

Roman Testudos prepare to sweep aside the onrushing barbarians. The Testudo was used when assaulting fortifications and other heavily defended positions to allow the legionaries to advance in the face of enemy missile fire

Classical warfare brings us to the battles of the Greeks and Romans – the cultures thought of as the wellspring of western civilisation: of philosophy and science, and of the arts such as we understand them today. Because the Greeks and Romans wrote histories of their exploits we know a great deal more about them than we do about their contemporaries, and most of what we do know of the wider world is pictured through the eyes of Greek and Roman historians. This is just as well, as it enables us to recreate the appearance and tactics of armies with reasonable confidence. We also have descriptions of actual battles, offering our first ever glimpse of how battles were planned and conducted.

The age of classical warfare begins with the wars between the Greeks and Persians starting with the revolt of the Greek cities of Ionia in the years following 500BC. The war that followed saw the triumph of the closely ordered and heavily armoured Greek infantry over the mixed bow and spear-armed armies of Persia. The Greek hoplite with his round, bronze-faced shield, body armour and long spear soon became the most feared and sought-after mercenary warrior in the ancient world. After the defeat of the Persians, Greek hoplites fought in the armies of the Persians themselves and ruled the battlefields of the eastern Mediterranean for the following two hundred years. During the Peloponnesian Wars the Greeks turned upon each other, in a struggle won by the Spartans.

The ultimate triumph of Hellenism came at the hands of a Macedonian rather than a Greek: Alexander the Great. Alexander's soldiers fought in a dense phalanx like those of the Greeks – but now they were armed with an even longer spear: the eighteen foot long sarissa, held in two hands. Such a cumbersome weapon required highly skilled warriors to wield it, and the Macedonians were certainly that. After crushing opposition in Greece, Alexander turned his mighty phalanx eastward against the Persians, defeating one army after another until all of the Persian empire lay in his grasp. Not content with conquering one of the largest empires of antiquity, Alexander pressed on to India, bringing a touch of Hellenic civilisation to the sub-continent. Following Alexander's death his vast empire broke apart into rival factions, but remained a world ruled by Greeks. For the next two hundred or more years Hellenic culture and language predominated throughout the lands once fought over by the Egyptians and Assyrians.

'In war, events of importance are the result of trivial causes.'

Julius Caesar

The rise to prominence of the heavily armoured infantryman was mirrored in the west where Greeks established colonies in Italy, Spain, Sicily and even the coast of France. Well organised, frequently state-equipped troops of this kind would come to dominate the wars between Rome and her rivals: at first the Etruscans and other peoples of Italy, and soon the Gauls, Spanish and Carthaginians. The Punic Wars between Rome and Carthage mark the beginnings of empire and provide us with inspiring accounts of battles won and lost. The brilliant Carthaginian general Hannibal humbled the might of Rome for years with his army of mercenaries and allies, but in the end none could stand before Roman determination and Italian resources. The Roman soldier of these times was essentially a militiaman, but a heavy infantryman for all that. Unlike the Greeks these Roman legionaries carried a heavy iron-shanked javelin: a weapon called a pilum designed for fighting other infantry at close quarters. Thrown just before the battle-lines clashed, the pilum was so heavy its iron tip would easily penetrate shield and armour and kill the man behind. Those not killed or wounded would find the pilum stuck in their shield and would be forced to abandon it and fight on unprotected against legionaries armed with sharp stabbing swords wielded from behind the protection of a wall of shields.

The Romans did not stop with the conquest of Carthage and Spain, but pressed on eastward against the old Hellenistic kingdoms. Now the new sword and pilum equipped legions faced a foe equally well-trained and at least as highly regarded – the sarissa armed troops of the Greeks. The clash between the two military systems ended with the triumph of the legion, but it was no easy victory and even today the debate goes back and forth over the merits of these rival ways of waging war. Whatever the case for the phalanx that had dominated warfare for hundreds of years, the legions marched east, the Hellenistic kingdoms tumbled or disintegrated, and the Roman empire lay upon the banks of the Euphrates. On the opposite side of the river lay Persia, now under the control of the Parthians, a nomadic people who had moved in and taken over from the former Greek rulers. The Parthians with their highly mobile cavalry-based armies were to prove something of a headache for the Roman heavy infantryman, whose weapons and tactics had evolved for fighting other infantry. The empires clashed repeatedly, and when the Parthians were succeeded by a resurgent Persian dynasty – the Sassanids – the fighting continued. Many times the Romans advanced into Mesopotamia, looting and burning cities, and many times the Persians drove them back almost to the Mediterranean coast.

It's impossible to put an exact date to the end of the classical age, but we may point to the growth in the cavalry arm as one of its characteristic features, together with the reduction of infantry to a secondary role. Plague and economic collapse nearly brought the Roman Empire to its knees in the 3rd century, but the Romans adapted and

PICKING A FIGHT

Roman legionaries were highly trained and adaptable soldiers – equally proficient with a variety of arms and quick to adapt to the weapons and armour of their enemies. Never more was this true than during the revolt of the Aedui in 21AD when Gallic troops led by Sacrovir, including a core of heavily-armoured gladiators, were confronted by the legionaries of Gaius Silius.

Tacitus tells us how these armoured leviathans fared in the face of legionary ingenuity.

"The ironclads' armour was proof against pila and swords, but the legionaries brought up their axes and pick-axes and hacked at armour and flesh as if demolishing a wall".

Roman Pugio, 1st Century AD
Roman soldiers often spent considerable amounts of money on decoration such as this.

soldiered on in the face of barbarian invaders including the Franks, Goths, Vandals and Huns. The empire was divided into a western half ruled from Rome and an eastern half ruled from Constantinople – otherwise known as the Byzantine Empire. Rome was sacked by Alaric the Goth in 410 and plundered by the Vandals in 455. In 476 the last Roman Emperor Romulus-Augustulus was deposed by Odoacer, a German warlord who has been fighting as a Roman general. But by then the proud legions were long gone and another age of warfare had begun.

Early in the Peloponnesian War the Spartan army, supported by its allies, advanced out of the Peloponnese and into Boeotia and the surrounding countryside. Its intention was clear: to send a message to Athens and her supporters that Sparta was the true master of Greece. As the Spartans progressed, contingents split from the army to hold strategic positions along the route, gather supplies, and take control of roads to and from the main cities. Some went unopposed, but others met resistance.

A small force consisting of Athenians and their allies was reported to be blocking the road to Boeotia. Although nominally allied to Athens, the Boeotians' loyalties were known to be suspect, and the Athenians wanted to demonstrate in full view of the enemy that it would be foolish to switch sides and oppose them.

Relying on their unshakable belief that they were by far superior to the Athenians in battle, the Spartans sent an equally small force to brush the opposition aside. The Spartan general Adrastus took command of a mixed force

comprising hoplites together with some lightly armed men. The hoplites included a Spartan phalanx as well as some of the most trusted of the allies.

THE SET UP

We know of the major battles of the Greek world, but many smaller conflicts are only mentioned in passing, and many more are likely to have gone unrecorded. Our game is an attempt to re-create just such a battle, and also to show that the Hail Caesar rules are not only about big games with hundreds of models!

As the Spartan army came into sight, and knowing they would be without cavalry, the Athenians formed a battle line of hoplites along the edge of a road with open ground to their front. This would allow their own cavalry to operate freely and give their missile-armed men a clear shot at the enemy as they approached. Part of the road was sunken and lined with trees in full leaf; this was used to full benefit by the Athenian commander during in the conflict, as we shall see.

MER 426BC

SPARTAN FORCES

Spartan division:
- Commander Adrastus
- 1 phalanx of Spartan hoplites
- 1 phalanx of Lacedaemonian hoplites
- 1 small unit of Helot skirmishers

Corinthian division:
- Commander Elpidios
- 2 phalanxes of Corinthian hoplites
- 2 small units of skirmishers with slings

ATHENIAN FORCES

Athenian division:
- Commander Demosthenes
- 2 phalanxes of Athenian citizen hoplites
- 1 phalanx of Elite hoplites (set up in ambush)
- 1 small unit of Black Sea archers

Boeotian division:
- Commander Archippos
- 2 phalanxes of Theban hoplites
- 1 unit of Boeotian light cavalry
- 1 small unit of skirmishers with slings

SPARTAN AND ATHENIAN FORCE STATISTICS

All commanders including the general have Leadership ratings of 8. The general has the standard re-roll rule in addition.

Type	Combat				Morale Save	Stamina	Special
	Clash	Sustained	Short Range	Long Range			
Spartan Hoplites	7	7	3	0	4+	6	Drilled, Stubborn, Elite, Phalanx, Immune to Blunders
Athenian Elite Hoplites (Heavy Infantry)	7	7	3	0	5+	6	Elite, Phalanx
Other Hoplites (Heavy Infantry)	7	7	3	3	5+	6	Phalanx
Helots armed with javelins and fielded as a small unit (Skirmishers)	3	2	2	0	0	4	
Slingers fielded as a small unit (Skirmishers)	2	2	2	2	0	4	
Black Sea Archers fielded as small unit (Light Infantry)	3	3	2	2	0	4	
Boeotian Cavalry fielded as small unit (Light Cavalry)	5	3	2	0	6+	4	

Note: All hoplites are armed with long spears and all have the phalanx rule as noted.

For this battle we decided to allow all the hoplite phalanxes a short ranged attack to represent outrunners in the Greek ranks. Thus the hoplites have a short range value of 3 rather than 3/0 as is usual for troops armed with long spears.

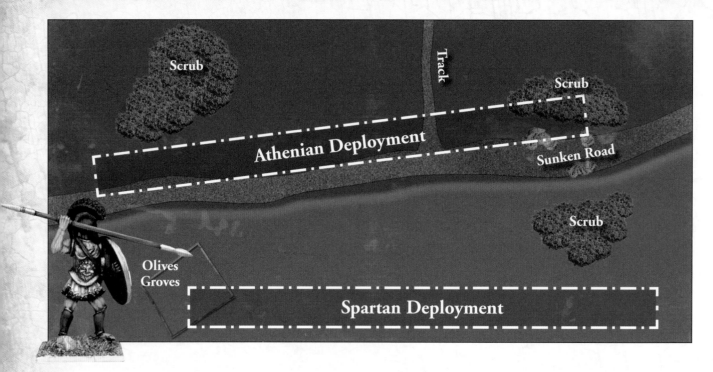

HOW IT WAS PLAYED

Seeing the Athenians' position clearly, their shields gleaming in the midday sun, the Spartans began to draw into a line, flanked by their lightly armed skirmishers. But as they approached the Athenians they moved their entire line quickly to the right where they perceived their enemy to be weakest. This kind of manoeuvre took other Greeks much longer to perform, but demonstrating their superior training and famous discipline, the Spartans' phalanx moved effortlessly as if of one mind and advanced towards the foe, eager for battle to be joined.

Reacting quickly to this sudden shift of the Spartan line, and in an effort to take advantage of the lingering of the Spartans' allies, the Athenians advanced quickly forwards. Meanwhile, the Boeotian allied cavalry on the Athenian right flank moved into the olive groves in front of them.

The other Greeks in the Spartan army noticed the Spartan phalanx ahead of them, and wanting to prove their worth, caught up with them at a quick pace. However, terrified by glimpses of enemy horsemen expertly navigating the olive groves ahead and coming right for them, the slingers on the Spartan left flank froze. Their want of training, experience – and some might say courage – betrayed them.

Letting loose a single poorly aimed volley of sling shot towards the cavalry, the skirmishers had already started to run as the enemy horsemen came within javelin range. No resistance was offered and no mercy was shown as the slingers were pursued and destroyed.

Meanwhile, unnerved by the Spartans' quick advance and the noise struck up by them as they sang, the main Athenian line became disorganised as some hoplites showed their bravery whilst others shamed themselves and froze in terror.

Now, the general Adrastus of the Spartans was obliged to hold back his men to allow his allies to catch up properly,

seeing that at the pace they were going the Spartans would otherwise be in danger of becoming surrounded. This allowed the other Lacedaemonian Greeks to come forward besides the Spartans and the helots to cover the phalanx's exposed flank.

As all students know the area around Sparta was called Lacedaemonia, and for this reason the Spartans bore the Greek letter equivalent to L (lambda) – an inverted V – as a device emblazoned upon their bronze-clad shields.

Witnessing the destruction of their slingers and seeing that the enemy cavalry were distracted as a result of their pursuit, one of the Corinthian phalanxes performed a masterful manoeuvre: wheeling to face the horsemen and advancing quickly towards them. Lightly armed out-runners broke ranks to engage the cavalry in the rear. This caused the Boeotian horsemen much consternation and soon forced them to break and flee from the battlefield altogether. For this brave act, the Corinthian hoplites were later honoured in Sparta.

The Athenian line now found its courage and formed a solid wall of men to oppose the Spartans. The archers they had recruited from the Black Sea coast moved to the front and trained their bows on the Spartans. By the luck of the gods not even they could find their mark. A small band of slingers saw the Corinthian phalanx's formation was in disarray and took the opportunity to try and strike at the hoplites' unprotected side. They only caused minimal injuries however.

Once again the contrast between the highly trained Spartans and the rest of the army showed itself. The Spartans advanced heroically towards the Athenians, but beside them their allies stumbled in the face of the enemy and were obliged to momentarily halt their ranks.

Now the Athenian trap was sprung! General Demosthenes, showing a remarkable tactical insight and no little cunning, had hidden some of the finest hoplites in Athens in the sunken lane. Ducked down low and hidden behind the trees, the Spartans were completely unaware of their presence. The Athenians sprang from their ambush and charged straight into the Spartans and their general. They were followed by a Theban phalanx, spears at the ready.

A very bloody combat was fought, with the Spartan commander in the thick of it. In the midst of the clash a brave Athenian named Miltiades struck Adrastus in the neck with his spear, inflicting a mortal wound upon him. The close-fought struggle took a heavy toll of both sides, with the Spartans fighting for the body of their fallen general and the noble Athenians refusing to give ground.

Seeing that battle had been joined, one Corinthian phalanx ran to the aid of the Spartans and charged into the Thebans who were pressing upon them. The other Corinthian phalanx again showed their bravery by charging at the Theban flank, taking the enemy by surprise and quickly breaking them. As their enemy fled, the Corinthians crashed through into the Athenian citizens behind, causing utter mayhem in their ranks and sending them in flight after their allies. Amidst the confusion the Athenian commander was badly wounded and dragged to safety.

Both sides now joined in earnest. Although the Athenian line was almost destroyed the elite phalanx refused to flee and continued to exchange deadly blows with the Spartans. The Black Sea archers showed their ferocity, drawing their axes and charging the Spartans. But, alas, the Athenians and their allies could not prevail against the Spartans and were soon broken and in flight. Skirmishers continued to pelt the Spartan line with missiles from a safe distance, but only caused a few casualties before they too melted away from the battlefield. Only the brave noblemen of Athens fought on. They were abandoned to their fate and surrounded, valiantly fighting until the last man.

So the battled ended with the mighty Spartans triumphant and the Athenian dead and wounded strewn upon the field. The way to Boeotia was now open, but an omen was foretold at this moment of victory – an omen that the Spartan's heard in grim silence: 'The war for Greece will not be won as easily as the road to Boeotia'.

The opposing lines clash and the casualties start to mount during the final moments of the battle

SPECIAL RULES AND SCENARIO

We decided to make the Spartan phalanx drilled, stubborn and elite (4+). We also decided to make the Spartans immune to blunders – treating the result as a standard 'fail' instead (which did happen during the game). It just seemed wrong to have a Spartan unit misunderstand orders or otherwise move unpredictably!

All hoplite phalanxes were treated as heavy infantry armed with long spears The Athenian elite unit was given the elite (4+) special rule the same as the Spartans, allowing it to potentially recover from disorder at the start of their turn.

The umpire secretly arranged for the Athenians to hide a single unit in the sunken road before the game. This unit could be placed on the board at the start of any Athenian turn, or would be placed automatically as soon as the enemy came within 6".

On this occasion Mike Perry and Alessio Cavatore donned loincloths to play the Spartans, whilst Alan Perry and Rick Priestley sauntered from the Agora to represent the Athenians. Steve May devised the scenario, provided both armies, recorded the game for posterity and took the photographs.

Cavalry chase the opposing skirmishers from the rough ground in the opening moves of the battle

Hoplites close up shoulder-to-shoulder forming a hedge of spearpoints

At the moment of impact warriors in the front rank stab furiously over the tops of their bronze-faced shields

PHALANX

Hand-to-hand combat defeats by up to 2 are treated as a draw.

The term phalanx properly describes a formation of Greek hoplites or pike-armed phalangites. In antiquity it was sometimes used to indicate any body of close fighting infantry. We created the following rule specifically to better represent the push, shove and sudden collapse of hoplite warfare, but it could be applied to any body of troops that you wanted to make especially resilient in the first rounds of hand-to-hand fighting.

Troops designated as phalanx treat any hand-to-hand combat defeat by up to a predetermined number of casualties as a draw. We generally set this level as 2, though there is no reason not to allocate different levels to represent troops who are more or less resistant. Units can even be assigned different values in the same battle if you wish – so long as you can remember which is which of course! We recommend sticking to 2, at least to begin with. So, a unit losing a combat by 5 casualties to 3, for example, would treat the result as a draw and would not have to take a break test. The same unit losing by 5 casualties to 2 would be defeated by 3 and would therefore have to take a break test with a minus 3 penalty to the result. Note that once a unit is shaken (i.e. once it has suffered casualties equal to its Stamina value – usually 6) it will be obliged to take a break test following a draw in any case. Where a phalanx unit is obliged to test on a draw because it is shaken, the full difference in casualties counts: for example, a phalanx unit losing a combat by 6 to 4 must take a test deducting 2.

Another view of the Greek cavalry. These light cavalry are armed with javelins and prefer to fight in open order.

Hoplite battles were decided by a clash of solid lines of armoured infantry. The Greeks had few cavalry or light troops, although the importance of these supporting units grew over time. Never the less the hoplite remained the most important part of all Greek armies until the time of Alexander

AN ENCOUNTER DURING THE ROMAN CONQUEST OF BRITAIN

Our battle takes place shortly after the death of the Roman governor Ostorius Scapula in 52AD. Taking advantage of the temporary lack of leadership, the Silures tribe have attacked and destroyed part of a legion engaged in building fortifications in their territory. (The Silures lived in what is now south Wales and the borders – the troops described by Tacitus were probably from Legio XX then based near Gloucester). Now the Silures are rampaging far and wide, ambushing Roman foraging parties and keeping the invaders pinned in their fortresses. The new governor Aulus Didius hurries to Britain at Caesar's command, but when he arrives his attentions are drawn northwards where Rome's ally Queen Cartimandua is fighting a civil war for control of the Brigantes. In the west the Silures will remain a troublesome thorn in the side of Rome for another twenty years.

Unrecorded by the pen of Tacitus, as Aulus Didius leads his legions northwards to the rescue of the beautiful but treacherous queen of the Brigantes, a mixed vexillation of legionaries and auxiliary troops embarks upon a punitive raid against a native settlement deep inside Silures country. This is a land of densely wooded valleys and treacherous bogs, of darkness, damp and druids. As the Romans march step-by-step, the wind stirs the shadows in the woods, the crows caw ominously overhead, and the sky is tinged the colour of blood.

OF MEN AND GODS

This game was devised as a multi-player scenario with the scene set and the game run by an umpire. Two avowedly depilated players took the role of the Roman commanders, whilst the three players sporting the most luxuriant moustaches – a necessary furnishing for any self-respecting Briton – represented the natives. The tabletop was set up to represent a narrow steep-sided valley lined with woodland as shown on the map. The table itself was nine feet by six with the Romans beginning at the western entrance to the valley edge as indicated. No Britons were placed on the table at the start of play, on the principle that their forces would remain hidden until discovered by the Romans or until they moved. Thus, at the start of the game, the Romans are unaware what dangers lurk before them. By the same token the Druidic temple is not placed on the table, being secluded deep within the woods at the head of the valley, and must either be discovered by the Romans or revealed by the Britons during the course of the game.

Each group of players was briefed separately by the umpire prior to the battle along the lines given below. The Britons elected to forego the option of conducting the game naked save for a daubing of woad, for which consideration the Romans were manifestly grateful.

'Battle followed battle. They were mostly guerrilla fights, in woods and bogs. Some were accidental - the results of chance encounters. Others were planned and calculated bravery'.

Tacitus Annals xii

THE ROMAN BRIEF

The Roman army consists of four divisions as follows:

General – Marcus Spandex, Praefectus castrorum
- 1 unit of legionaries
- 1 unit of raw legionaries
- 1 unit of auxiliaries
- 1 small unit of auxiliary archers

Cenicus Dodius – in charge of the cavalry
- 2 units of auxiliary cavalry
- 1 small unit of Numidian light cavalry

Maximius Flaatus
- 1 unit of legionaries
- 1 unit of raw legionaries
- 1 unit of auxiliaries
- 1 small unit of auxiliary archers

Dipso Maniacus Vino
- 1 unit of legionaries
- 1 unit of raw legionaries
- 1 unit of auxiliaries
- 1 small unit of auxiliary archers

All Roman commanders apart from Dipso Maniacus Vino have a Leadership rating of 8. Marcus Spandex has the General's re-roll rule and is therefore entitled to re-roll a single command test each round. Dipso Maniacus Vino turns up scandalously drunk. His Leadership value is therefore determined randomly at the start of the Command part of each turn. Roll a dice: a roll of 1=7, 2-5=8 and 6= 9.

The Roman force is engaged in a punitive raid. The Silures have committed sundry outrages against the majesty of Rome. Standards of Legio XX were lost to the enemy during a recent attack. It is your duty to avenge this disgrace and restore the Legion's pride. Scouts have located a tribal centre in a steep-sided valley. The table represents this valley. It is dawn. As you enter the valley the sight of grazing animals confirms the enemy have been caught napping. Progress up the valley, looting, taking captives and finding and recovering the lost standards. Your objectives are, in order of priority:
- Crush any opposition!
- Recover the lost standards of Legio XX.
- Loot and destroy native settlements.
- Capture woman and children, and drive away livestock.

THE ROMAN ARMY

All commanders including the general have Leadership ratings of 8 apart from Dipso Maniacus Vino who has a randomised Leadership rating as already noted. The general has the standard re-roll rule in addition.

Type	Clash	Sustained	Short Range	Long Range	Morale Save	Stamina	Special
Roman Legionaries armed with pila and swords (Heavy Infantry)	7	7	3	0	4+	6	Drilled, Elite (4+), Testudo
Raw Roman Legionaries armed as above (Heavy Infantry)	6	6	3	0	4+	6	
Auxiliaries with spears (Medium Infantry)	6	6	3	0	5+	6	
Auxiliary Archers fielded as small unit (Light Infantry Archers)	3	3	2	2	6+	4	
Cavalry Auxiliaries with spears/javelins (Medium Cavalry)	8	5	3	0	5+	6	
Numidian Cavalry fielded as small unit (Light Cavalry)	5	3	2	0	6+	4	Feigned Flight

Roman legionaries are armed with pila and archers with bows. No special rules apply to spear/javelin armed troops and spears are not considered long spears.

THE BRITONS' BRIEF

This force is divided into three commands: a division of infantry, cavalry and chariots representing the local chief's household troops, a large division of infantry, cavalry and chariots representing local tribes, and a smaller division of druidic warriors. The local chieftain controls the villagers, hunters and lookouts as explained below.

General – Bagotrix, Chieftain of the Valley
- 4 Warbands
- 1 unit of Skirmishers with slings
- 1 unit of Chariots
- 1 unit of Cavalry

Catubatrenus
- 4 Warbands
- 1 unit of Skirmishers with slings
- 2 units of Chariots
- 1 unit of Cavalry

Alibongus – the Druid
- 2 units of Druidic Fanatics
- 1 unit of Skirmishers with javelins

Celtic Villagers
- 1 group of Villagers
- 1 group of Hunters
- 1 group of Sentries
- 1 Herdsman

All Briton Commanders have a Leadership value of 8 and Bagotrix has the general's re-roll rule allowing him to re-roll one command result each turn. Alibongus the Druid is a commander but also has up to 3 attacks (as opposed to the more usual 2).

THE BRITONS

All commanders including the general have Leadership ratings of 8. The general has the standard re-roll rule in addition.

Type	Combat				Morale Save	Stamina	Special
	Clash	Sustained	Short Range	Long Range			
Warband armed with swords and javelins (medium infantry)	9	6	2	0	5+	6	Wild Fighters (3 re-rolls)
Druid Fanatic Warband (medium infantry)	9	6	2	0	5+	6	Wild Fighters (3 re-rolls), Fanatic, Frenzied Charge
Skirmishers with javelins fielded as a small unit.	3	2	2	0	0	4	
Skirmishers with slings fielded as a small unit	2	2	2	2	0	4	
Cavalry armed with javelins (light cavalry)	7	5	3	0	6+	6	
British Light Chariots	6	5	4	0	4+	6	
Celtic sentries with bows (tiny)	1	1	1	1	5+	1	
Celtic villagers (tiny)	1	1	1	0	0	1	
Hunters armed with javelins and fielded as small unit (skirmishers)	2	2	2	2	0	4	

Britons are armed with swords and javelins throughout, apart from the sling-armed Skirmishers. The Celtic sentries occupy the lookout post, which is treated as a building, adding +2 to their Morale save. The villagers are armed with whatever comes to hand. The herdsman has no stats and is simply slain if caught, if he reaches the villagers he is absorbed into their unit.

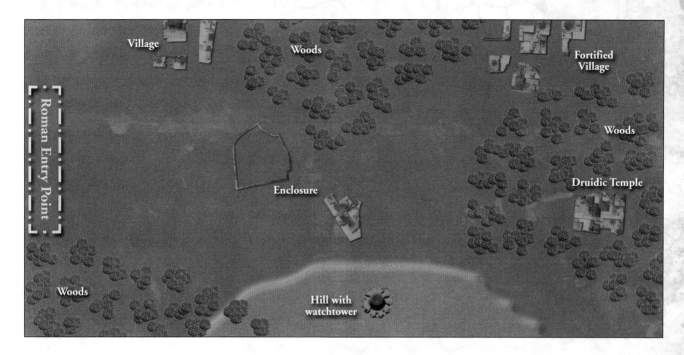

It is the dawn of a great festival day and the tribes are gathering to celebrate in fine style with food, drink and raucous song. Recent victories against the hated Romans have furnished the proceedings with a number of impressive trophies in the form of legionary standards. The Britons have also captured several legionaries who will be sacrificed on the druids' altar during the evening. The site of the gathering is the valley before you with its secret druidic temple hidden deep inside the eastern woods. Many druids have already assembled around the temple. None dare approach whilst the priests perform their blood-curdling rites. Meanwhile, all the neighbouring tribes are travelling towards the valley and are expected to arrive shortly. Within the valley itself the ordinary folk tend to their animals, whilst the women and children prepare for the evening's feast in their rude huts. Sentries take their place in the lone lookout post.

At the start of the game only the herdsman and the lookouts are placed on the table. The villagers are assumed to be inside their huts pursuing their rude crafts in preparation for the day ahead and are therefore not placed on the table. They can do nothing until warned by the herdsman or until attacked by the Romans. Chieftain Bagotrix and his household warriors are camped around the stockaded village at the head of the valley and are not placed onto the table until the alarm is given. Until then they can do nothing. Catubatrenus and the tribes are approaching the valley and will arrive at the south-eastern corner of the table on the appropriate dice roll made from turn 2 onwards. Until the alarm is given their default order is to move to the stockaded village and join Bagotrix. The druids are hidden deep within the woods. Neither the druids nor their temple are placed on the table at the start of the game. Alibongus, the druidic forces, and temple can be placed on the table at the start of any Briton turn after the alarm has been given. Until then they can do nothing.

The Briton objectives are as follows:
- Firstly to raise the alarm! How to do this is described below.
- Subsequently – to head-off the Romans and defeat them.

Set up the table along the lines shown on the accompanying map. We considered the animal enclosure to have no significance other than helping to set the scene. It can be missed off if preferred or treated as rough ground if you want to make life harder for the Romans. The temple and track leading to it are not placed on the table until the druid division is activated.

The Romans have the first turn and are allowed to bring one division onto the table each turn, entering along the western edge. Troops entering the table are placed within 6" of the table edge and cannot move further that turn. Should there not be room to place some or all of the units in a division (because troops already deployed have failed to move) then newly arriving units will have to wait until the blockage is cleared.

Herdsman. Once the Romans are on the board the herdsman immediately spots them. The Britons can then move the herdsman either towards the village to warn the villagers or towards the lookout post to give the alarm. The herdsman does not need a commander. He is moved by giving orders against a Leadership value of 8, treating him as a tiny unit. He always moves at least once each turn. If moved over by the enemy he is slain instantly without fighting and no hand-to-hand combat is initiated. If the herdsman reaches the village before the Romans he warns the villagers (see villagers). If the herdsman reaches the lookout post the alarm is sounded (see lookout post). We put him about 15" from the village – i.e. within 3 moves distance.

Lookout post. If there are Romans within 12" of the lookout post at the start of any Briton turn the alarm is sounded automatically. If the herdsman or villagers move into touch with the lookout post the alarm is automatically given. If Romans choose to attack the lookout post either by ranged fire or hand-to-hand combat the alarm is automatically given at the start of the following Briton turn assuming the lookouts have not been destroyed in the meantime. Should the lookouts be destroyed before they give the alarm then they are

Roman legionaries and auxiliaries in the thick of the fighting

unable to do so. Otherwise, if there are Romans within 24" of the lookout post at the start of any Briton turn roll a dice, on the score of 4, 5 or 6 the alarm is sounded. Finally, if any Roman unit progresses further east than the line between the lookout post and the animal enclosure the alarm is automatically given at the start of the following Briton turn regardless of whether the lookouts have been destroyed or not – this is as far as the Romans can possibly get without being spotted.

Villagers. If the herdsman reaches the village before the Romans the villagers deploy as a tiny unit and can be placed within 6" of the village. Subsequently they can be given orders with a Leadership value of 8 and always make one move. Should the villagers reach either the stockaded village or the watchtower the alarm is given automatically. If the village is attacked before its inhabitants are warned, then the villagers deploy automatically as a unit that has been charged in combat – they are caught by surprise and cannot evade or make closing shots.

Hunters. Some villagers are off hunting in the northern woods. They will deploy at the edge of the northern wood next to the village at the start of a Briton turn once the village is attacked. They do not need a commander and are ordered with a Leadership value of 8.

Stockaded village. Bagotrix and his division can deploy into the open area to the east of the village as soon as the alarm is given. If the alarm is given at the start of a Briton turn they

can be given orders as normal. The village itself can be occupied and defended by a single unit of infantry if desired – it is lightly defensible with a Morale bonus of +1. The stockaded village is where the Roman standards are displayed – surrounded by a great pile of captured arms and armour.

Druidic Temple. The Britons can place the temple and the druidic division in the clearing in the woods at the start of any turn once the alarm has been sounded. They must be deployed if the Romans move into the surrounding woods and if they have not already done so. At the druidic temple will be found Roman captives awaiting sacrifice.

Neighbourng tribes. Catubatrenus's division of neighbouring tribes will arrive on the table on the dice roll of a 4, 5 or 6 made at the start of each Briton turn. If they have not arrived by the time the alarm is given they automatically arrive the following turn. They are deployed into the south-eastern corner of the table between the eastern woods and hill and move from the board edge with orders as usual. They get one free move on the turn they deploy – sufficient to place them on the table regardless of their Leadership roll. If the alarm has yet to be given the division's orders must be to move to the stockaded village and camp next to Bagotrix's division.

Herd. The herd of cattle is placed on the table at the start of the game and automatically moves 6" per Briton turn down the valley, away from the Romans, until captured. The herd does not need orders to move – it always moves once per turn. The herd cannot be moved through by troops from either side. Don't make the herd too big or it will hinder progress– it needs to have about the same footprint as a unit of troops. The Romans can capture the herd by any Roman unit moving into touch, at which point the herd will start to move back towards the Roman starting edge (it being assumed some troops have been detailed to drive the cattle away). The herd can be recaptured in the same way. Once the herd has left the table it has been successfully driven off.

Plundering. The Romans can plunder or attempt to destroy either village, the watchtower, or temple if they have a unit in touch at the end of any Roman turn and no enemy within 12". If they plunder they will automatically find legionary standards and Roman prisoners, and are assumed to take any civilians present captive along the way. If they choose to destroy a location they are assumed to have set the buildings on fire and these become uninhabitable from that point on.

The game ends once one side is broken, or by the end of the evening at the umpire's discretion in which case he must pass judgement on the players' efforts. If the Britons are broken then the Romans are free to fulfil any outstanding objectives. If the Romans are broken then any objectives already fulfilled count in their favour, whilst any remaining troops will be forced to withdraw. Overall, this is a tough one for the Romans who must coordinate their forces both to explore the valley and take on any enemy that appear. Roman success must therefore by judged in light of the fact that their raid was unlucky to take place on the same day as a great festival and gathering of tribes.

HOW IT WAS PLAYED – OR ALIBONGUS REVEALS ALL!

Our Roman players surveyed the narrow tree-hemmed valley with evident trepidation before deploying their cavalry division along the northern portion of the western board edge facing the village. The only option remaining to the Britons was to move the herdsman – who was evidently feeling the effects of the damp upon his arthritic limbs that morning as he only managed a single move, placing him firmly in danger of being trampled by the advancing Roman cavalry. The cattle, meanwhile stumbled down the valley, no doubt catching the scent of horses or possibly the garlicky whiff of their riders.

The Romans deployed their main infantry division next, under the command of Spandex, positioning the battlelines further south, with the division's flank resting upon the adjoining woodland. Fearing the sudden appearance of Britons the Romans very sensibly took the precaution of deploying some light troops into open order along the edge of the woods. The Roman cavalry meanwhile appeared to lose their way in the morning mist (rolling a 10 for their move) and so held their ground. Spandex's legions marched resolutely forward a single move.

The Briton player began his second turn by rolling for the arrival of the neighbouring tribes without success. The herdsman wheezed forward another move leaving him mere inches short of the village and some 20" or so from the Roman cavalry. In their turn the Romans deployed their second infantry division under the inebriated command of Dipso Maniacus Vino, whilst Spandex formed a defensive line to the south of the village.

A band of Roman archers found themselves within bowshot of the Britons' look-out post and cast a few arrows in its direction without any effect other than to arouse the notice of the sentries. The Roman cavalry finally sprang into action, rolling three moves and trampling over the gasping herdsman as they launched themselves upon the village. The villagers deployed into a defensive line, but were quickly massacred, leaving the Romans in possession of the village, no enemies nearby, and therefore one objective achieved. A search of the buildings revealed them to be empty and the Romans led the women and children off into captivity.

The alarm was raised at the start of the Britons' following turn (because the Romans had shot at the look outs) and the neighbouring tribe also decided to show up with an auspicious dice roll of a 6. The chieftain's own household division deployed around the stockaded village. The Hunters deployed on the edge of the wood and, spying the Romans pillaging their village, proceeded to attack the opposing cavalry with their javelins.

By this time the Romans were starting to get an idea of how many enemy they were facing and decided to draw their troops together into a tighter defensive line. The final Roman infantry division moved onto the table edge behind Spandex's troops, whilst the unpredictable Vino (Leadership 9 this turn) merrily led his men forward in a futile attempt to capture the Britons' cattle. Meanwhile the Numidian cavalry skirmished with the Hunters around the village, though with little consequence. Whilst the Hunters remained within 12" the Romans were unable to set fire to the village, so the Britons were satisfied to keep things bogged down.

The Britons moved forward rapidly in their turn, with the foremost warbands, cavalry, and chariots crowding into the narrow open space along the valley floor. Catubatrenus's division showed remarkably enthusiasm (three moves) and spilled into the area between the watchtower and eastern woods. Meanwhile Bagotrix dispatched a portion of his command through the northern woods. This allowed him to make room in the centre and gave him a chance to get behind the flanks of any potential Roman advance. As the woods were only passable to troops in open order the warbands were obliged to open their formation to enter.

The Romans responded by advancing to the edge of the animal enclosure in an attempt to form a solid defensive line between the northern and southern woods. Spandex's

Briton chariots seen against a background of the Welsh hills. Chariot ponies were small, hardy beasts not unlike modern day Welsh hill ponies

division took up a convincing position to the north. Sadly Vino chose this moment to blunder, and the intended advance of his division resolved itself as a two move retreat to his rear! This left a yawning gap in the Roman line which the cavalry successfully plugged with a double move. Meanwhile, the rearmost Roman infantry division failed to move at all. At this point is was all looking a bit of a shambles for the Romans, although Spandex's troops continued to maintain a tenable position around the general.

The Britons were determined to mount a head-on assault towards the Roman lines, but managed only a steady shamble forwards (one move) in the north, whilst in the south the advance stalled altogether. The Romans responded by drawing their line back into a tight formation with infantry in good mutually supporting positions. A unit of Roman archers found itself within range of the enemy skirmish screen and had the satisfaction of seeing the Britons turn and run before a volley of arrows (a 6 'to hit' resulting in a break test that the skirmishers failed).

The Britons saw that matters would be settled in the centre and decided to reveal their secret weapon – the dreaded druidic warriors and their fearsome leader Alibongus. The sudden appearance of the Celtic temple and its fanatical devotees did little for the fighting spirit of the Romans whose confidence had visibly plummeted as each enemy division took its place on the field. To have called these latest foes half-naked savages would have been a distinct exaggeration; for they were proudly skyclad to a man, not least the raving madman at their head: the druid Alibongus. The druids ran forward as bereft of fear as of trouser, elbowing their way past friendly units in the front of the Briton army. The cavalry moved up to support them. The Britons had now formed a credible line between the northern woods and the southern hill. The opposing infantry forces had drawn into charge reach – though only just.

Somewhat unnerved by the appearance of the fanatical warriors the Romans pushed the Numidian cavalry forward and proceeded to pepper the naked Celts with javelins. Roman archers, who had deployed into open order ahead of the legions, added their own missiles to the barrage. Both druid units suffered a casualty each as a consequence, but the

Roman archery failed to halt their advance (failing to score the 6's needed to initiate a break test). On the positive side the Romans had managed to move their remaining infantry back into formation, and now stood in a solid battleline that would be tough for the Britons to breach.

In the Britons' turn Alibongus declared his charge, and with the 'frenzied charge' rule giving them three moves on a successful order both units of druids hurled themselves upon the opposing Romans. The archers in front of the first unit of fanatics evaded back through the legions to their rear, and the chargers flew onwards into the massed ranks of heavy infantry. It had been a long charge though – almost 18" in fact – and the rest of the Celtic army predictably failed to keep pace. The fanatics were on their own. Against a battleline of well-supported legionaries they would be lucky to survive. To make matters worse Catubatrenus' tribesmen hung back altogether (Catubatrenus failed his first order, leaving the whole division standing). Suspicions were cast upon the loyalty of Catubatrenus and his warriors – had they been bought off with Roman gold? The Roman players were certainly happy to claim as much!

Each unit of fanatics found itself in a separate combat. In the south the dice showed little favour to either side. The fanatics with nine attacks and benefiting from their charge bonus and re-rolls landed eight hits, but the Romans managed to save six. They needed 4's to save so this was better than average. Two casualties were marked on the Romans. In reply the Romans and their supports managed to hit with five of their attacks. Average again as the legion was supported by a single auxiliary unit. The fanatics enhanced save (+1 Morale save until shaken) was cancelled out by the legionaries' pilum bonus (–1 Morale save in the first round). However, the gods were with the fanatics that day and they saved three hits. They needed rolls of 5 or 6. Two more casualties were marked on the fanatics bringing their total to three including the casualty suffered in the previous turn from bowfire. Result – two casualties scored each – a draw! The Roman line had held.

In the north the other unit of fanatics was joined by Alibongus, bringing their total number of attacks to twelve of which ten landed hits on the Romans. A fistful of 1's and 2's

The Romans draw into a tight defensive line in the face of the Britons' relentless advance

drew a groan from the Roman players. No fewer than eight casualty markers were placed by the legion. However, the legion was supported by a raw legionary unit to its rear and a unit of auxiliaries to its flank. The Roman player had thirteen dice by way of reply (needing 4's to hit). Once more the dice showed their disfavour with a mere four hits, two of which the fanatics saved (needing 5's – their +1 fanatic bonus being cancelled out by the legionaries' –1 pilum). Two casualty markers were placed next to the fanatics, bringing their total to three including the missile casualty suffered in the previous turn. With a loss by '6' the already shaken Romans needed a roll of 11 or 12 to avoid breaking and not surprisingly they failed. The legion was removed and both supporting units were obliged to test. They only needed to score 9 or more to avoid destruction (as neither unit was shaken, unlike the unlucky legionaries) but both failed to come up with the goods and both units took to their heels and fled (and were therefore removed from the table). The Celtic players were jubilant. The pride of Rome had been brought low by a bunch of savages wearing nothing but a fancy haircut!

As the Roman units were removed Alibongus declared his intention to make a sweeping charge into the only Roman unit still standing in front of his fanatics. This was a unit of auxiliaries. Because sweeping charges are worked out right away the Romans once more took up the dice – and once more the Romans were destroyed in a single round – suffering six casualties in return for two and rolling a miserable 5 for their break test. It had been an incredible run of luck for Alibongus – he had led his fanatics against no fewer than four enemy units and broken them all. The fanatics had suffered five casualties and so were not even shaken. In his post combat move Alibongus led his men back to the Celtic lines – not wanting to be crushed by the Roman cavalry in the following turn. The opposing Roman division had been broken (Spandex's troops) and the division behind had been given a mauling. The auxiliaries were from Maximius Flaatus' division.

The Roman turn saw both players battling to restore a crumbling line. The Roman cavalry now held the gap

formerly occupied by Spandex's troops but could only draw close enough to skirmish ineffectively. However, in the south the remaining unit of fanatics was easily beaten and destroyed. The Britons having lost their initial clash value, charge bonus and re-rolls, the Romans' superior endurance and heavy armour won the day.

At last the main warbands of Bagotrix and Catubatrenus advanced purposefully upon the Romans. The warbands which had moved through the northern woods began to emerge behind the Romans' flank. But Alibongus had the Romans in sight. With the frenzied charge rule still applying he was obliged to charge once more. So – with one casualty short of a shaken unit – the fanatics charged upon the Roman ranks. The fanatics had been careful to move back into support with their cavalry in the previous turn, but alas the horsemen failed to keep pace and were unable to join the fight. Once more the fanatics were on their own.

This time it was a legionary unit of Maximius Flaatus' division with two supports that faced the stark naked madmen. But Alibongus (for indeed it was Alan Perry whose talented paws wielded the dice that day) knew his luck was in and Flaatus (in the guise of Paul Sawyer) sensed that destiny had betrayed him. Flaatus threw himself to the forefront of battle, but for all his efforts the Romans lost by two casualties to four. With a diffident toss (for which this player is justly famous) the Roman commander rolled his break test and the cursed cubes turned up a double 1. Any roll of a 4 or more would have seen him all right – but no. Nor was the agony quite over yet, for both supporting units also turned tail and ran – with rolls of 3 and 4 respectively. Truly the gods had spoken, and rather frankly too.

At the point the Roman army broke and the invaders were defeated. It had been an astounding battle, won not so much by the savagery of Alibongus' fanatics as the timidity of the Romans who had failed dice roll after dice roll and finally collapsed in terror. The Britons celebrated by jeering at their opponents' dice rolling deficiencies until the kindly umpire intervened to lead the weeping Romans to a consolatory beer.

Late Roman infantry deploy in the face of barbarian cavalry. Following the collapse of the empire in the 3rd century, the old-fashioned Roman legions disappear to be replaced by infantry armed with spears and flat, oval shields much like their barbarian opponents

The Roman Empire suffered a long period of disintegration and civil wars during the middle and late third century, resulting in a complete breakdown in the old system of closed borders protected by modest legionary forces. The causes of this disaster stem from the pressures exerted by powerful and numerous invaders all along Rome's northern and eastern frontiers. The old military system proved unable to respond effectively, at least not until hordes of barbarians had rampaged through Roman provinces, plundering and sowing devastation in their wake. In the west these invaders were chiefly German tribes such as the Franks, Saxons, and Alamanni. Along the Danube there were the Sarmatians and Goths. In the east there was the additional threat posed by a resurgent Persian empire under the newly founded Sassanid dynasty. The Sassanids were far more ambitious, and much better organised, than the Parthians they supplanted. Sassanid Kings saw themselves as the heirs of Xerxes and the Achaemenids of old, destined to restore the Persian empire to its former glory.

As a result of these repeated invasions and almost continuous warfare, Emperors were forced into an increasingly military roll as the leaders of armies. Successful generals found themselves elevated to the purple by their troops – not always willingly if their biographers are to be believed! Rival Emperors – in reality rival armies – split the old Roman Empire apart. Gaul and Britain became independent as the Gallic Empire. In the east the Palmyrans took over a substantial part of the old Hellenised Near East. At first they did so nominally on behalf of Rome, later as rivals. Amidst this anarchy the old military systems soon broke down as forces were hastily mustered to meet new threats. New, larger and more mobile armies were to emerge, but the cost far exceeded anything the Roman state had ever endured before. In order to pay for these vast armies, civic society, the economy and imperial government were all reorganised from the top down. A huge bureaucracy of tax gatherers and civil servants was created, and a new caste of Emperors – half-educated, pragmatic military men from Illyria – was ushered to the fore.

For the ordinary people these were tough times. In the third century they had been burdened by repeated invasions. If they lived near the fighting zones they would have suffered from the wholesale requisition of supplies to meet the rapacious needs of the army. From the fourth century onwards citizens became legally bound to their lands or trades, and they were taxed even more heavily than ever before. Agricultural workers, artisans and tradesmen became little more than serfs in service to a militarised and increasingly centralised state. In the west, cities declined in importance as people fled to the relative safety of the countryside. Banditry became rife as farmers abandoned their lands – unable to endure both rising taxes and periodic pillaging. Everywhere populations declined – a situation not helped by a plague that took hold after 251 and recurred periodically over the next 20 years, carrying off the Emperor Claudius Gothicus amongst its victims. The resulting manpower shortages were made up to some extent by the large-scale settlement of alien – mostly German – tribes on otherwise abandoned land. The prosperity and relative freedom of the days of high empire were ended forever.

By the time the Romans had regained control of all the lands from Britain in the west to the Euphrates in the east, their armies had changed completely. These changes had begun as a response to the invasions of the previous decades, when it was necessary for forces to become increasingly mobile in order to meet and defeat barbarian hordes that had already penetrated the frontiers. The old fashioned, heavily armed legionaries disappear during these upheavals. They were replaced by a mix of border guards spread thinly across the frontiers and field armies, which were held in reserve to deal with invaders. The border forces were called limitanei and their role was to garrison the new fortifications and hold out whilst the field armies – the comitatenses – turned up to offer battle. In time the limitanei became bound to the area they were expected to defend – a kind of hereditary militiamen/farmers rather than professional warriors.

The field armies included the remnants of the old legions. These retained little of their predecessor's qualities aside from their names, and were reduced in size to about 1,000 men apiece compared to about 5,000 in a traditional legion. Gone were the familiar segmented armour and oblong scutum of the legionary, replaced by mail armour and oval shaped shields. Infantry now carried spears: weapons more suited for use against horsemen than the old Roman pilum, and easier to manufacture in the many new armouries established to supply the burgeoning armies. Where required, a cheaper and easier to produce replacement for the pilum was created called the 'martiobarbulus' – dart of Mars. This was a short, lead-weighted javelin that could be thrown prior to contact. Several of these darts could be carried in addition to an infantryman's spear. However, the real strength of the Roman army no longer lay with its infantry, but with heavily armoured horsemen. Often these troops were Germans – and frequently they were men born outside the Empire who had been recruited en masse to serve in the new armies. Throughout all ranks, Roman armies increasingly consisted of barbarians who were, in many cases, barely distinguishable from their enemies.

During this period the main foes of the Romans were the German tribes that, in the west, included Saxons, Franks and Alemanni. These were not necessary new peoples, but more likely new names for confederacies that had fought against the Romans for centuries. Along the Danube frontier a new enemy emerged in the shape of the Goths – a large and powerful Germanic nation that had moved eastwards into the lands north of the Black Sea. In time the Goths came under pressure from the Huns, forcing them south and westwards into conflict with the Roman Empire. This enforced migration was to lead to the great military disaster at the Battle of Adianople in 378 when the Emperor Valens and an army of over 40,000 men was destroyed by Gothic cavalry. Further east still, Rome's principle opponent remained the Sassanid Persians. Here the Romans enjoyed periodic success as well as suffering their fair share of setbacks. The Emperor Julian the Apostate succeeded in defeating the Persians at the very gates of their capital Ctesiphon in 363, but was subsequently killed during the retreat to Roman controlled Mesopotamia. His successor was forced to buy off the Persians – a tactic that was to become habitual during the fifth century and beyond into the days of the Byzantine Empire.

By the fifth century the Huns had subdued the Goths and together they invaded the Roman east, causing widespread devastation and panic. Hun armies captured Armenia and rampaged through Syria. West of the Black Sea they rode though Thrace and into Italy and Gaul. By the mid fifth century Attila the Hun was so feared that the Romans and Visigoths put aside their differences to fight against him and his mostly Ostrogothic allies. The result was the Battle of Chalons of 451 where the power of the eastern invaders was dealt a mortal blow. Gibbon refers to this as the 'last victory achieved in the name of the Western Roman Empire.'

The adoption of Christianity by Constantine ended an ambiguous position where the genii of Roman Emperors were effectively worshipped as state gods. At the end of the third century this had led to the bloody persecution of Christians who refused to make the appropriate – and legally enforceable – sacrifices both to the traditional Roman gods and to the genius of the Emperor. From the time of Constantine's triumph at the Milvian Bridge in 312 Roman armies would adopt the Christian Chi-Rho symbol, and battle standards would increasingly become icons bearing images of Christ and the saints. Henceforth Rome would become the embodiment of the church, rather than its antithesis.

Cavalry became an increasingly important part of Roman armies from the mid-third century. By the reign of Constantine the cavalry were placed under their own commander in each of the Empire's provinces - the Magister Equitum.

GO MEEK INTO THE DESERT 260AD

A BORDER CLASH BETWEEN ROMANS AND PERSIANS

It is AD260. Several years ago, the Sassanid Persians, under their Shahanshah (King of Kings) Shapur I, invaded the Eastern provinces of the Roman Empire. Last year, betrayed by his advisors, the ageing Roman emperor Valerian was captured by Shapur. In the wake of this calamity, and with the Emperor Gallienus battling to put down rebellions in the West, the Roman armies of the East, led by Marcus Clodius Ballista, praefectus praetorio (Praetorian Prefect), are struggling to organise themselves to defend the empire, and expel the invaders.

Ballista sent a scratch force of legionaries and auxiliaries, commanded by Lucius Domitius Aurelianus to defend the twin cities of Zeugma and Apamea, but whilst marching there they bumped into a much larger force of 'reptiles', commanded by Hamazasp, a vassal of Shapur, and were forced to retreat, fighting a series of delaying actions. The action described here is one of those.

THE WARGAME

Elephants! When it came to formulating the rules for Hail Caesar we recalled a recent convention where we had seen a gorgeous Sassanid Persian army that included three of these magnificent beasts, and all very beautifully presented and painted. We contacted the army's owner who turned out to be Dr Phil Hendry. Some readers will have seen pictures of Phil's many armies in the pages of the wargames press, on his own website, and in various books about ancient wargames. To our delight, Phil agreed to come down to Nottingham and to bring not only his Sassanids, but also his contemporary Imperial Romans.

The game was played in John Stallard's gaming room, and the battle was arranged to take place on the day before the popular Partizan wargames convention in Newark. As a result the local hotels found themselves choc-a-bloc with wargamers who had come up for the event. Word of our battle soon got round, so before long we had gathered quite a crowd. Still – the more the merrier! Around the table we had: Rick Priestley, Henry Hyde and Duncan Macfarlane commanding the Sassanids, and Phil Hendry, Paul Sawyer and Colin Speirs commanding the Romans. As both Rick and Paul were old hands at Hail Caesar, the rest being initiates, these two players elected to co-umpire the game with the impartial assistance of Alessio Cavatore, who also took notes for this report. Guy Bowers arrived a little later with his camera, and photographed the action for posterity whilst offering much hearty advice to both sides. John Stallard was our host for the occasion, ensuring that refreshment and conversation flowed in equal abundance.

THE TABLE

We first intended to borrow Alan Perry's majestic desert terrain modular boards to play the game on, as John's terrain is more appropriate to the luscious green of Albion. However, Phil told us that he had his own terrain designed to go with the very armies we would be using. In fact he would be displaying a game at the Partizan convention the following day, so he had come prepared with armies, scenery, dice, the lot! We therefore decided to use Phil's terrain as well as his armies. It was very interesting to see Phil's solution to putting on an attractive yet easily transportable wargame. It consists of a light-khaki tablecloth, which Phil has covered in green textured dots of various sizes to resemble desert scrub. A number of polystyrene hills are placed on top, some tall palm trees, a little oasis and a circular tower (from Monolith Designs), and everything is painted to match the tablecloth.

The bases of Phil's models are also painted to match the terrain, so when they are deployed on the field they meld perfectly with it. In the end, with this simple yet clever use of colour, Phil has created a portable battlefield for his armies that is nicely themed, inexpensive and very easy to transport and store. It looks good in the pictures too!

THE ARMIES - ORDERS OF BATTLE

THE SASSANIDS

1st Division – cavalry:
- Division Commander – Army General *Hamazasp*
- 3 units of Savaran Cataphract (two units have kontos, all three units have bows as well).
- 1 unit of Sassanid light cavalry

2nd Division – horse archers:
- Division Commander
- 2 units of horse archers (one Parthian one Arab)

3rd Division – war elephants:
- Division Commander
- 3 Elephants

4th Division – infantry:
- Division Commander
- 4 units of mixed spearmen/archers
- 2 units of skirmishers

SASSANID STATISTICS AND SPECIAL RULES

All commanders including the general have Leadership ratings of 8. The general has the standard re-roll rule in addition.

Type	Combat				Morale Save	Stamina	Special
	Clash	Sustained	Short Range	Long Range			
Elephant with howdah and crew	4	3	1	1	4+	6	Elephant
Savaran Cataphracts with kontos and bow (Cataphracts)	9	6	3	2	4+	6	
Savaran Cataphracts with bow (Cataphracts)	9	6	3	2	4+	6	
Sassanid light cavalry with javelins (Light Cavalry)	7	5	3	0	6+	6	Feigned Flight
Parthian/Arab Horse Archer (Horse Archers)	6	3	3	3	6+	6	Feigned Flight, Parthian Shot
Sassanid infantry (Medium Infantry with spear and bow)	6	6	3	3	5+	6	
Skirmishers with javelins and fielded as small units (Skirmishers)	3	2	2	0	0	4	
Sassanid infantry (Medium Infantry)	6	6	3	0	5+	6	

The rules for the various weapons carried apply – these are shown in the description of the unit rather than noted as special rules. Note that the mixed spearmen and archer units are not given the long spear rule.

THE ROMANS

1st Division – infantry left:
- Division Commander –
  Army General *Lucius Domitius Aurelianus*
- 2 cohorts of auxiliary infantry
- 1 cohort of auxiliary archers
- 1 scorpio unit (light artillery)
- 1 unit of auxiliary 'expedita' (skirmishers)

2nd Division – infantry right:
- Division Commander
- 2 cohorts of legionaries from Legio II Traiana Fortis
- 1 cohort of auxiliary archers
- 1 scorpio unit (light artillery)

3rd Division – infantry reserve:
- Division Commander
- 2 cohorts of legionaries (one from Legio II Traiana Fortis and one from Legio XII Fretensis)
- 1 cohort of auxiliary infantry

4th Division – cavalry:
- Division Commander
- 2 alae of heavy cavalry
- 1 ala of light cavalry (Moors)
- 1 ala of light cavalry (camels)

DISPOSITIONS

All of the Roman infantry was deployed around the watchtower, having already taken position to defend the oasis from the approaching Sassanid army.

The Roman cavalry division started the game off the table. We assumed they were looking for more water for their mounts, as the little oasis near the tower had barely enough water for the men. As the dust of the approaching Sassanids was spotted a messenger had been sent out to summon the cavalry with all haste. This division would therefore enter the table on the roll of a 4+ in Turn 2, 3+ on turn 3, 2+ on turn 4 or automatically on turn 5. It would appear in the gap between the two hills on the Roman left flank.

The entire Sassanid army was assumed to be just outside the opposite table edge and needed to be ordered onto the table starting on turn 1. They were going to go first.

OBJECTIVES

The two armies were fighting for control of the oasis outpost. The first side to break would be driven from the field. Otherwise, the side deemed by the umpiral committee to have the most decisive presence around the oasis at the close of play would be declared the winner.

ROMAN STATISTICS AND SPECIAL RULES

All commanders including the general have Leadership ratings of 8. The general has the standard re-roll rule in addition.

Type	Combat				Morale Save	Stamina	Special
	Clash	Sustained	Short Range	Long Range			
Auxiliary Infantry with spears and javelins (Heavy Infantry)	7	7	3	0	4+	6	
Auxiliary Archers (Medium Infantry Archers)	5	5	3	3	5+	6	
Scorpio (Light Artillery)	1	1	2	2	0	3	
Expedita with javelins fielded as small unit (Skirmishers)	3	2	2	0	0	4	
Legionaries with spears and javelins (Heavy Infantry)	7	7	3	3	4+	6	Drilled
Heavy Cavalry Ala (Heavy Cavalry)	9	6	3	0	4+	6	
Moorish Cavalry Ala (Light Cavalry)	7	5	3	0	6+	6	Feigned Flight
Camel Ala (Light Cavalry)	7	5	3	0	6+	6	

The rules for the various weapons carried apply – these are shown in the description of the unit rather than noted as special rules. Note that none of the spearmen were given the long spear rule.

Sassanid Entry Point

Palm Trees

ROMAN DIVISION II

ROMAN DIVISION I

Scrub

Tower

ROMAN DIVISION III

Roman Cavalry Entry Point

HOW IT WAS PLAYED

The Sassanid army appeared on the horizon – infantry division to the extreme left, elephants in the centre and horse archers on the right scouting ahead of the mighty Savaran division led by the Persian general Hamazasp, otherwise known as Shah Henry. However, it seemed that the cataphracts, true to their reputation of not being the most nimble of troops, were delayed and therefore failed to appear on the Persian right. This was due to Shah Henry failing a command roll, re-rolling it because of his general special ability and failing once again. Plainly it was not to be.

Taking advantage of the fact that the enemy's strongest division had failed to arrive, the Romans made a very brave decision that would shape the entire game. The Roman general ordered his infantry to advance as fast as possible against the enemy, with the idea of smashing them apart with his legionaries before the slow-moving Savaran could join the fray. The first and second division advanced boldly towards the Sassanids and a missile exchange erupted between the skirmishers at the fore of 1st division and the horse archers facing them. The Romans jubilantly managed to force the opposing Arab cavalry to retire under a barrage of javelins!

The second turn saw the Sassanid Savaran cavalry division once again fail to reach the battlefield. At this point Henry was considering a quick trip to The Gushnasp Fire-temple at Shiz to get his dice blessed in the holy flame of Zarathushtra. The horse archers and elephants, nervously aware of both the big gap on their flank and the rapidly advancing Roman infantry, decided to hold their ground. They proceeded to pepper the skirmishers with bow fire, successfully driving away their lightly armed opponents. Meanwhile, the massed ranks of Sassanid infantry on the Persian left seized the moment and charged down at the oncoming legionaries in an altogether unexpected show of bravery. Predictably, they bounced right off the solid ranks of legionaries, but only after a few hurried prayers to Mithras and some fortunate dice rolling by the Romans.

In the Romans' turn, Paul's efforts to bring his cavalry division onto the field proved no more successful than Henry's, leaving the Roman left flank and Persian right very empty indeed (as befits a desert after all). The Roman infantry continued with their relentless advance in the centre, driving away the horse archers who used their Parthian Shot special rule to retire past the elephants and reform beside their Arab counterparts. On the Roman right, the legionaries pressed on against the Sassanid infantry, and even the auxiliary archers joined the fray with credible results. Advancing steadily behind, the Romans' reserve division also began to slowly close the distance with the enemy.

Finally, in the Persians' turn the Sassanid general arrived onto the field to the resounding cheers of his underlings, the braying of trumpets, and calls for celebration. He inspected his army and saw that the elephants and Parthians were busily destroying the remaining Roman skirmishers with a volley of well-aimed arrows. A little beyond them, his infantry were engaged with a numerically inferior enemy division that was never the less cutting the Sassanid spearmen to pieces with typical Roman efficiency, bringing the fighting to a bloody stalemate.

It was now the Romans' turn, and at last Paul's cavalry also arrived, and just in time to protect the legionaries' now dangerously exposed left flank. The gallant horsemen immediately started to ride towards the enemy cataphracts, plainly unimpressed by tales of the Savarans' much-vaunted superiority. The Roman infantry in the centre pushed on and, after sending the Parthians scampering for the hills with a shower of javelins, closed in against the elephants. Surely now these exotic monsters would charge and scatter their foes.

The Romans on the right flank finished off a couple of units of Persian spearmen, but emerged from the confrontation shaken. They therefore stopped to lick their wounds and allow the reserves to catch up. Sadly, the reserve division also halted its advance when called upon to move. Perhaps they imagined that the enemy infantry had been adequately dealt with. Their commander, Colin, seemed to have caught the highly contagious 'dice plague' that had earlier wrought such havoc amongst the Paul and Henry's divisions.

And then the moment of decision was upon us, as the Sassanid cataphracts spied the approaching Roman cavalry and spurred their steeds into a thunderous charge, kontoi at the ready. The two units of Roman heavies decided to meet them head-on and countercharged. We could almost feel the earth shaking under the hooves of the horses and their armoured riders.

The elephants chose to withdraw rather than charge the enemy infantry, possibly waiting to see the outcome of the cavalry clash. The remaining Persian infantry units also followed their example. All eyes turned to the right, to the cloud of dust rising from the big cavalry melee on the flank.

Alas, once that dust had settled there was nothing left of the Roman equites, who were taught the harsh lesson of what happens when you charge with two units against three units of superior troops well supported by friends. Paul Sawyer's dice had obviously studied the odds in advance and decided that resistance was pointless, turning what was always going to be a tough fight into a total and immediate collapse. This was a disaster for the Romans as the Sassanid cavalry were now poised to wipe out their whole left wing and advance upon the Romans in the centre from both front and flank at the same time.

Sensing that time was of the essence, the Roman infantry closed the distance with the retreating elephants and spearmen, ensuring that the Persians had nowhere to retreat to in the following turn other than by abandoning the battlefield. This was a calculated risk. The Romans would try and break the enemy army by annihilating the elephants and what was left of the infantry division. If they managed to do that, they would have won the game without having to fight the deadly cataphracts again. This was a brave and risky move, because it left the entire Roman line with its left flank exposed to the enemy cavalry.

At last the Persian cavalry arrive and quickly find themselves engaged with their Roman counterparts

Roman infantry defend the oasis. Nice shields! Despite repeated attempts to move them, the division remained unengaged at the end of the game

Well, there's certainly a lot of them! The Persian infantry come under attack from their Roman opponents

The final moments of the Roman cavalry division as the Persian cataphracts prepare to sweep all before them

In order to buy time for the infantry to finish the job, what was left of the Roman mounted troops, the two units of light cavalry, declared a charge against the exposed flank of the lead cataphract unit. What these hot-heads (and the players commanding them) had forgotten is that the cataphracts, even though they are as slow as infantry, are still a cavalry unit, and were therefore able to respond by turning to face the charging lights. Let us draw a piteous veil over the carnage that ensued. Following this bloodbath the unit of cataphracts, still practically untouched, pursued the fleeing Moorish cavalry right into the flank of the unit of Roman auxiliaries who were facing the elephants. The next turn did not look too promising for the Romans.

And indeed the rest of the Savaran turned left and rolled up the flank of the Roman first division, even charging some units in the rear. In an attempt to charge the already engaged auxiliaries, the elephants finally issue their trumpeting challenge only to fail to make contact with the beleaguered infantry by a few inches. That would teach them to be so cautious. The Sassanid infantry still held back as they had suffered many casualties already, and to lose a unit at this stage would break a division and potentially bring defeat upon the Persians even at the moment of victory.

As it turned out the elephants would have made no difference, as the auxilliaries were trampled into the ground by the all-conquering cataphracts. The Roman general was crushed underfoot as he tried to lead his men in a desperate last stand.

It has to be said that many armies would have lost heart at this stage, but the Romans were determined to carry on whilst their army remained unbroken. If the second division could turn and charge the exposed elephants and destroy them, while at the same time the reserve division could finally move off the blocks and reach the remaining Sassanid infantry, victory could still be theirs. Just.

The legionaries had a great start, managing to charge the elephants, but then the goddess Fate decided the outcome of the battle, as she so often does. The hurried closing shots by the few archers in the elephants' howdahs managed to find their mark and caused the charging legionaries to take a break test. Colin rolled a spectacular double 1, at which point not only the nerve of the Romans, but also that of the players, broke without any chance for recovery. The Roman army abandoned the field in defeat – *Romanes eunt domus!*

"I write these few lines in the family journal lest we are all murdered by these accursed barbarians. Maximus Effluvium, the magister of the house left many hours since, riding with great speed under the cover of darkness, taking with him only Dacius and Tervix. With the help of the Lord, they will be able to reach the fort, and the garrison commander will send help.

The enemy's scouts have continued to haunt the fields through the night. We fought them off for a while, but we are no warriors, and Lucius was killed defending the young magister who has also been wounded. At the first light of dawn, a troop of cavalrymen joined the foe, perhaps the vanguard of a larger raiding force to come. They have sacked the outbuildings and slaughtered all those who tried to resist. Now the few of us that are left: Lady Apollonia, her sons and daughters, and a handful of us slaves, have taken shelter on the second floor and pulled up the ladders.

I can hear them smashing everything apart downstairs. The lady has barely managed to bring the Lares and Penates with her, so the heathens have by now stolen all of our remaining valuables. It is only a matter of time before they burn us out or demolish the house. May the Lord protect us."

"I've made my way to the rooftop, to see if I could spot any trace of rescue. The barbarians shot at me with their curved bows, but luckily I ducked for cover just in time. The brutes were preparing to storm the house when we heard the bugle calls in the distance. Never before has the sound of a tuba or cornu felt so welcome! The Huns around the villa immediately turned their attention to this new challenge and most of them rode off towards the west. I clambered to the top of the roof and from there I could see in the distance the banners of the rescue force advancing along both roads. Our valiant legionaries are coming! I pray that they manage to defeat the enemy and get here before the fiends set fire to the villa!"

THE WARGAME

Our game represented one of the many unrecorded raids against Roman outposts and colonial settlements west of the Danube during the fifth century AD. The game itself was played in Alan Perry's legendary wargame room, using Alan and Michael's extensive collection of late Romans and assorted barbarians (in this case Huns and Goths).

THE TABLE

For this battle we settled for a 10 foot x 6 foot table, with the scenery arranged as shown on the following maps. The key features were the Roman villa and the fords along the river

THE ARMIES - ORDERS OF BATTLE

The Huns

1st Division – holding force, deploys on table:
- Division Commander
- 1 unit of Goth infantry (heavy infantry, pilum)
- 2 small units of Hun cavalry (light cavalry with bows and javelins)
- 1 tiny unit of Hun scouts, ransacking the villa (skirmishers armed with bows)

2nd Division – Hun main force, arrives Turn 3 on 4+, Turn 4 automatically, from East or South road):
- Division Commander (General)
- 1 unit of Hun Noble cavalry (cataphracts, kontos and bows)
- 2 small units of Hun cavalry (light cavalry with bows and javelins)

3rd Division – Hun main force, arrives Turn 3 on 4+, Turn 4 automatically, from East or South road):
- Division Commander
- 3 small units of Hun cavalry (light cavalry with bows and javelins)

4th Division – Goth main force, arrives Turn 3 on 4+, Turn 4 automatically, from East or South road):
- Division Commander
- 1 unit of Goth infantry (heavy infantry, pilum)
- 2 units of Goth cavalry units (cataphracts)

5th Division – Hun flanking force, arrives Turn 4 on 4+, Turn 5 automatically, from West road):
- Division Commander
- 3 small units of Hun cavalry units (light cavalry with bows and javelins)

HUN STATISTICS AND SPECIAL RULES

All commanders including the general have Leadership ratings of 8. The general has the standard re-roll rule in addition.

Type	Clash	Sustained	Short Range	Long Range	Morale Save	Stamina	Special
Hun scouts with mix of bows and javelins (tiny unit of Skirmishers)	1	1	1	1	0	1	Must remain in the villa and attempt to set fire to it
Hun Nobles armed with kontos and bows (Cataphracts)	9	6	3	2	4+	6	
Hun cavalry armed with with javelins and bows (Light Cavalry fielded as small units)	5	3	2	2	6+	4	
Goth Infantry with heavy throwing spears (Heavy Infantry with pilum)	7	7	3	0	4+	6	
Goth cavalry (Cataphracts)	9	6	3	0	4+	6	

The rules for the various weapons carried apply – these are shown in the description of the unit rather than noted as special rules.

The Romans

1st Division – infantry centre/right:
- Division Commander (General)
- 1 unit of elite legionaries (heavy infantry, drilled, elite 4+, long spears)
- 1 unit of legionaries (heavy infantry, drilled, long spears)
- 1 unit of legionaries (heavy infantry, drilled, long spears), with 1 small sub-unit of Skirmishers (javelin-armed skirmishers)
- 2 units of Scorpios (light artillery)

2nd Division – infantry left:
- Division Commander
- 1 unit of legionaries (heavy infantry, drilled, long spears)
- 1 unit of legionaries (heavy infantry, drilled, long spears), with 1 small sub-unit of Skirmishers (javelin armed skirmishers)
- 1 small unit of Infantry Archers unit

3rd Division – cavalry:
- Division Commander
- 1 unit of Cataphract cavalry (cataphracts, drilled, kontos)
- 1 unit of Heavy cavalry (heavy cavalry)
- 1 small unit of Light cavalry (light cavalry)
- 1 small unit of Horse Archers (horse archers)

ROMAN STATISTICS AND SPECIAL RULES

All commanders including the general have Leadership ratings of 8. The general has the standard re-roll rule in addition.

Type	Combat				Morale Save	Stamina	Special
	Clash	Sustained	Short Range	Long Range			
Elite Legionaries with long spears (Heavy Infantry)	7	7	3/0	0	4+	6	Drilled, Elite 4+
Legionaries with long spears (Heavy Infantry)	7	7	3/0	0	4+	6	Drilled
Sub-unit of Skirmishers armed with javelins (small unit)	3	2	2	0	0	4	Sub-unit
Archers (small unit of Light Infantry)	3	3	2	2	6+	4	
Scorpio – bolt-throwing engines (Light Artillery)	1	1	2	2	0	3	
Roman Cataphracts with kontos (Cataphracts)	9	6	3/0	0	4+	6	Drilled
Roman Heavy Cavalry (Heavy Cavalry)	9	6	3	0	4+	6	
Roman Light Cavalry with javelins (small unit of Light Cavalry)	5	3	2	0	6+	4	
Roman Horse Archers (small unit of Horse Archers)	4	2	2	2	6+	4	

The rules for the various weapons carried apply – these are shown in the description of the unit rather than noted as special rules.

"How great are the dangers I face to win a good name in Athens."

Alexander the Great

DISPOSITIONS

The entire Roman force started the game on the table and was allowed to deploy anywhere within a foot of the western edge.

After the Romans had deployed, the Huns were permitted to position the holding force (1st division) anywhere east of the river. The scouts were placed within the villa where they were busily engaged in looting. They would remain here until the villa was fired or recaptured.

The remaining Huns were formed into two separate groups: the main force and the flanking force. These were kept off the table at the start of the game.

The three divisions composing the main force were approaching from the south-east and therefore would be allowed to arrive at any point on the eastern table edge or along the south-east road. The players declared where each of their divisions would enter the table. In order to determine when they would arrive, it was agreed that at the beginning of the Hun turn 3 the players would roll a dice for each of their divisions. On a roll of 4+ that division could be ordered onto the table that turn. On a result of 1-3 the division was delayed and would instead arrive at the beginning of the following turn (turn 4).

The flanking force, which we imagined to be engaged in a wide encircling manoeuvre, would arrive at any point on the

western table edge (right behind the Romans!) on a 4+ on turn 4. Failing that, the flanking force would arrive automatically on turn 5.

The map shows the initial deployment, with the Goths blocking the ford in the middle of the table and the Hun cavalry ready to harry any unit attempting to cross at the northern ford. The Romans' strongest infantry division deployed in column on the central road; their lighter infantry division in column on the northern road, and the cavalry spread out in front of both infantry columns. Clearly the Romans intended to send the cavalry to capture the crossing points before more Huns could turn up to defend them.

OBJECTIVES

The battle began with some roguish barbarians busy razing, burning and pillaging in the fields around the Roman villa. At the end of every Hun turn, these sinister types would attempt to set the main villa on fire by rolling two dice. On turn 1, they will succeed only on the roll of a double six. On turn 2 they'll need a double five or double six. On turn 3 a double four, five or six, and so on until they will need any roll of a double from turn 6 onwards.

In order to prevent this, the Romans must enter the villa with an infantry unit and then hold it for an entire Hun turn. If successful, this would make the villa secure and the Romans would win the game.

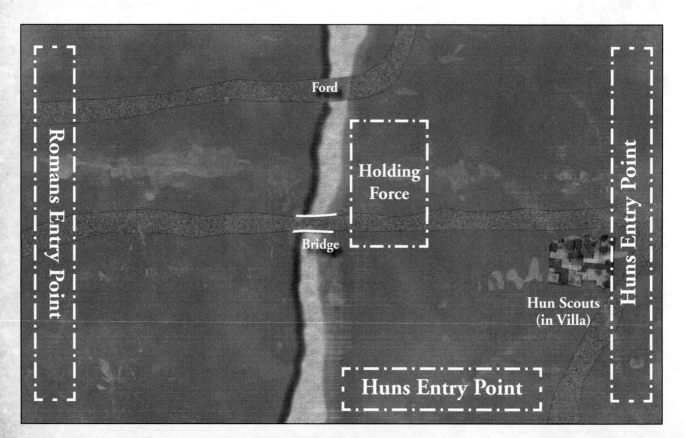

Roman infantry advance towards the villa with the artillery train to the rear

HOW IT WAS PLAYED

The Romans (under the command of Michael Perry and Steve May) made as inauspicious start as it is possible to imagine. The cavalry units screening the force advancing along the north road began the game with a splendiferous blunder, and decided to run away for two entire moves. Maybe their horses took fright when they caught the scent of the Hun ponies, and perhaps of their riders too – or of the raw meat kept under their saddles to 'mature'. The Roman infantry got caught up in the mass of bolting horses, and understandably they hesitated as well, advancing only thanks to their excellent training and superb discipline (i.e. the 'drilled' rule). The cavalry and infantry on the central road kept pace. One could only picture them looking in dismay at the mayhem to their left.

The Huns (led by Rick Priestley and Alan Perry) had deployed the Goth infantry to hold the ford in the centre. Cavalry had been positioned to deny their enemy the crossing at the northern ford. As the Romans were so timid in advancing, the barbarians had little to do but cheer and taunt the Romans for their cowardice, which they did with great enthusiasm. The Hun scouts around the villa, however, failed to set it on fire. Maybe they had found their way into the villa's cellar!

The second turn was as different from the first as it could possibly be. The Roman cavalry commander, possibly swayed by the pleading of the villa's owner, sent his cataphracts forward at full pelt. The cataphracts bounded towards the enemy, crossed the ford and crashed straight into the Goths on the other side. Inspired by this glorious charge, the Roman infantry on the north road advanced rapidly and reached the western bank of the north ford. Here they faced off against the Huns on the other side of the river, who were by now looking distinctly less confident. The Roman cavalry in the north recovered their nerve and came up in support of the infantry. In the wake of the cataphracts, the 'heavy infantry'

division in the centre advanced steadily. The 'Drilled' rule ensuring a steady advance in spite of poor dice rolls.

The following combat saw the levelled kontoi of the cataphracts wreak havoc amongst the Goth infantry. The Goths gave ground in disorder and were chased by the Roman cavalry. The central ford was securely in Roman hands and the route to the villa was open!

Worried by the turn of events in the south, one of the Hun cavalry units covering the north river crossing moved to support the beleaguered Goths. The other took careful aim and shot at the Roman skirmishers who were just about to enter the ford. The sudden flight of Hunnic arrows appeared to send the poorly armed skirmishers into a panic (a couple of 6's obliged them to take a break test). Predictably, the skirmishers turned tail and ran (failing their test and breaking).

The combat in the centre went a bit better for the Goth infantry during this round, and they inflicted heavy casualties on their opponents. Never the less, the barbarians were forced to give ground together with the supporting Huns. Still nothing appeared to be happening at the villa – a few bars of raucous song drifted drunkenly from its general direction.

In the Roman turn the cataphracts returned to the fray, now accompanied by a light cavalry unit that had moved forward to support them. Once again, the Roman cavalry slammed into the Goths and Huns. At the same time the Roman infantry in the centre reached the ford. In the north the Romans crossed the river to engage the screening Huns with short-range missile fire, forcing them to retreat.

The combat in the centre ended with the complete annihilation of the Goths and Huns, leaving the cataphracts

Roman cataphracts storm across the river and charge the Goths on the other side

exhausted and badly mauled. They took a sixth casualty and were therefore shaken. The Romans were now in control of the field. This was a perfect turn for the Romans, and if the Hun main force failed to turn up at the first opportunity the game could have been very short indeed.

Luckily for the barbarians, the second and fourth divisions arrived from the south-east. The second division (Huns), led by the general, advanced steadily to meet the bloodied cataphracts. The fourth division (Goths) decided that perhaps they had forgotten something in the baggage train. Another blunder! They therefore remained off the table. At this stage the last unit of the Hun holding force was obliged to retire (as their division had now lost two units out of three and was therefore broken). This seemed the sensible thing to do in any case, and they proceeded to fall back, taking a few shots at the advancing Legionaries as they did so. And no, of course, there was still no sign of flame or smoke at the villa. Things did not seem to be going well for the barbarians.

The Roman cataphracts and their supporting light cavalrymen wisely decided to fall back and wait for the Roman infantry to cross the river and join them. In the north, the infantry division and the rest of the Roman cavalry continued to advance while exchanging arrows with the retreating Huns.

Thankful for this moment of respite, the Hun general consolidated his position northwards of the villa. The third (Hun) division arrived on to the table from the south and took up a position opposing the Romans. Bizarrely, the Goths once again failed to turn up on the table... perhaps some Roman gold had found its way into the hands of their chieftains? We imagined the Hun general sending a few messengers back with very clear instructions to his Goth allies. To compound this, there was no trace of the Hun flanking force, and – needless to say – no fire was set in the villa.

In their turn the Roman infantry advanced slowly. The Roman cavalry commander rode to the tired and wounded cataphracts to deliver a powerful speech, reminding them that the civilians in the villa were just the same as their loved ones waiting for them at home, or perhaps hinting at the vast amounts of Italian wine that was being wasted on uncouth palates. With such words, and a tolerable roll of the dice, he managed to rally them so that they were once again ready to fight. Seeing this formidable unit recover, the Hun players muttered grim oaths to their dark gods, but the pious Romans were not to be daunted by pagan threats.

In their own turn the Huns were greatly relieved by the timely arrival of both the flanking force on the western edge and of the Goth division in the east. Plainly, the Goths had been 'convinced' by their master's messengers that it was in their interest, and in those of their home villages, that they join the action promptly.

Suddenly the situation looked less rosy for the Romans, with three fresh enemy divisions lining up around the villa, and the dust of the flanking force rising behind them. The Roman artillery, bringing up the rear of the advance, was at this very moment in the middle of the ford and looking distinctly vulnerable.

During the following turn the two battle lines around the villa straightened up for the unavoidable clash. Aside from the inevitable exchange of missiles and insults, little serious damage was done whilst the rival forces manoeuvred in preparation for the deciding conflict. The Roman artillery scrambled across the ford and successfully unlimbered, pointing their machines backwards to cover their rear against the Huns' flanking force. Then, during the following two turns all hell broke loose, bringing the game to an abrupt and spectacular end.

The main Roman line pushed on towards the beleaguered villa. Their horse archers rode ahead with the intent of tempting some of the impetuous Huns and Goths into an uncoordinated charge, thus breaking up their line. The ruse was somehow successful. A unit of Hun heavy cavalry charged the horse archers. The horse archers proved too slow to flee away and were caught and massacred. The blood-mad Goths chased them and crashed into the Roman line behind. Unfortunately the accompanying Huns hesitated and didn't charge in with the Goths. This delay proved the undoing of the barbarians. The long spears of the Roman infantry took the edge off the Gothic charge, and the supporting Roman troops annihilated their enemies with ruthless efficiency.

Next it was the turn of the Roman heavy cavalry, together with the now much refreshed cataphracts, to charge the remaining Huns. The ensuing cavalry battle lasted long enough for the Roman infantry to catch up and add their weight to the fight. There was nothing the Huns could do, caught flat-footed by the legionaries and pinned by Roman cavalry. Many of the Hun units were destroyed or routed, and the Romans advanced upon the villa. The few barbarians who were still harassing the household proved too drunk to resist, much less to set anything on fire, and were quickly put to the sword. The lady of the house and her family and entourage were saved! The Romans had won the day.

THOUGHTS AND CONCLUSION

Before the game we decided to give all Roman legionaries the long spear rule. It seemed reasonable that troops would have chosen that weapon, knowing they were going to face an army of cavalry. However in game terms it was felt that applying the rule to all the legionaries had made them too effective against the Hunnic cavalry. In hindsight, we thought it would probably be better to give some of the heavy infantry plain spears or throwing spears instead of long spears. However, the accompanying force lists give the legionaries long spears as that is how our troops were equipped for the battle.

The Hunnic attempt to burn the villa – whilst affording much hilarity on the part of the Roman players – was probably not the way to do it. A binary random roll is always dangerously fickle when it comes to setting a time limit on a game. A better routine would have been to roll a dice each turn and accumulate the score towards a total – say 25 – which would have given a more predictable time limit for the Romans to mount their rescue. However, as it was, things turned out reasonably well, at least from the Roman point of view.

It had been an entertaining game with plenty of highs and lows on both sides, even if most of the lows ended up in the Huns' camp. In fact, we fought this battle twice, the game described being the second of the encounters. The Huns won the first battle so quickly and so convincingly, destroying the Roman cataphracts as they crossed the ford, and holding the river against all-comers, that we decided to play it again. The Romans' success in the final game may be partly put down to experience, as the players did a much better job of capturing the bridges and securing them the second time round. The Huns, on the other hand, were perhaps a little over confident after their initial victory, and therefore too willing to confront the Romans with the holding force alone rather than falling back and awaiting reinforcements.

The charge of the Goth heavy cavalry! Roman infantry stand firm, making good use of their long spears against the enemy horsemen

THE DARK AGES

The disintegration of the Roman Empire during the fifth and sixth centuries heralded the beginnings of the Dark Ages in Western Europe. Where the Romans had once held sway now there were any number of barbarian tribes fighting over the spoils. These movements of peoples from one end of Europe to the next give us that other term for the first phase of these turbulent years: the migration period. Britain was abandoned by the legions and was soon to become a battleground between the native Britons, Saxons, Angles and Jutes. The Vandals moved southwards from Germany through France and into Spain where they set up a kingdom together with the Alans. Elsewhere Franks moved into France, the Lombards into Italy, and Goths into Italy and eventually Spain. The Vandals moved on to North Africa, capturing Carthage and establishing an empire that dominated the western Mediterranean.

Popular culture dubs these violent times the Dark Ages, reflecting a lack of reliable historical record, generally low literacy levels and widespread cultural poverty. However, despite this paucity of ready information, as wargamers we are at liberty to colour the bare facts and raise savage armies of shaggy mail clad barbarians to carve out new kingdoms amongst the remnants of the Roman West. Nor are we are entirely ignorant of what warriors of the day looked like or how they fought. Wherever they came into contact with the remnants of civilisation that still persisted under the auspices of the Christian Church and the Byzantine Empire these barbarians never failed to make their mark. The Vandals certainly made a

name for themselves when they sacked Rome in 455, whilst the Norse became so well-established in the armies of the Eastern Emperors they gave their name to the 'Varangian' Guard – Varangians being Rus warriors of Nordic descent. Elsewhere, barbarian troops were recruited into the service of Rome, even rising to command armies against other barbarians.

General trends in warfare had already started to emphasise the mounted arm in late antiquity, and this came fully to the fore with the collapse of Roman authority. Many of the invading barbarian armies had at their core heavily armed cavalry riding sturdy horses, now commonly shod with iron for the first time, and carrying men who rode with the aid of stirrups. Both of these developments helped to improve the effectiveness of the mounted arm. Where the preceding age had seen the rise of the heavy infantrymen, the Dark Ages saw the eclipse of infantry by mobile, heavily armed cavalry.

Not all of these rampaging barbarians were horsemen by any means, especially in the West and North where Saxons and Franks, and later Danes and Norse, continued to fight largely on foot in massed ranks much as their ancestors had. But where they found themselves opposed to cavalry, such peoples soon adapted to mounted warfare: the Franks evolving into the knights of Charlemagne for example. In the East the principal invaders were themselves horse-riding nomads such as the Huns, Bulgars, Avars, Pechenegs, and other steppe peoples. Soon they too settled into lands that had once formed part of the Roman Empire as well as parts of the Near East and Eastern Europe.

Vikings are a popular wargames army – the term is usually applied to Danish raiders, but could equally refer to warriors of the many Scandinavian kingdoms of the Dark Ages.

Gothic infantry – these early Goths fought in dense warbands much as their ancestors had for hundreds of years.

The greatest threat to stability in the Eastern part of the Roman Empire came not from the nomads of the northern steppes, but from the deserts of the South. After years of warfare between the Sassanid Persians and the Byzantine Empire, as the Eastern Roman empire is now usually known, both found themselves under attack from a new and vital force: the Arabs. Inspired by religious fervour, the Arabs emerged from their deserts in the seventh century and quickly conquered much of the Roman east and all of the Persian Empire. They went on to take over North Africa and eventually Spain before overreaching themselves as they advanced northwards to France. At the battle of Tours in 732 the Arabs were decisively defeated by the Franks, led by Charles Martel. In the reign of Charlemagne the Franks fought for dominance in northern Spain, eventually achieving control as far as the river Ebro. The boundaries of the Christian and Muslim worlds had been established.

The Byzantines continued to exert considerable influence both militarily and culturally, even though their armies were often under funded and always hard-pressed on all fronts. Unfortunately, Constantinople was often divided by religiously motivated discord. Schisms within the Orthodox church would continue to dog the remnants of the Roman East until its final collapse a millennium later. The Byzantine armies now combined hard-hitting cavalry with well armoured infantry armed with long spears and various kinds of lighter missile-armed infantry. Such armies are popular amongst wargamers because they are well documented and offer a mix and variety of troops that is appealing. But, in truth, the age of the legion had passed, and for the most part the foot now found themselves in a supporting or defensive role. When the Byzantine general Belisarius undertook the re-conquest of North Africa at the behest of the Emperor Justinian it was his heavy cavalry supported by Hun allies who met and defeated the Vandals. Half a millennium later, on the eve of the Middle Ages, it was the mounted knights of William of Normandy who would overcome the mail-clad infantry of the Saxons, affirming once more the supremacy of the mounted arm.

Most wargamers will tend to choose their favourite theatre of operations and collect, perhaps Anglo-Saxons to oppose Vikings, or Carolingian Franks to oppose the Moors. Others will choose to base their games upon the conquests of Islam and its

enduring battle with the Christian empire of Byzantium. All of these, and many more besides, have something to offer the wargamer inspired by wars fought amongst emerging nations whose descendants are, for the most part, recognisable today.

Y GODODDIN

The early history of post-Roman Briton is shrouded in myth, but some of the events of those times are preserved in the writing of Bede, the Anglo-Saxon Chronicle, and in surviving Welsh medieval poetry. The Y Gododdin is ascribed to the bard Aneiran and is an account of a battle between the men of the Britonnic kingdom of Gododdin and the Angles of Deira. This clash takes place at a place called Catraeth, which is usually assumed to be Catterick. One stanza gives this account of the fighting.

Men went to Catraeth with a war-cry,
Speedy steeds and dark armour and shields,
Spear-shafts held high and spear-points sharp-edged,
And glittering coats-of-mail and swords.
He led the way, he thrust through armies,
Five companies fell before his blades.
Rhufawn His gave gold to the altar,
And a rich reward to the minstrel.

Although the poem survives only in a medieval copy, it is thought to refer to events of the late sixth or early seventh century and was probably composed shortly afterwards at the beginning of the seventh century. The leader of the men of Gododdin is supposed to be their King – the enigmatically named Mynydogg Mwynfawr. Even Arthur gets a mention, possibly the earliest reference to this most mysterious of British rulers.

He fed black ravens on the rampart of a fortress
Though he was no Arthur.
Among the powerful ones in battle,
In the front rank, Gwawrddur was a palisade.

THE BATTLE OF BRUNANBURGH 937AD

Here, King Athelstan, leader of warriors,
ring-giver of men, and also his brother,
the aetheling Edmund, struck life-long
glory in strife around 'Brunanburh'...

'The Song Of Brunanburgh',
The Anglo-Saxon Chronicle

One of the largest battles of the Viking Age, the Battle of
Brunanburgh, saw Athelstan the King of England and
Edmund, his younger brother, defeat Olaf Guthfrithsson,
King of Dublin, Constantine II King of Scots, and Owen I,
the King of Strathclyde. Olaf, Constantine and Owen's
alliance was also supported by numbers of Irish, Cornish
and Welsh mercenaries.

Athelstan was an astute politician who had already unified
most of England and Wales under his sway, including the
much-disputed territory of Northumbria. To the Scots and
the kingdom of Strathclyde he was an ever-growing threat.
Constantine had already run foul of Athelstan's authority
twice before, but in 937 he allied himself with his neighbour,
Owen of Strathclyde, and Olaf the Viking King of Dublin.
Together these forces invaded Athelstan's territory.

The combined armies converged at a site the exact location
of which is still the subject of much debate. The stage was set
for one of the bloodiest battles of its time. The alliance's
forces numbered perhaps 10,000 men of which almost half
were Vikings. The Saxons mustered somewhere in the region
of 8,500 men. For the time these were large armies indeed.

The opposing armies advance into shouting range and exchange obscenities. The air turns blue with bloodthirsty oaths.

154

The Song of Brunanburgh makes great play of the number of different contingents at the battle, referring to it as "the conflict of banners."

As for the battle itself, it started with a dawn attack by the alliance against a defensive position adopted by the smaller English army. The fighting raged all day. The Song of Brunanburgh describes the battle thus:

"The field grew dark with the blood of men from the time when the sun moved over the earth in the hours of the morning until that noble creation sank at its setting."

According to Egil's Saga the battle was close and hard fought with many casualties on both sides, including a great proportion of the nobility and their retainers. For the alliance, the Song of Brunanburgh accounts five young Kings and seven of Olaf's earls slain, plus a host of seamen (Vikings) and Scots. On the Saxon side, Althelstan's two

cousins, two prominent bishops, two senior eoldermen plus a multitude of 'lesser' men were lost. Amidst the slaughter, the Scots and Welsh were eventually broken and the Saxons closed in on the Vikings' flank, finally routing them. Constantine fled north across the border and Olaf escaped back to his ship with a small group of his hird. The remnant of the alliance's army was cut to pieces and England was saved from another large scale Viking invasion.

Postscript –Brunanburgh was not as decisive as it at first appears considering it was such a large and bloodthirsty battle. Athelstan reigned for two more relatively peaceful years and enjoyed his position as arguably the most powerful man in Europe. Edmund succeeded him only to face Olaf's return a year after Athelstan's death. Olaf re-established the Viking Kingdom of York and, although he was killed a year later, it took 14 years of hard fighting to finally secure Northumberland as part of England forever.

BRUNANBURGH THE WARGAME

The arrival of Hail Caesar at Beast Towers, the home of Gripping Beast Miniatures, caused much excitement. Here was the perfect excuse to refight one of the largest battles of the Viking Age in Britain: the Battle of Brunanburgh. Furthermore, the alliance of forces at Brunanburgh presented the perfect set-up for a four-player game: the Saxons of Wessex and Mercians on one side, and the Vikings and assorted Celtic types on the other.

We set up the table and laid out the armies before deciding who would take command of the forces. All expected that Gripping Beast owner and undisputed Beastmaster Andy 'Lord' Sherwell would take the part of Athelstan as an exalted position and fine moustache entitled him. In fact, much to everyone's relief, Lord Sherwell gallantly gave up his command to gestir Ken Pearce and volunteered to umpire instead. It has to be said that things do generally go better when Lord Sherwell isn't actually playing. Darren Harding would naturally lead the Vikings as Olaf Guthfrithsson and Martin Gibbins opted for the Mercians of Edmund. This left Roger Jenkins to manage the Celtic hotchpotch that was Constantine and Owen's forces.

ORDERS OF BATTLE

THE SAXONS

The Saxons are divided into four separate divisions for purposes of command. With two players taking the role of the Saxon army, Athelstan and Egil came under the control of Ken as overall commander, and the Mercians and Eorl fell to Martin.

Athelstan's Contingent (Wessex)
- Athelstan, King of England (General)
- 3 units of Saxon Thegns (28 models) and Ceorls (28 models) in combined formation (3 large units with 56 models in each).

Egil's Viking Contingent
- Egil Skallagrimsson – Icelandic adventurer, warrior and poet (commander)
- Egil's Vikings – Vikings (small unit of 24 models).

Edmund's Contingent (Mercia)
- Edmund, brother of Athelstan (commander)
- 3 units of Saxon Thegns (32 models) and Ceorls (32 models) in combined formation (3 large units with 64 models in each)

Mounted Contingent
- Eorl (commander)
- 2 units Mounted Saxon Thegns (standard units with 12 models in each).

SAXON FORCES							
Type	Combat				Morale Save	Stamina	Special
	Clash	Sustained	Short Range	Long Range			
Saxon Thegn (Heavy Infantry)	7	7	3	0	4+	6	Combined Formation
Saxon Ceorl (Medium Infantry)	6	6	3	0	5+	6	Combined Formation
Combined Thegn/Ceorl units fielded as single large unit	9/8	9/8	4	0	4+/5+	8	Thegns and Ceorls fight as a combined unit
Mounted Saxon Thegns (Medium Cavalry)	8	5	3	0	5+	6	
Egil's Vikings fielded as small unit (Heavy Infantry)	5	5	2	0	4+	4	Tough Fighters

THE VIKING ALLIANCE

The Viking army is divided into four divisions with Olaf and Eric's troops commanded by Darren, and Constantine and Owen's troops by Roger. Owen was made commander of the Welsh unit representing the mercenaries who were in reality a mix of troops of which the Welsh were a part.

Olaf's Contingent
- Olaf Guthfrithsson, King of Dublin (General)
- 3 units of Viking Hird (24 models) and Bondi (24 models) in combined formation (4 standard units with 48 models in each)

Eric's Contingent
- Eric (commander)
- Viking Hird (24 models) and Bondi (24 models) in combined formation (standard unit with 48 models)
- Gall Gael – Viking Men of the Isles (standard unit of 32 models)

Constantine's Contingent
- Constantine, King of Scotland (commander)
- Pictish Warriors (large unit with 60 models)
- Scots-Irish (standard unit with 40 models)
- Lowland Scots Thanes (32 models) and Lowland Scots (32 models) in combined formation (large unit with 64 models)

Owen's Contingent
- Owen, King of Strathcylde (commander)
- Welsh teulu (30 models) and priodaur (30 models) in combined formation (large unit with 60 models)

Type	Combat				Morale Save	Stamina	Special
	Clash	Sustained	Short Range	Long Range			
Viking Hird (Heavy Infantry)	7	7	3	0	4+	6	Combined Formation
Viking Bondi (Medium Infantry)	6	6	3	0	5+	6	Combined Formation
Combined Hird/Bondi units fielded as single standard unit	7/6	7/6	3	0	4+/5+	6	Hird and Bondi fight as a combined unit
Gall Gael (Medium Infantry Warband)	9	6	2	0	5+	6	Frenzied Charge
Pictish Warriors fielded as a large unit (Medium Infantry)	8	8	4	0	5+	8	
Scots Irish (Medium Infantry)	6	6	3	0	5+	6	
Lowland Scots Thanes (Heavy Infantry)	7	7	3	0	4+	6	Combined Formation
Lowland Scots Spear (Medium Infantry)	6	6	3	0	5+	6	Combined Formation
Combined Thanes/ Spear units	9/8	9/8	4	0	4+/5+	8	Scots Thanes and Spears fighting as a single large combined unit
Welsh Teulu (Heavy Infantry)	7	7	3	0	4+	6	Combined Formation
Welsh Priodaur (Medium Infantry)	6	6	3	0	5+	6	Combined Formation
Combined Teulu/ Priodaur units fielded as a single large unit	9/8	9/8	4	0	4+/5+	8	Teulu and Priodaur fight as a combined unit

ALLIANCE FORCES

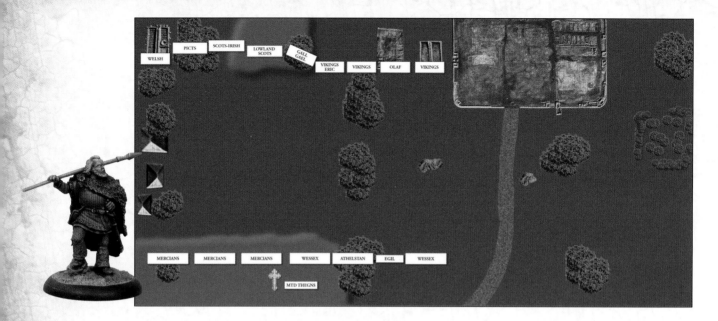

The size of our units was drawn from research by Professor Guy Halsall of York University applying a ratio of roughly 1 figure to represent 20 men. Some of the factions known to have been at the battle were absorbed into similar units for convenience, notably the various mercenaries. We also took the liberty of adding extra figures here and there to enhance the appearance of the armies – and because we had them!

Note that the models come from our extensive collections and are based to our own preference for deep ranks. These correspond nicely to the four deep 'warband' formation for the most part, but we didn't worry too much about the unit depths, concentrating on keeping the frontages within the usual tolerable limits.

The stats have been given for all the individual units that were actually fielded as combined formations. The stats for individual unit are all for standard sized units. The stats given for the combined units are for the size as fielded in our game, hence all but the Viking Hird/Bondi units have the stat bonuses for large units added.

In addition to the special rules listed all infantry units were allowed to use the Close Ranks special rule to represent the famous shield wall, a tightly drawn formation presenting a wall of shields to the enemy.

COMBINED FORMATION
It was a common practice in the Viking Age for higher status warriors, being better trained and armed, to occupy the front ranks of battlefield formations. We decided that we wanted to reflect this directly in the game in some fashion. After due consideration we came up with what we called a *combined formation* rule. The combined formation rule allows what would otherwise be two infantry units to join together into a single combined unit with the better troops at the front and the others behind them. In our case most of the units combined in this way qualified as 'large' as a result. The combined unit fights exactly as the superior troops in its front ranks until such time as the unit becomes *shaken* after which it fights exactly as the inferior troops in its rear ranks. Where different stats apply these are both given in the army

roster, e.g. Morale Save 4+/5+ meaning the unit has a save of 4+ until it becomes shaken, after which its save drops to 5+. Bear in mind that where heavy infantry and medium infantry are combined this does mean the unit counts as heavy infantry at the start of the game but medium infantry once it becomes shaken. This may affect it in other ways: for example, vulnerability to missile fire.

COMMANDERS IN COMBAT
To simulate a more heroic (read blood-thirsty!) approach to personal combat, we decided to increase the risk of a commander suffering death or injury in hand-to-hand fighting. We also wanted to emphasise the risks and tension of personal combat in an age when it was the fate of individuals that so often dictated the course of history. Therefore, we decided that instead of rolling just once each round to determine if a commander fell casualty in hand-to-hand fighting, a roll would be made for every single attack made by the commander that round. Thus a commander making three attacks would have to roll a pair of dice three times, and any score of 10, 11 or 12 on any of the rolls would indicate that he had fallen casualty. A commander making two attacks would roll twice and would fall casualty on rolls of 11 or 12. A commander making a mere single attack would roll once and fall casualty on a 12 as usual.

This drastic increase of risk for commanders making multiple attacks, and especially for the generals with their potential three attacks, might reasonably make some players reluctant to commit their full quota of attacks to a fight. Any nervousness expressed by the players when committing their attacks proved a marvellous opportunity to employ one of the many colourful period insults that our crew had so far mastered. A list – slightly ameliorated for the benefit of sensitive readers – is included at the end of this account.

DOUBLE MOVE
To represent the attack of the allied Viking and Scots army onto the static position of the Saxons we decided to give the alliance side two Command segments in their first turn, so they would effectively get two chances to move their army in their first turn of the game.

The action in full swing on the Saxons' left flank

HOW IT WAS PLAYED

Newly self-appointed umpire Lord Sherwell ran through the scenario tweeks and extra special rules that we would be using. A brief pause to stock up on the infamous *Beast strength* coffee (no tea here) and we were off.

Viking and Scots Double First Turn. As per the scenario, the Vikings and Celtic types took advantage of their bonus move and, knowing that it would immediately be their move again, Olaf and Constantine signaled an all out advance into the teeth of the enemy. One paltry stumbling move later and the two commanders were ready to try again. This time they needed to proceed with some caution. In theory they could just about make a successful charge if their order rolls were good enough, but should something go wrong they could end up with a very raggedy battle line – universally acknowledged to be 'A Bad Thing'.

Faced with the awesome might of Athelstan and his bodyguard, Olaf opted to advance cautiously maintaining his line. On the right flank Constantine decided that the Mercians were not going to leave the hill come-what-may, so he reasoned that the Scots and Welsh might as well go and get them. Some decidedly average dice rolling later and the Vikings managed to advance slowly, but kept their line. Over on Constantine's flank, Roger's erratic rolling enabled the Scots to press on despite the complete lack of support from their Welsh allies who resolutely refused to budge. A few rounds of Viking Age insults later and it was over to the Saxons.

Saxon Turn One. Athelstan decided to meet the oncoming Vikings but wasn't quite ready to engage. He advanced his main units to form an imposing battle line while sending Egil's 'friendly' Vikings out towards the right flank. As he advanced, Athelstan tried to order his mounted reserve onto the table as he could see a potential hanging flank by Constantine's contingent. Unfortunately, the distance was just too far and Ken failed the modified roll. Edmund did the sensible thing by holding steady on the ridgeline, choosing to spend his time practicing for the next round of insults.

Althelstan issued his orders and moved his troops to within javelin range of the Vikings arrayed to their front. Ken rolled a number of 6's prompting a test by the centre Viking unit which fell back in good order. It was not exactly devastating, but if Olaf could not repair his line the Saxons might be able to launch a supported charge on their next turn.

Viking Turn Two. Despite the minor setback, Olaf was all Viking enthusiasm as he sounded the charge. Apart from the unit that had been hurled back by the previous turn's rain of Saxon javelins, the Vikings didn't need to be issued an order as they all used their initiative. With a clash of shield and sword, the Viking charges all hit home. However, on the other flank Constantine found himself plagued once more by truculent supporters (and Roger's dice). His instruction to charge towards the hill resulted in a stumble one move forward, with units coming to rest mere yards from the Saxons. Maybe the insults were getting to the Celts. Even their javelins missed.

The Saxons cling to their ridge line where they enjoy an uphill advantage. In the foreground, the Mercians charge at the shambling Celts

Olaf, Eric and Athelstan all hurried to join the combats. The Saxons elected to close ranks to form a shield wall. This was a sensible decision seeing as the Vikings were fronted by Hird and supported on the left, whereas Egil's troops hadn't quite extended the Saxon line. Add to that Olaf's three attacks and you have a formidably offensive unit. Even with their shield wall reducing casualties thanks to the improved Morale save the Saxons were driven back disordered.

Saxon Turn Two, On the Saxon army's left flank, the disorganised Celtic advance was too tempting a target for the Mercians. Martin used his troops' initiative to charge down from the commanding position on the hill into the vulnerable unsupported Scots and Welsh.

In the centre, the cavalry reserve attempted to move on from behind the hill and attack the Gall Gael. This they did successfully. Heedless of the Gall Gael's fearsome reputation the cavalry charged forward. As the units clashed the cavalry's commander joined in the fight. Good man!

With the majority of the units committed this round of combat was shaping up to be the pivotal moment in the battle. Which is why at this point we had another swift round of Viking Age insults! See useful list following this account.

With oaths, exhortations and defamatory remarks complete, the Saxons on the left flank punished the Teulu for advancing without sufficient support: inflicting eight unsaved casualties and leaving the Welshmen shaken. At the other end of the battle line, and in complete contrast, Egil's Vikings took five casualties. This caused them to become shaken as they were a small unit, yet they managed to merely give ground in good order.

In the centre the Saxons just couldn't make any headway against the Gaels, and after a flurry of dice rolling were giving ground disordered. This was not a good omen for the main

event: the continued combat between Olaf and his Hird, and Athelstan and his Hearthguard. As you would expect from two great units with maximum support, the combat generated quite a few dice rolls, and thanks to some good rolling by Olaf the Saxons finished the round shaken. And then it all went horribly wrong. A confident Ken rolled for his break test and got a 'three'. Olaf roared as the Saxon king fled the scene surrounded by his humiliated retainers. And then it got worse. As Athelstan had thrown his full weight into the combat, the Vikings, using our modified rules for risks to commanders in combat (see notes) had a good chance to kill or wound the Saxon King. This they did and left the King not only fleeing the table, but also severely wounded into the bargain. Cue the Viking horns.

Following up this victory, the Vikings moved up into support for the final combat of the turn. A small measure of calm was restored as the Saxon shield wall managed to save nine of the ten Viking hits and the combat ended in a draw.

A slightly longer than normal round of insults preceded turn three, and it has to be said that most were directed at Ken for losing Athelstan, and that the most cruelly cutting came from the umpire! Lord Sherwell was not at all amused by the Saxons' performance.

Viking Turn Three. The hapless Constantine got things off to a flying start by blundering his first order, following which the Scots retreated. With very little other movement it was straight on to combat.

On the far left the Vikings hammered Egil's smaller unit. No doubt inspired by the great man's poetry (and infamous bad temper) Egil's boys merely gave ground in good order once again. They ended the combat still fighting, but shaken. In the next combat along, Olaf, his blood now well and truly up, battered the Saxon shieldwall, but to no avail. The exertion of the previous round must have had an effect, as the Vikings ended up taking three casualties and giving ground together with their supporting unit. Darren was just about to move on to the next combat when Ken reminded him that Olaf had taken part in the combat and so was potentially a casualty. With icy stare, Darren passed some dice to Ken who, completely unphased, proceeded to wound Olaf! It was a small consolation for the Saxons.

Darren vented his anger on the next combat along where Eric's Vikings crushed the now unsupported Saxons. In their sweeping advance, the Vikings smashed into a unit of Saxon cavalry and an immediate round of combat was fought. The surprised cavalry were forced to give ground disordered. To finish the round off, the Gall Gaels battered a lone Saxon unit who ended the turn shaken but just holding on.

Saxon Turn Three. There were no initiative moves and with all the commanders committed to combat (except doddery Constantine) there were no orders either. Matters therefore proceeded straight into combat. On the Saxons' far left the Mercians inevitably overwhelmed the remains of the Teulu and managed to kill the Welsh king in the process.

The Gall Gaels broke the Saxon unit in the centre and advanced to threaten the flank of the Mercians on the hill. In the other combat in the centre, the Vikings shattered the Saxon cavalry and looked set to turn in on the Saxon's left flank.

In the large combat on the Saxon's right, Olaf's unit formed shield wall around the wounded Olaf as the Saxons looked to avenge their king. Against the supported large unit Olaf's shield wall was not good enough, and the Vikings were forced to give ground disordered.

Vikings Turn Four. With the various commanders wounded or locked in battle, only Constantine issued an order, declaring a charge against the Mercian held hill. Constantine's orders were obeyed only up to a point and the Picts were left stranded at the foot of the hill. Olaf's hird were shattered during the combat that followed and Olaf hobbled from the field.

Saxon Turn Four. The field was littered with shaken units and the pace of the game began to slow as the participants mentally prepared their excuses and sharpened their best insults for the beckoning post game session. The only action occurred when the Mercians were unable to resist charging down the hill into the unsupported Constantine. Constantine's troops were overwhelmed and gave ground disordered ending the turn shaken.

Viking Turn Five. By this time the players were sensing that matters were coming to a conclusion with both armies worn out by the fight and commanders locked in battle or incapacitated. Over on the Viking right Constantine's troops broke and fled the scene. As Edwin's Mercians followed up the dice revealed Constantine dead.

Saxon Turn Five. Final turn as everyone bar the rampant Edmund was spent. After crushing Constantine, Edmund had used his advance to position himself for a charge onto the Scots' flank, which he now made. The result? The Scots

were shattered. But by now so were the players. The Battle of Brunanburgh was over.

Hands were shaken and bonhomie flowed in excess. The players decided that the field belonged to the Mercians. Had the Saxons done enough to destroy the Viking threat? And at what cost with Athelstan mortally wounded? Certainly the Celtic fringe had been put in its place. Perhaps Edmund may even have a chance of taking Athelstan's place as King of all England. But what was certain was that the players had had a jolly good game and that had Lord Sherwell insisted on playing it would have been all so very, very different.

A NOTE ON PERIOD INSULTS

"You are the bride of a Svinafell Troll, as people say, and every ninth night he treats you like a woman."

Njal's saga

As we all know, wargaming can – if played in the right and proper spirit – get a bit rowdy. What better way to enhance the educational value of an evening's entertainment than to revive the use of long-forgotten insults? We are all true champions of the Viking Age, a time when the well-honed put-down was considered high art. Here are some examples to throw your opponent's way.

> Idiot
> Goat Dung (alternatively employ any animal of your choice – though *Goat* usually works)
> Pig (or indeed Goat) *Filth*
> Fox Tail
> Fox Beard
> Halfwit
> Buffoon

The above are all from the *Colloquy of Aelfric Bata* circa 1000AD, England.

> Raven Starver (a coward)
> Stench Weasel (a practitioner of poor personal hygiene)
> Womanish (a coward, be careful here...)
> Pot Licker (a greedy fellow)
> Nithing (a worthless individual)
> Warlock (an oathbreaker)

The above are assorted favorites in common use.

And finally we leave you with this 10th century Latin insult.

> *Canis calum in tuo naso!*

There are many, many more. Sadly some of the most entertaining are, if anything, too vulgar to inflict upon an unsuspecting reader. For further examples, we therefore leave you to your own research.

THE MIDDLE AGES

The Hundred Years War was a long running conflict between the English and French crowns to establish authority over large parts of what is today France. The battles of this period established the supremacy of the largely infantry based armies of the English over the feudal knights of France – but even so - it was an age when the mounted knight was surely at his most flamboyant!

The Middle Ages will forever be associated with knights in armour and their retainers wielding bows and pole arms. Here are the warriors who fought on behalf on the kings and nobles of feudal Europe, the recognisable predecessors of the peoples and nations of modern times. Once we consider the wars of the medieval period we enter an historical realm that is increasing well recorded and understood, where the names and stories of many of the warriors of the day are known to us, and where battles are often described and discussed by contemporary writers. It is still a world unlike our own in many ways, though visible remnants of it endure in the ecclesiastic architecture of churches and monasteries as well as in the castles and fortresses of overlords and monarchs.

The age of medieval warfare may be said to begin with the Norman Conquest of Saxon England, and with the annexation of Byzantine Anatolia by the Turks. These events followed on from decisive battles, both were fought at the extreme boundaries of Christendom, and both were to shape the future development of world history. They took place about the same time too: the Battle of Hastings in 1066 in the West and the Battle of Manzikert in 1071 in the East. Of course, these are arbitrary dates really, and they do not in themselves signify any great or immediate change in the evolving story of warfare. None the less, it is convenient for us to mark the eleventh century as the beginning of our chosen era. As for its end, we shall settle upon the development of effective gunpowder weapons during the final years of the

Norman Knights such as these did not only subjugate the Saxon kingdom of England, they carved out a substantial empire that included the south of Italy and Sicily. The Normans also fought as mercenaries in Byzantine and Armenian service. The Norman adventurer Bohemond, Prince of Taranto was one of the leaders of the First Crusade and the Prince of Antioch. He campaigned in Greece and the Levant against the Byzantines and Muslims.

The Wars of the Roses were civil wars fought for control of the English crown between two rival branches of the Plantagenets, the Houses of York and Lancaster. The battle of Tewkesbury in 1471 was a decisive victory for the Yorkist King Edward. The war lasted until 1485 when the last of the Plantagenets, Richard III, was slain at the battle of Bosworth and crown passed to the House of Tudor.

fifteenth century. In England the death of the last of the Plantagenet kings, Richard III, at Bosworth Field in 1485 marks the transition to early modern times with the accession of the Tudors. It was the final victory upon British soil gained by the charge of heavily armoured knights.

If the preceding era had witnessed the triumph of the armoured horsemen then the Middle Ages were to see the almost universal triumph of the mounted knight and the rapid evolution of armaments and tactics by way of response. As the centuries progressed the armour of the knight advanced from the mail coat of former years to a mixture of mail and plate, and eventually to the sophisticated and beautiful articulated harness of the fifteenth century. But the knights and heavily armoured men-at-arms were not to have it all their own way. Infantry soon found ways to counter the supremacy of the mounted arm. In their wars against the English the Scots spearmen adopted the dense schiltron formation bristling with spears. Elsewhere the refinement of the crossbow placed a weapon capable of defeating the thickest armour into the hands of the common man. In Europe the crossbowman was to become a mercenary for hire, the universal soldier ready for battle and siege alike. The English appreciated the value of missile power more than their contemporaries. In the hands of the English archer the long bow – or war bow to give it its proper name – was to become a battle-winning weapon.

The armies of Western Europe evolved around knights and their retainers, the archetypical warriors of a feudal society. To the east the Arab world retained its own traditions, based in part around mobile, lightly armed cavalry and missile-armed infantry. The two cultures clashed in the long series of wars known as the Crusades, thereby providing wargamers with one of the most colourful themes of the Middle Ages. Here we introduce the armies of the Saracens with their flowing robes and armies of swift horsemen, worthy opponents to

pitch against the mail-clad knights of Christian kings. Although the Crusades in the East are the best known, the Knights of the Teutonic Order also campaigned in the North against the pagan Prussians and Livonians of the Baltic coasts. In Eastern Europe there were other foes to fight including fierce Mongol hordes and the increasingly powerful Ottoman Turks who displaced the Seljuk Sultanate of Rum from the fourteenth century onwards. The Mongols devastated Hungary and only withdrew following the death of the Khan and subsequent in-fighting between rival Mongol factions.

All these make fascinating subjects for wargames armies, whether your interest is in the early part of the period with its predominance of mail-clad knights, or the later years and more sophisticated armies that combined different types of foot and mounted troops together. Gunpowder weapons first make an appearance in Western European armies of the fourteenth century in the form of simple bombards. At first they are siege weapons and play little part in field battles, but soon artillery pieces begin to make their mark, with mobile, wheeled carriages introduced around the turn of the fifteenth century.

It was to take another half century or so for improvements in technology to furnish the humble infantryman with a practical handgun, and not until the end of the century that such weapons began to rival the traditional bows and crossbows in effectiveness. But by then the medieval era – the age of feudal lords, kings and the church of Rome – was drawing to a close. New forces were at work in the world. Protestantism would champion the many over the few: the common man over the nobles and established clergy. The printing press would bring knowledge and literacy to a whole new class of Europeans, and wealth and power would devolve down from the old feudal masters. It was a time of change, the first dawn of a new age that would be dominated by science and reason. It was an age in which the knight in armour was starting to look an anachronous figure indeed.

Gunpowder weapons first appeared upon the battlefields of Europe during the Middle Ages in the form of simple bombards. These weapons made their presence felt during sieges and would soon make their appearance upon the battlefield.

THE ROAD TO DAMASCUS 1148AD

THE BATTLE OF THE BARADA RIVER 24TH JULY 1148

The County of Edessa in the Holy Land was the first Crusader state to be founded and its fall in 1144 triggered the Second Crusade. Initially the idea of the crusade was simply to recapture Edessa itself. King Louis VII of France and Konrad III of Germany set out separately, travelling across Europe to the Holy Land. After reaching Constantinople the armies joined forces at Lopardium and then campaigned both together and separately eastwards.

Konrad, King Baldwin III of Jerusalem and Patriarch Fulcher of the Templars met at Jerusalem where they were later joined by Louis. There it was decided that Edessa, having been lost and re-taken twice already, wasn't in any condition to be conquered again. Instead, the Crusaders decided to launch their attack upon Damascus. This was surprising considering that Damascus had hitherto been an ally of the Crusader states, but none the less the allied army prepared to advance upon the city.

The combined Crusader forces marched north east towards Damascus. On reaching the fertile and irrigated suburbs they turned north to cross the Barada River, thereby circumnavigating the city's substantial walls in order to approach at the weakest point in the defences. A force of militia and local Turkoman tribesmen tried to stop the Crusaders amongst the walled orchards, narrow lanes and irrigation canals that lay beside the river. This worked for a while and the attackers were held at bay, but eventually the bloody confrontation went in favour of the Christians. This is the action that our game attempts to recreate.

THE SETUP

The exact sizes and make up of the forces involved are not known. We do know that the three Crusader armies approached the Barada River with Baldwin's troops in front, Louis in the centre and Konrad bringing up the rear, so that

is how we arranged the allied forces. We substituted Hospitallers for Templars as these are what we had to hand. This force started the game at the hilltop village of Mizzah (see map) and its objective was to reach the opposite side of the board between the river and the Quanawat canal with at least three quarters of its units intact.

The small Muslim blocking force is there mainly to hold up the invaders until the relief force from the city under Mu'in al-Din Abu Mansur Anur arrives on the Christians' right flank. The Muslim players were allowed to arrange the blocking force up to half way across the table using any terrain features for defence. Anur began the game with one of his divisions marching down the road from the city in column. He would roll randomly thereafter for reinforcements, two divisions at a time, arriving on any roll of a 4+.

The approach of the Frankish army causes some consternation in downtown Damascus

THE CRUSADERS – ORDER OF BATTLE

King Baldwin III of Jerusalem's contingent:

DIVISION 1
- 1 x unit of mounted Hospitallers
- 1 x unit of mounted Knights
- 1 x unit of Turcopoles

DIVISION 2
- 1 x unit of foot Knights
- 1 x unit of Armenian spearmen
- 1 x unit of Armenian archers
- 1 x unit of crossbowmen
- 1 x unit of archers.

King Louis VII of France's contingent:

DIVISION 3
- 2 x units of mounted Knights
- 1 x unit of Turcopoles

DIVISION 4
- 2 x units of spearmen
- 2 x units of crossbowmen.

Konrad III 'King of the Germans's contingent:

DIVISION 5
- 1 x unit of mounted Knights
- 1 x unit of mounted Armenian Knights
- 1 x unit of Turcopoles

DIVISION 6
- 3 x units of spearmen
- 2 x units of archers.

CRUSADER STATISTICS AND SPECIAL RULES

All commanders including the general have Leadership ratings of 8. The general has the standard re-roll rule in addition.

Type	Combat				Morale Save	Stamina	Special
	Clash	Sustained	Short Range	Long Range			
Hospitaller knights with lances (Heavy Cavalry)	9	6	3/0	0	4+	6	Eager, Tough Fighters, Stubborn
Crusader knights with lances (Heavy Cavalry)	9	6	3/0	0	4+	6	Eager, Tough Fighters
Turcopoles with bows and spears, fielded as small units (Light Cavalry)	5	3	2	2	6+	4	Feigned Flight
Foot knights and Spearmen (Heavy Infantry)	7	7	3	0	4+	6	
Archers and Crossbowmen (Heavy Infantry)	6	6	3	3	4+	6	

The rules for the various weapons carried apply – these are shown in the description of the unit rather than noted as special rules. Note that none of the spearmen were given the long spear rule.

THE DAMASCANS – ORDER OF BATTLE

Blocking Force:

DIVISION A
- 4 x units of Turkomans

DIVISION B
- 1 x unit of dismounted Ghulams
- 1 x unit of Militia
- 2 x unit of archers
- 1 x unit of Napfa.

Mu'in Al-Din Abu Mansur Anur's Relief Force:

DIVISION C
- 1 x unit of Ghulams
- 3 x units of Turkomans

DIVISION D
- 1 x unit of Ghulams
- 3 x units Turkomans

DIVISION E
- 1 x unit of Ghulams
- 3 x units of Turkomans
- 1 x unit of camels

DIVISION F
- 2 x units of Ghulams
- 2 x unit of Bedouin cavalry

DIVISION G
- 3 x units of Militia
- 1 x unit of Fanatics

DIVISION H
- 1 x unit of Fanatics
- 1 x unit of Militia
- 1 x unit of archers
- 1 x unit of skirmishers

DAMASCAN STATISTICS AND SPECIAL RULES

All commanders including the general have Leadership ratings of 8. The general has the standard re-roll rule in addition.

Type	Clash	Sustained	Short Range	Long Range	Morale Save	Stamina	Special
Dismounted Ghulams (Heavy Infantry)	7	7	3	0	4+	6	
Damascan Militia (Medium Infantry)	6	6	3	0	5+	6	Levy
Turkomans with bows fielded as small units (Light Cavalry)	5	3	2	2	6+	4	Feigned Flight
Archers (Medium Infantry)	5	5	3	3	5+	6	
Napfa-armed Skirmishers (small unit)	3	2	2	0	0	4	Napfa – any units taking casualties must make a missile break test with a –1 penalty. Napfa range is 6".
Fanatics (Medium Infantry)	9	6	3	0	5+	6	Fanatic, Wild Fighters.
Ghulams armed with bows and spears (Heavy Cavalry)	9	6	3	2	4+	6	
Camels armed with bows and fielded as small unit (Light Cavalry)	5	3	2	2	6+	4	
Bedouin with spears and fielded as small units (Light Cavalry)	5	3	2	0	6+	4	
Skirmishers with javelins fielded as small unit (Skirmishers)	3	2	2	0	0	4	

The rules for the various weapons carried apply – these are shown in the description of the unit where applicable rather than noted as special rules. Note that none of the spearmen were given the long spear rule.

HOW IT WAS PLAYED

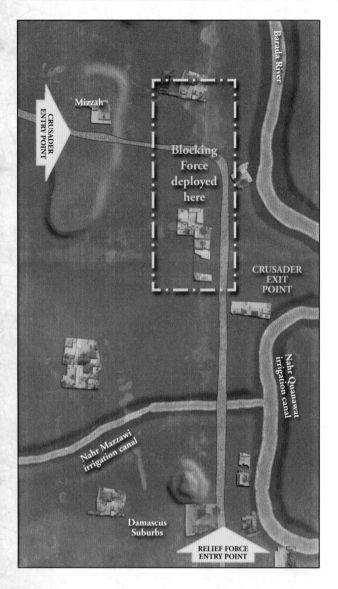

It all looked very pleasing and easy for the Crusaders as they surveyed the sparse opposition behind the crumbling walls of the suburbs below their own positions at Mizzah. Indeed, the Hospitallers, knights and Turcopoles of Baldwin raced off – almost uncontrollably – in pursuit of a unit of Turkoman light cavalry that dared to approach their lines. Baldwin's infantry proved to be much slower on the uptake. In their turn the blocking force stood firm while Anur's reinforcements dragged their feet (and hooves) on the road.

The Hospitallers made short work of one unit of Turkomans, but ended up trapped and shot at by a second unit. This forced them to retire to the Northwest, far away from their comrades arrayed on the slopes below Mizzah. Meanwhile, Baldwin's knights and Turcopoles advanced across the plain and tried to engage the enemy infantry behind their walls. Shots were exchanged to little effect. Louis' force now arrived very slowly behind the main advance, advancing on to the battlefield with a single move. The first two divisions of Anur were now all on the table, but were also making slow progress.

There then followed a catastrophe for the blocking force. Baldwin's knights charged headlong into the elite unit of dismounted Ghulams who were straddling the main road between two orchards. In the ensuing combat the Crusaders inflicted heavy casualties. The Ghulams routed, taking with them their two supporting units of archers. The Crusaders pressed forward, hitting the Muslim militia in the flank with a sweeping charge and destroying them in a single round of fighting. This left only three units of Turkomans and a tiny unit of Napfa between the entire Crusader horde and its objective on the far side of the table. As the knights' pursuit of the enemy militia had carried them into the middle of all these units, they received a heavy pounding from flame and arrows in the

Anur's infantry march onto the table to confront the rampaging Crusaders

The Crusaders begin to advance from their initial position on the hills behind Mizzah

following turn. The Germans now arrived up the hill heading towards Mizzah, while the rest of the infantry struggled to make their way off the high ground and onto the plain. More of Anur's reinforcements arrived and their commander diverted them off the road to sweep towards the Crusaders' vulnerable looking flank.

Baldwin's cavalry withdrew from the village under a hail of missiles that came from every direction. The Hospitallers finally returned from their pursuit of the enemy and rejoined their friends. Their early and over enthusiastic charge had taken them out of the battle for several turns. Konrad's German infantry formed column and pushed their way past their sluggish allies still struggling to descend the hill, with the German/Armenian cavalry thundering down into the plain to protect the army's right flank. At last the first of Anur's divisions arrived at a point where they could do some damage, and quickly formed line opposite Konrad's cavalry. A unit of Turkomans who were somewhat ahead of the rest of their division were shaken during a preliminary encounter, but in return they did some damage to Baldwin's Turkopoles, who had taken up a position upon his right flank.

Frankish crossbowmen prepare to see off the heathen

Sustained casualties and a lucky shot from the village sent Baldwin's knights recoiling into the column of German infantry behind. Meanwhile, the French infantry shook themselves into line to face the threat upon the army's right flank. It was well that they did, for a single arrow hit from a Ghulam unit the other side of the irrigation canal sent the Armenians knights in full flight never to be seen again, leaving the German knights and the whole flank very exposed (a break test was forced from a roll of 6 which also inflicted a casualty, and the poor Armenians rolled snake eyes – double 1!). The Crusaders were momentarily dismayed by this unexpected loss. They needn't have worried, for in the combat that followed between the German knights in company with French infantry and Ghulams together with a Turkoman unit it was the Crusaders who came up trumps, killing the enemy commander and routing half the division.

Baldwin's infantry eventually got their act together and pushed down into the plain to attack the last enemy infantry still defending the suburbs and the road to their objective. The three original Turkoman units, like mosquitoes, kept plugging away at the Hospitallers, successfully holding them at bay. By now more of Anur's troops were arriving, but even a rapid advance was going to find it difficult to stop the Christians' reaching the opposite table edge, which was their ultimate aim.

Seizing their moment, Baldwin's knights struck out for the objective, forcing back the blocking Turkoman units to the very edge of the table. But the Turkomans hung on and successfully recoiled the Hospitallers with missile fire in their turn. There was heavy pressure now on the Crusaders' right flank with many of Anur's troops joining the fray against the German horse and French foot. But the blocking force had gone and there was next to nothing stopping Baldwin, Louis and Konrad's forces from gaining their goal. So it was

determined to be a Crusader victory, as was the real battle. The Christians might have won that battle, but the subsequent siege and campaign proved a complete disaster – but for now it was victory indeed!

COMMENTS ON THE SPECIAL RULES

The Crusader knights were rated as *eager* – which means they would automatically move at least once when given a charge order against an enemy within range. They were also given the *tough fighters* rule, allowing them to re-roll one missed combat attack each round. This was to give the knights an edge over their Ghulam opponents in addition to that afforded by their lances (–1 morale save when charging/countercharging). The Hospitallers were also made *stubborn*, allowing them to re-roll a failed morale save when taking casualties.

Both the Turcopoles and their adversaries the Turkoman light cavalry were given *feigned flight*, allowing them to move out of combat and therefore avoid getting pinned down by the heavier cavalry.

The Damascan militia were rated as *levy*, obliging them to roll a 4+ to shake off the effect of disorder. The napfa armed unit was treated as a small unit of skirmishers armed with short ranged missile weapons – but it was decreed than any unit suffering casualties from *napfa* would be obliged to take a break test with a –1 modifier. The Fanatics were given the *fanatic* rule, boosting their morale save by +1 until shaken, and the *wild fighters* rule, allowing them to re-roll up to three failed hits in their first round of combat only. As it was this unit failed to reach combat.

Another valiant Crusader falls victim to the accursed Saracens, or possibly the temptations of the Communion wine...

A hail of arrows falls upon these daring horsemen in an attempt to drive the Turkomans back to their lines

What a scorcher! Napfa-armed skirmishers rain fire and destruction upon the Frankish knights...

Ghulams advance apace with Turkoman horse in close support

APPENDIX I: DESIGNER'S NOTES

The Hail Caesar rules are a development of Warlord Games' Black Powder wargame that covers warfare of the eighteenth and nineteenth centuries. Hail Caesar is a broad set of rules covering the earliest warfare through to battles of medieval times. Many of the underlying procedures and mechanisms have therefore changed in order to more properly represent wars of the ancient and medieval world. As a result, even though the structure of the Hail Caesar game is the same as Black Powder, players of Black Powder will find many differences of detail and emphasis. Thus, regardless of whether players are familiar with Black Powder or not, it is best to consider Hail Caesar as an altogether new set of rules. These notes are intended to give an idea of the design aims and process of development of Hail Caesar.

Our over-riding concern was to create a game that looked and felt like a conflict of ancient times. Black Powder emphasises the sweep of battle, the predominance of musketry as the main arm, and the sudden and decisive consequences of moving to close quarters to deliver the *coup de grâce*. None of this seemed quite right for battles of the ancient world, where manoeuvre often amounted to 'keeping in line', where missile fire was usually secondary to close quarter fighting, and where hand-to-hand combat could be a protracted affair. To address this change of emphasis the basic move rates were reduced to roughly half those of Black Powder, and the stamina value of units (the number of casualties units can take before being shaken) was doubled (from three to six for standard sized units). The affect of shorter moves is to keep the army more closely together as a body, reducing the potential for broad sweeping manoeuvres and emphasising cohesion. The effect of increased stamina is that it introduces more granularity into the system for inflicting and recording casualties, allowing for overall less effective shooting as well as prolonged hand-to-hand fighting. In short, these changes make ancient battles more of a 'grind' for the opposing armies, though hopefully no less nail biting for the players.

As the rules for Hail Caesar started to take shape it soon became necessary to define various types of troops. The ancient and medieval worlds were far more diverse in this respect than the era of the musket. In Black Powder, unusual weaponry and native types are mostly treated as exceptions and special cases. The proliferation of differently armed and equipped warriors of ancient times forces Hail Caesar to address armaments and fighting styles as part of the core rules. This has been tackled by creating a variety of different functional types of troops from the get go: for example, heavy, medium and light cavalry. These types have standard game values and, in some cases, specific armaments and formations rules. The same principle applies to infantry, artillery and chariots. The overall effect is that rules that would be treated as 'special' or exceptional in Black Powder, and consequently covered in a separate section away from the main text, are integrated into the body of the rules. This does tend to make the rules themselves a little longer, but this is perhaps to be expected from a game where these essential qualities in troop types are often key to an army's fighting style.

The core command system is common to Black Powder and Hail Caesar, and forms the backbone of game play. Units, or groups of units, are given orders and a test is made to see whether they act upon their instructions. If this is successful, units will act as ordered within the number of moves allowed to them. Units can potentially move not at all, once, twice or three times depending on the result of their dice roll. This system replaces the predictable fixed movement of most wargames. Variable move distances reflect the decisiveness of commanders, the determination of troops, and the limited ability of troops on the ground to understand what is happening around them.

Moves are not calculated from the number of metres a man could theoretically move over some pre-determined fixed time. Troops may sometimes be rooted to the spot from turn to turn whilst others bound across the battlefield with relative ease. This idea is based upon a view taken about behaviour of armies in battle, rather than theoretical drill manoeuvre rates on a parade ground. Thus, a determined commander seeing an opportunity, leading troops who are eager, and communicating an order successfully through his command structure, can mount a cavalry charge that takes his forces straight into the heart of the enemy. Conversely a timid commander who is unsure what to do, leading troops who are poorly motivated, whose instructions may be lost, delayed or misinterpreted, might do nothing at all while the enemy close upon him.

Players of Black Powder will notice that the role of free moves has been extended in Hail Caesar. Modifiers to the command rolls have also been reduced to that for distance only. These changes draw the emphasis away from the use of marching columns along roads to facilitate the movement of troops, artillery, baggage and supplies. Taken together with the reduced move rates, the overall result is to encourage a steady advance and more cohesive battle plan. This might feel odd to players who have grown used to the sudden re-deployments of Black Powder. However, it better represents the measured movement to contact characteristic of many larger ancient battles. This does not affect the potential for relatively rapid manoeuvres with mounted troops, especially in smaller scenario-driven games. This is further emphasised by the introduction of a faster pace for light cavalry and horse archers in open order. A side benefit of the reduced moves and more compacted battle formations is that it becomes possible to play on tables four feet wide using the measurements given. In Black Powder it is generally necessary to reduce the standard moves to do so.

Shortening move distances changes the way the initiative and proximity rules work within the game. In the case of initiative this is because units entitled to move on their initiative (i.e. within 12" of the enemy) are now much less likely to be within 'charge' range of a target (a single charge move is now 9" for cavalry and 6" for infantry, rather than 18" and 12" as in Black Powder). The drive to combat is therefore slowed down, and will often involve a turn of preliminary contact at short range before the opposing sides clash. This results in a game that feels more like a fight between ancient armies, where the combatants are dense blocks of heavy infantry arrayed facing each other. A second important consequence of the reduced move is the way it interacts with the proximity rule. Because the proximity rule affects a unit's movement within 12" of the enemy it does not normally come into play in Black Powder except where units are within charge range or critical distance for musketry. However, in Hail Caesar this affects movement as opposing armies approach each other, forcing units to 'face up' to the enemy in front of them. To reflect its new found importance the proximity rule is defined more tightly, and the overall affect is to guide units into mutual combats, or to ensure that units avoiding combat move away from their enemy rather than attempting to slip around their formations or through gaps in their lines.

Although move distances have been reduced overall, shooting ranges have been kept about the same with bow fire set at 18". This distance is not based on a ground scale as such. If one assumes a typical standard sized unit to be equivalent to a Roman cohort, it is theoretically possible to retro-calculate an approximate ground scale based on the number of men occupying the unit's frontage. However, as far as we are concerned a single model could equally easily represent almost any number of actual combatants from perhaps as many as a hundred to just one. This presumed ratio is not necessarily constant, and may vary from one game to another. With that in mind, the ranges for long-ranged missile shooting are set relative to the movement distances and the size of tabletop we would expect a game to be played over. In fact, we did start out with shorter ranges, but found the results unsatisfying. Although more realistic on a representational level, this approach proved less convincing in terms of results, so missile ranges were promptly increased to a degree that gives credible results and looks and feels right.

Rather than dealing with shooting as such, the rules cover 'ranged' fighting; which is judged to include conventional bow fire; similar shooting with long ranged weaponry such as crossbows, slings, staff slings and artillery; and a closer exchange that can include skirmishing with hand-to-hand weapons as well as thrown weapons such as spears, javelins, throwing axes, darts, stones and so forth. These two distinct styles of ranged fighting are allocated separate values. Almost all troops have been given some short ranged attack ability (up to 6") representing both thrown weapons and troops skirmishing ahead or out of the main body where historical precedent suggests it. This allows for the representation of troops whose fighting methods are essentially 'non-contact', especially light cavalry, horse archers and skirmishers.

Players familiar with Black Powder will know that disorder results from a volley of musket fire on any roll of a 6 to hit. This is fine for musketry and cannon fire, which one naturally expects to be decisive and dramatic. However, it didn't feel at all right when it came to the exchange of the hand-hurled missiles, arrows and sling stones typical of pre-gunpowder warfare. This gave us reason to reconsider how to utilise disorder in the game. Hence, disorder in Hail Caesar has been incorporated into the break test results for both ranged attacks and hand-to-hand combat. Missiles can still disorder troops, but this is far less likely than in Black Powder. On the other hand, with prolonged combats more common in Hail Caesar, disorder often results from a hand-to-hand combat break test.

The rules for hand-to-hand fighting did need to be refined to allow for longer fights and for the participation of adjoining units in a way that reflected their fighting qualities. To make this more workable additional guidance on unit frontages is given compared to Black Powder. However, we were keen to keep the same sense of flexibility that so strongly characterises the original game. The changes ensure that combats are resolved one on one where appropriate, together with supporting units if present. In Hail Caesar the supporting units contribute to the fighting with their own attacks, unlike in Black Powder where they simply add a modifier to the result. Furthermore, troops are given a separate supporting value based on their close ranged fighting ability, enabling us to create troops that are more or less effective as supports.

At last we satisfied ourselves that our framework was solid. Many enjoyable games were played. New ideas and robust observation flowed forth. At this stage we had to decide whether to restrict our game to a limited time period, or produce a more broad based set of ancient rules that would allow us to fight all kinds of engagements from the Bronze Age to the medieval period. We felt it would be unrealistic to try and cover every aspect of every army of the ancient and medieval world in detail. To attempt such a thing would be very much against the spirit of the original Black Powder game, where players are encouraged to freely adapt rules to suit individual wars, campaigns and encounters. Our own games had concentrated heavily on Roman armies of the first century AD, and in particular the conquest of Britain. This stemmed from our personal interests and collections as much as anything. Although many other games were fought using armies as diverse as New Kingdom Egyptians and medieval Crusaders, we felt it would be foolish to try and reduce the whole of three thousand of years of history into a rigid formula. Rather, Hail Caesar gives a good selection of rules that we have used, and leaves players to adapt the game as they wish to reflect the capabilities and distinctions between specific opposing forces. Having said that, the selection of rules given is reasonably comprehensive in the generalised way intended.

In keeping with Black Powder we abandoned any attempt at assembling our opposing armies by means of army lists or points values, preferring to match our forces to the scenario and players. This does not preclude the use of army lists and points values of the kinds commonly used by some game rules should players wish to do so. Some suggestions about how to adapt the copious army lists produced for other games are included in a separate appendix together with a couple of army lists by way of example.

APPENDIX 2: USING SMALLER MODELS

Although Hail Caesar has been developed to enable us to play games using our own collections of 28mm sized models, it is perfectly possible to play using armies of any size or scale. In essence the size of the models is merely an aesthetic choice. Indeed, it would be possible to play with card counters or wooden blocks were one so minded. The key factor is the unit frontages. Unit depths are much less important, being essentially the depths required to mount the models in a satisfying manner. Thus, if you have armies of 20mm sized models, 15mm, 10mm or 6mm, so long as they are arranged into units with the frontages indicated in the rules you can play without further modifications.

Players may feel that units of the frontages indicated are rather large for smaller sized models. This is more apparent at 15mm and smaller sizes where many more models are required to 'fill' the base area. In this case we'd suggest reducing dimensions as shown below.

It is possible to have more regularity in unit frontages with smaller models, and the frontages given have been rounded off to take advantage of this. There is no reason why players shouldn't adopt their own system should they prefer, for example standardizing to a 100mm frontage if so desired. So long as the proportions of standard to large and small sized units are retained all will be well.

If using smaller models on a small tabletop, players may wish to reduce the move distances and shooting ranges too. Our own experiments with 10mm sized armies have been played successfully using the standard distances upon a four-foot wide table. We did not find it necessary to reduce distances; however, it would be a simple matter to reduce all measurements in proportion. This is left to players to arrange to suit their own armies and tabletops.

28mm models as shown throughout this book are preferred by the authors and contributors because they are a pleasing size both to paint and display. The number of manufacturers who offer models in this size has grown apace over recent years, and the range available covers almost every conceivable part of the ancient era. Whilst the majority of companies can supply metal miniatures, some are also able to offer plastic kits, and these are becoming increasingly popular with gamers in the ancient period. The actual size of a 28mm model does vary somewhat from one manufacturer to another, so it is always best if you can see the models before buying. However, a little variation in height and bulk is to be expected amongst real warriors, and so it is amongst their miniature counterparts.

Some players prefer smaller sized models for various reasons. For some it is lack of space, for others it is cost, and for many it is simply that they enjoy the spectacle of massed hordes. Of course, if your models are to be smaller then so must the corresponding terrain be smaller, and this does enable the modeller to represent a more varied and interesting portion of topography as well as larger settlements and more substantial buildings. A Sumerian ziggurat in 28mm would fill a tabletop, but in 6mm it can be represented convincingly and still leave room for the battle to rage below.

Of the commonly available smaller sizes 15mm is the most popular and well supported by manufacturers, 10mm is growing in popularity, and 6mm is an established size with a strong following. Just as many 28mm models are not exactly 28mm tall, so these smaller sizes are also 'nominal' and often a little larger in practice. It is also possible to buy 25mm models. This size was once almost universal, but has been largely superseded by the larger 28mm models. Whatever your preference, you will find plenty of choice, and a group of like-minded enthusiasts prepared to champion the virtues of their chosen size and style.

20mm is not a common size for metal miniatures, but is very readily available as 1/72nd scale plastic models. In practice, as with all these nominal sizes, the actual height of the models varies, and most 1/72nd models come in about 23-24mm tall. Although these sets are moulded in a soft plastic that is a bit 'bendy' they represent fantastic value for money. The number of sets available has skyrocketed over the last few years and the standard of design and moulding has advanced a thousand-fold since the old Airfix sets of the 1960's.

UNIT SIZES FOR 15MM AND SMALLER SIZES				
Type of Troops	Formation	Standard	Large	Small
Infantry	2 deep battle-line	120-160mm	240-300mm	60-90mm
Warbands	4 deep warband	120-160mm	240-300mm	60-90mm
Phalanx	4 deep phalanx	120-160mm	240-300mm	60-90mm
Cavalry	2 deep battle-line	120-160mm	240-300mm	60-90mm
Light Chariots	Single line	120-160mm	240-300mm	60-90mm
Light Artillery	Single line	60-90mm	120-160mm	30-40mm

APPENDIX 3: A BRIEF GUIDE TO ARMY LISTS

Wargames enthusiasts have fought battles with model armies of the ancient era for many decades now. The majority of games are fought between friends in their own homes and at local wargame clubs where suitable tabletops can be accommodated more easily. Over the years there have grown up national and even international competitions, during which players meet to fight battles with others of like mind: comrades in spirit if otherwise strangers. The need to ensure players from different towns, and even different parts of the world, can participate on an equal footing has led to the widespread use of army lists to select opposing forces. An army list assigns points values to the various units available to each particular army, and will generally provide strict guidelines as to how many such units of each type can be included. This enables players to build their armies to a standardized 'points value' with proportions of troop types that reflect generalised historical practice and ensure that all armies are comparably effective for purposes of tournaments.

No ancient general ever mustered an army on this basis. A fair and even fight against a randomly determined enemy was probably the last thing on Caesar's mind when he advanced upon the Gauls. Nor can one quite imagine Alexander the Great marching his armies to the banks of the Granicus, peering over the waters upon the massed ranks of his opponent, and muttering, 'So it's Persians today then – and I see they have maxed out on cavalry.' The Hail Caesar game as played by its creators does not utilise army lists. It relies upon the fact that the authors know enough of their armies, and their history, to field forces that are convincing in the context of a game. However, that is not to say the authors are unfamiliar with army lists or their usefulness. Even for experienced gamers, a thoughtfully constructed army list provides a useful overview of an army's make-up and effectiveness.

Players who are interested in army lists for Hail Caesar will be reassured to know that a series of publications is in progress. Army lists will soon be available for all the most popular armies and many of the osbscure ones too! Players who have armies already can, of course, field them as selected using whichever army lists they currently use. For example, if players already have armies created for Warhammer Ancient Battles (WAB) or built to conform to WAB army lists, these will be perfectly playable in Hail Caesar so long as allowances are made for organising the army into divisions and fielding the appropriate number of commanders.

By way of example we have constructed two army lists representing the Roman army of the first and second centuries AD and Britons of the period of the Roman invasion. These are quite general lists and we would certainly not feel constrained by them when constructing a scenario. A force might be completely atypical for any number of reasons. The lists given merely demonstrate a principle, and are intended to reflect the broad character of a field army of the nations and time concerned.

ROMAN ARMY 1ST-2ND CENTURIES AD	
Infantry 50%+	At least half the units in the army must be made up of infantry.
Cavalry up to 25%	No more than a quarter of the units in the army can be cavalry.
Legions 50%+ of infantry	At least half the infantry units in the army must comprise Legionary units of one type or another.
Artillery	There must be at least three Legionary units for every artillery unit fielded, and no more heavy or medium artillery than light artillery units in total.
Divisions 4 units+	Divisions must contain at least four units and be led by a commander.

'Give me a safe commander – not a rash one!'

Augustus Caesar according to Suetonius

EARLY IMPERIAL ROMAN – TROOP VALUES

All commanders including the general have Leadership ratings of 8. The general has the standard re-roll rule in addition.

Unit	Clash	Sust	Short	Long	Morale Save	Stamina	Special	Points Value
Heavy Infantry Legionaries armed with pila and swords.	7	7	3	0	4+	6	Drilled, Testudo.	32 points per unit.
Extra to upgrade Legionaries to veteran no more than half in total	7	7	3	0	4+	6	Drilled, Elite 4+, Testudo.	+3 per unit
Reduction to downgrade Legionaries to raw recruits – no more than half in total.	6	6	3	0	4+	6		-5 per unit
Medium Infantry Auxiliaries with spears.	6	6	3	0	5+	6		23 points per unit
Light Infantry (LI) Auxiliaries with spears/javelins.	5	5	3	0	6+	6		20 points per unit
Medium Infantry Auxiliary Archers	5	5	3	3	5+	6		24 points per unit
Light Infantry Auxiliary Archers.	4	4	3	3	6+	6		21 points per unit
Reduction to field LI Archers as small unit.	3	3	2	2	6+	4		-6 per unit
Infantry Skirmishers armed with javelins and fielded as small unit.	3	2	2	0	0	4		11 points per unit
Infantry Skirmishers armed with slings or bows and fielded as small unit.	2	2	2	2	0	4		12 points per unit
Medium Cavalry (MC) Auxiliaries spears/javelins.	8	5	3	0	5+	6		27 points per unit
Extra to give MC kontos instead of spears/javelins – 1 unit only	8	5	3	0	5+	6	Kontos	+3 per unit
Light Cavalry (LC) Auxiliaries armed with javelins and fielded as a small unit.	5	3	2	0	6+	4		17 points per unit
Extra to upgrade LC Auxiliaries to Numidians – 1 unit only.	5	3	2	0	6+	4	Feigned Flight	+2 per unit
Light Cavalry Auxiliaries armed with bows and fielded as a small unit.	5	3	2	2	6+	4	Feigned Flight	21 points per unit
Light Artillery Scorpion bolt thrower.	1	1	2	2	0	3	Drilled	18 points per unit
Medium Artillery Onager	1	1	0	3	0	3		20 points per unit
Heavy Artillery Ballista	1	1	0	3	0	3		23 points per unit
Commanders	1 Commander must be provided per division. All commanders including general have Leadership 8.							Free
Extra to upgrade general to Leadership 9.	The general can have Leadership 9 at the following extra cost.							+25 points

Notes: One unit of light cavalry can be fielded as camel mounted troops if desired – such troops were known only in the east. As eastern legionaries were notoriously soft at least 1 unit of Legionaries must be fielded as raw recruits if camels are included.

ANCIENT BRITON ARMY 1ST CENTURY BC – 1ST CENTURY AD

Infantry 50%+	At least half the units in the army must be made up of infantry.
Cavalry and/or Chariots up to 50%	Up to half of the units in the army can be cavalry and/or chariots.
Warbands 50%+ of infantry	At least half the infantry units in the army must comprise medium infantry Warbands.
Divisions 4+ units.	Divisions must contain at least 4 units and be led by a commander.

'He learned that Alexander, having completed nearly all his conquests by the time he was thirty-two years old, was at an utter loss to know what he should do during the rest of his life, whereat Augustus expressed his surprise that Alexander did not regard it as a greater task to set in order the empire which he had won than to win it.'

Augustus Caesar according to Plutarch

ANCIENT BRITON ARMY – TROOP VALUES

All commanders including the general have Leadership ratings of 8. The general has the standard re-roll rule in addition.

Unit	Combat				Morale Save	Stamina	Special	Points Value
	Clash	Sust	Short	Long				
Medium Infantry (MI) Warband armed with swords and javelins	9	6	2	0	5+	6	Wild Fighters (3 re-rolls)	28 points per unit
Extra to field MI Warband as large unit.	11	8	3	0	5+	8	Wild Fighters (3 re-rolls)	+7 per unit
Extra to field one standard-sized MI Warband as Fanatic	9	6	2	0	5+	6	Wild Fighters (3 re-rolls), Fanatic	+1 per unit
Skirmishers with javelins fielded as a small unit	3	2	2	0	0	4		11 points per unit
Skirmishers with slings fielded as a small unit	2	2	2	2	0	4		12 points per unit
Skirmishers with bows fielded as a small unit – 1 unit only.	2	2	2	2	0	4		12 points per unit
Medium Cavalry armed with spears/javelins – 1 unit only.	8	5	3	0	5+	6		27 points per unit
Light Cavalry armed with javelins	7	5	3	0	6+	6		25 points per unit
Light Cavalry armed with javelins and fielded as a small unit	5	3	2	0	6+	4		17 points per unit
British Light Chariots	6	5	4	0	4+	6		27 points per unit
Commanders	1 Commander must be provided per division. All commanders including general have Leadership 8							Free

APPENDIX 4: RULES SUMMARY

SEQUENCE OF PLAY

1. Play alternates between the opposing sides, first one player (blue) and then the other (red) and so forth: blue, red, blue, red, etc until the battle is over.

2. The scenario will likely dictate which side goes first. Otherwise, the players can agree which side is to take the first turn, or roll a dice to decide randomly.

BLUE TURN

1. **Blue Command:** movement is executed by initiative and/or orders.

2. **Blue Ranged Attacks:** ranged attacks are worked out against enemy within range.

3. **Hand-to-Hand combats are resolved:** both sides take part in any engagements.

RED TURN

1. **Red Command:** movement is executed by initiative and/or orders.

2. **Red Ranged Attacks:** ranged attacks are worked out against enemy within range.

3. **Hand-to-Hand combats are resolved:** both sides take part in any engagements.

MEASURING

1. Players are free to measure at all times.

2. Distances are usually measured base-edge to base-edge except for issuing orders.

3. When issuing orders the distance from commanders is measured from the head of the commander model to the nearest base edge of the unit receiving the order.

COMMAND – GIVING ORDERS AND MOVING BY INITIATIVE

1. All initiative moves must be made before orders are given. Individual initiative moves can be resolved in any convenient sequence, but each unit must complete its move before another is allowed to do so.

2. Orders are issued by one commander at a time. Each commander must finish giving orders before another begins. Moves are enacted in their entirety as soon as orders are issued. Where orders are given to multiple units, units can move in any sequence, but each unit must complete its move before another is allowed to do so.

3. Commanders can only issue orders to units in their own division, and similarly units can only receive orders from the commander of their division.

4. Units making moves on initiative cannot also be given orders. Units can move either by initiative or by orders – not both.

5. Units engaged in combat, whether fighting or supporting, cannot be given orders and cannot move using initiative.

6. Units that are disordered cannot be given orders and cannot move using initiative. However, note they are still entitled to a free 'retire' move if they belong to a broken division.

7. Units from broken divisions are allowed a free 'retire' move if they fail their order or where no order is issued. They are allowed this move even where disordered and therefore unable to receive an order or use initiative. Such units can be moved at any convenient time after all initiative moves are complete, and must be moved if they have not already done so by the time their commander has finished issuing orders.

FRAMING OF ORDERS

1. Orders must be framed in good time without conditions or vagaries.

2. A unit can only be issued one order in any turn

3. If a unit is to charge then the order must specify 'charge' and must indicate the target or targets.

4. If a unit is to change formation then the order must specify the formation change.

5. Units will always try to obey their orders in so far as they can and in the most direct and straightforward way possible.

TEST AGAINST LEADERSHIP

1. To determine if an order is successful, roll two dice and add the scores together to get a result of between 2 and 12.

2. If the result is equal to the commander's Leadership rating, or 1 less, then the unit is permitted one move as per its instructions.

3. If the result is 2 less than the commander's Leadership rating, then the unit is permitted two moves as per its instructions.

4. If the result is 3 less than the commander's Leadership rating, then the unit is permitted three moves as per its instructions.

5. If the result is greater than the commander's Leadership rating then the order is failed. The unit does not move unless it has a free move. The commander cannot issue further orders unless he is also the army's general in which case he is entitled to a single re-roll each turn.

6. The army's general is allowed to re-roll a test to issue an order once in the Command part of each of his side's turns. Should he do so then the second result stands, even if it is worse than the first or a blunder.

7. If a result of 12 is rolled when testing to issue an order, then the order is failed and the result is a blunder. If the general blunders the dice can be re-rolled if he has not re-rolled already that turn.

DIVISION ORDERS

1. Units from the same division can be given a single order so long as they form an interlinked group with no units separated by more than 6".

2. When giving a division order, all units must be given essentially the same order. This does not prevent individual units being instructed to change formation if that is consistent with the broad intent of the order; for example to allow light troops to form a skirmish screen, or for units to pass through terrain they could not otherwise enter.

3. Where a division is ordered to charge an enemy, then units unable to charge will attempt to support fighting units where possible. This is judged to be following their orders as best they can.

4. Units moving as a division must still form an interlinked group with no units separated by more than 6" after they have moved. I.e. the division has to stay together and cannot move off in two separate directions. Note that this restriction overrides any order given.

REDUCTION IN LEADERSHIP FOR DISTANCE

1. If the distance from the commander to the unit he wishes to give an order is 12" or greater, then his Leadership rating is reduced by 1 for every full 12" distance between them. Exceptions to this rule are noted below.

2. No modifiers for distance are applied to the following units unless they form part of a division as noted below:
   • Skirmishers in open order
   • Light cavalry in open order
   • Horse archers in open order

3. When issuing orders to a division, the distance penalty is applied in respect of the unit that is the greatest distance from the commander and to which a penalty is normally applied (i.e. not an exception as noted above). However, any penalty applies to all the units in the division including those that are normally exempt. This means all units test against the same value when acting as a body.

FREE MOVES

1. A unit in column formation moves once if it has failed its order.

2. A tiny unit will move once if it has failed its order.

3. A baggage, carriage, wagon or comparable unit will move once if it has failed its order and is also on a road or track.

4. Some units have a special rule entitling them to a free move if they fail their order – specifically drilled and eager units.

5. Units from broken divisions can move once if they fail an order or if no order is attempted, even where disordered. They must use this free 'retire' move to attempt to leave the battlefield.

BLUNDERS

1. Any roll of a 12 (double 6) made when issuing an order is a blunder. If the commander is also the army's general then this can be re-rolled so long as the general has not already used his re-roll that turn. However, a re-rolled result always stands even if it is worse than the original and even if it is a blunder.

2. To resolve a blunder roll a dice and consult the blunder chart.

D6	BLUNDER
1	**Uncontrolled flight!** The unit turns round to face its rear and then makes two full moves into its facing quarter. The unit will move even further if necessary to clear the position of friends. Once it has moved, the unit suffers 1 casualty to represent loss of life and equipment suffered during the ignominious stampede.
2	**Back!** The unit moves backwards one move to its rear quarter whilst continuing to face the same direction.
3	**Drift left.** The unit makes one move to its left quarter.
4	**Drift right.** The unit makes one move to its right quarter
5	**Forward!** The unit makes one move to its front and will charge if facing enemy within one move's distance and which the unit is otherwise allowed to charge.
6	**Uncontrolled Advance!** The unit makes three moves to its front. The unit will charge if facing enemy within three moves' distance and which the unit is otherwise allowed to charge

6. Units making an evade move are also entitled to move once, even if their order is failed. This is not strictly speaking a 'free move' as it happens outside the move part of the turn, but is included for the sake of completeness. See Evades.

ORDERS TO OFF-TABLE UNITS

1. Units yet to enter the game can be given orders.

a. If the commander is also off the table then no distance penalty applies. If the whole division is off the table it can be given a division order without applying distance penalties.

b. If the commander is on the table then measure the distance to the table edge where the unit or division will enter.

2. Units that have left the table can re-enter by being given orders so long as they are not shaken or units from broken divisions.

a. If the commander is on the table then measure the distance to the point on the table edge where the unit left the battle.

b. If the commander has also left the battle no distance penalties apply to any units that are off-table.

3. Units entering or returning to the table always move 6" onto the table as their first move.

4. A division moving onto the battlefield might not be able to fit all of its units onto the table at once. Any units following from behind are still assumed to have been moved long with the rest of their division, and will automatically move onto the table once there is room for them to do so.

MOVEMENT RATES OF UNITS

MOVING UNITS TABLE	
Infantry, Elephants, Wagons and Baggage, Man-portable Artillery, Cataphract Cavalry, and Heavy Chariots.	6"
Light Chariots, and Cavalry other than Cataphracts, Light Cavalry in open order, or Horse Archers in open order.	9"
Light Cavalry in open order and Horse Archers in open order.	12"

MOVEMENT AND PROXIMITY TO ENEMY

1. Except where governed by the proximity of enemy, units are free to move in any direction or orientation so long as no model moves more than the distance allowed.

2. Formed units that have enemy within 12" and to their front, even if only partially, are governed by the proximity rule as noted below. The following enemy units are exceptions and are ignored.
   - Commanders
   - Artillery units

- Tiny units
- Non-combatant units including wagons and baggage
- Any units within buildings or fortifications
- Any units in open order can be ignored by choice.

3. Formed units facing an enemy within 12" can only move towards or away from that enemy whilst continuing to face.

a. A formed unit 'faces' an enemy if the enemy lies directly in front of its centre frontage.

4. Formed units that have an enemy within 12" to their front quarter but are not actually facing an enemy within 12", must face towards an enemy as they move. The enemy unit faced must lie within no more than three moves distance.

5. Units in open order that have enemy within 6" of any part of them are affected by proximity as noted below.

6. Whilst there are any enemy within 6" a unit in open order can only move either towards or away from the closest enemy.

MOVING THROUGH OTHER UNITS

1. Units are not allowed to move through opposing units. Units can move over opposing commanders freely.

2. Units cannot normally move through friends engaged in combat, but are allowed to do so if moving to join the engagement either as supports or by charging.

3. Units can move through friends only where it's possible for the moving unit to completely clear their position.

4. Units can move through friends without penalty if:
   - Either, both or all units are skirmishers or other infantry in open order.
   - If both or all units are light cavalry in open order and/or light chariots in open order and/or horse archers in open order.
   - Where only a minor portion of either or all units is moved through. This is determined as any part of the unit that does not include the centre-front/leader position.

5. Where units cannot move through friends without penalty, they can still move through so long as they can clear their friends' position; however, each unit involved takes a test for disorder. Roll a dice for each unit. On the score of a 1, 2 or 3 the unit becomes disordered.

MAN-HANDLING ARTILLERY

1. Mobile light artillery moves at infantry rate. Any unit that moves more than once cannot also shoot in that turn.

2. Mobile forms of medium or heavy artillery can only move a maximum of once per turn, and cannot move and shoot in the same turn.

FORMATION CHANGES

1. All changes to formation must be indicated when giving orders or stated aloud when using initiative.

2. Changes to formation take up one entire move except as noted below. Those units noted below can change to or from open order and then make one non-charging move, the whole counting as a single move.

   - Skirmishers
   - Light infantry
   - Light cavalry
   - Horse archers
   - Light chariots

3. A unit can only make one formation change in the Command part of any turn.

4. Skirmishers, horse archers and tiny units are restricted to open order or column. Light infantry, light cavalry and light chariots can adopt open order if they wish. Other infantry and cavalry can only adopt open order where they could not otherwise move without penalty. Other units cannot adopt open order.

SQUARES

1. A square cannot move and the only order it may be given is to change formation. It may not change formation and then move further in the same turn.

MOVEMENT OF COMMANDERS

1. Commanders move 24" per turn regardless of how they are mounted, and suffer no movement penalties in respect of their mounts, it being assumed they are capable of dismounting where appropriate.

2. Commanders can join a unit that is fighting hand-to-hand combat within 12" in any turn, including opposing turns, up until the point that hand-to-hand attacks are struck.

3. Commanders are ignored for purposes of determining initiative, proximity of enemy, calculating targets for shooting, and in most other circumstances as described in the body of the rules.

4. Commanders can move freely through units from their own side, and can be moved through freely by troops from their own side. If a friendly unit moves on top of a commander the commander model is moved sufficiently far to allow the unit to take up its position.

5. Commanders cannot move through enemy units, although they can move through other commanders from either side freely.

6. A commander who is moved into by an enemy unit must join a friendly unit within one move's distance, otherwise he becomes a casualty and is removed as dead or captured.

TERRAIN

1. Terrain rules are regarded as part of the scenario and can be freely adapted to suit. The following rules reflect our usual practice, but are often varied as the occasion demands.

2. **Woods.** Infantry in open order, cavalry in open order and commanders can move through woods. The movement of open order cavalry is reduced to infantry speed. Other troops cannot move through woods except by means of roads or tracks.

3. **Rough Ground.** Infantry in open order, cavalry in open order and commanders can move through rough ground without hindrance. Other troops are restricted to a maximum of one move. A unit moving into rough ground completes that move and moves no further. A unit already in rough ground at the start of movement makes one move only.

4. **Linear obstacles.** Hedges, walls and ditches are often considered decorative elements or used to mark boundaries of other features such as woods, rough ground, or buildings. However, they can also be treated as obstacles in their own right. Where so treated, infantry in open order, cavalry in open order and commanders can move over linear obstacles without hindrance. Other units must surrender one entire move to cross a linear obstacle. Where substantial obstacles are treated as impassable to wheeled vehicles – this is up to the players/umpire to determine.

5. **Rivers.** Small rivers can be treated as linear obstacles. Larger rivers can only be crossed at a ford or bridge.

6. **Buildings.** Buildings are arranged into blocks sufficient to allow entry to a standard sized unit plus a tiny unit, or as the players prefer. Only infantry can enter or assault a building, although light artillery can be deployed in or on buildings at the start of the game if desired. An artillery piece deployed in this manner is regarded as immobile. To enter an unoccupied building a unit must move into touch with the perimeter and then expend one move to move inside. The unit is then arranged within the building or built-up area as required. To leave a building measure from a point on the perimeter.

SHOOTING AND SKIRMISHING AT A DISTANCE

1. Units with a ranged attack value can make attacks during the ranged attacks part of the turn. This represents both skirmishing and shooting. Two separate values are indicated: short range and long range.

WEAPON RANGE	
Javelins, darts and other thrown weapons	6"
Slings	12"
Bows, crossbows and staff slings	18"
Light artillery	24"
Medium artillery	36"
Heavy artillery	48"

2. Short ranged attacks are made at ranges of up to 6". Long ranged attacks are made at ranges of greater than 6" up to the distance shown for the weapon carried.

3. Formed units automatically make their attacks against the closest target they can see within their own front quarter measuring from the unit's centre-front position. Where several enemy units present themselves as potential 'closest' visible targets, attacks can be divided as the players see fit. Artillery is an exception to this rule as noted below.

4. Units in open order must direct their attacks against the closest visible enemy. Where portions of the open order unit lie closest to different enemies then attacks are divided between them as the players see fit.

5. Artillery units must shoot at the closest enemy target if such a target presents itself within half the weapon's maximum range. However, if no enemy target presents itself within half maximum range, the artillery unit can shoot at any enemy target within its frontal arc. Light artillery can make up to one move and shoot in the same turn. Medium and heavy artillery cannot move and shoot in the same turn.

6. Artillery units are also allowed to shoot overhead at targets they can see, so long as there is 6" of clear ground in front of both shooter and target. Other units are not permitted to shoot overhead.

7. Units already engaged in hand-to-hand combat, whether as fighting units or supports, cannot make ranged attacks.

8. Units with long ranged attacks are also allowed to shoot during other parts of the turn, or during the opposing side's turn, by means of closing shots or traversing shots as noted separately.

9. The following targets can be ignored in favour of a more distant target if the player wishes:
   - Targets in open order formation.
   - Artillery targets.
   - Wagons, carts, baggage and such like targets.
   - Targets that are only partially to the front quarter of the attacker.
   - Targets that are only partially within sight of the attacker.

- Targets occupying buildings or within cover.
- Targets visible through narrow gaps (narrower than the unit's own formation and minimum 3" in the case of artillery).

Working Out Ranged Attacks

1. Roll the number of dice equivalent to the unit's ranged attack value. Any dice scoring 4, 5 or 6 once any modifiers have been taken into account are 'hits'. Dice failing to score hits are 'misses'.

2. Regardless of any modifiers that apply, dice rolls of 1 are always misses and dice rolls of 6 are always hits.

3. If the dice roll required to score a hit after modifiers have been taken into account is 5 or less, then a missile break test is initiated if any dice rolls a 6.

4. If the dice roll required to score a hit after modifiers have been taken into account is 6, then a missile break test is initiated if two or more dice roll 6s.

5. The following modifiers apply to the dice scores rolled.

Closing Shots

1. If a formed unit of a kind indicated below is charged to its front, it is allowed to shoot at the charger with any weapons that have a long range attack value. A unit in open order can shoot in this way at chargers coming from any direction, so long as it has a long range attack value.

- Infantry
- Cavalry
- Elephant
- Chariot
- Light artillery

FORMATION MODIFIERS FOR RANGED ATTACKS

Ranged Attack Value	Formation Modifiers
None	**Column or Testudo.** Units in column or testudo cannot make ranged attacks.
1 Dice	**Square.** Attacks in square are limited to one dice only.
2/face	**Buildings.** Units occupying buildings are limited to a maximum of two dice from any one face up to their ranged attacks value in total – see the rules for buildings.

'TO HIT' MODIFIERS FOR RANGED ATTACKS

Dice Score	Situation
–1	**Attackers are shaken and/or disordered.** This applies if the attacking unit is either shaken, disordered, or both.
–1	**The target is partly obscured, in open order, artillery or baggage.** This applies if the target is partly obscured, or in open order, or artillery or wagons and other baggage.
–1	**The target is formed heavy infantry being attacked by enemy to their front quarter, or formed cataphract cavalry regardless of the direction of attack.** Note that some unusual formations count as front all round in which case the penalty applies all round too, for example the testudo as described on page 105.
–1	**Closing Shots.** This applies to units shooting at enemies as they charge home.
–1	**Traversing Shots.** This applies to units shooting at enemies as they traverse their front.
–1	**Long Range Shots.** This applies at all shots at ranges of over 12".

2. A unit making closing shots cannot react to the enemy charge by either countercharging or evading, except in the case of units that have the special Parthian Shot rule, which are allowed to both shoot and evade.

3. Work out attacks once the chargers have moved, using the shooter's long ranged attack value. Apply any casualties and take any break tests required as a result of shooting.

Traversing Shots

1. A unit is allowed to shoot at an enemy target that crosses its front within 12". This can occur either during the opposing players turn or, more rarely, during a sweeping advance following hand-to-hand combat in any turn.

2. Only units armed with long ranged weapons can make traversing shots.

Morale Saves

1. Units hit by ranged or hand-to-hand combat attacks must test their morale to determine if hits are converted to casualties.

2. Roll a dice for each hit suffered. If the score of any dice is equal to or more than the unit's Morale Save value that hit is negated or 'saved' and has no effect. If the dice score less than the unit's Morale Save value the hit is converted to a casualty upon the unit.

3. Casualties must be recorded on each unit in some appropriate manner, as the players prefer.

4. Morale Save values are modified in some situations as indicated on the table below. These will increase the save value in some circumstances (positive modifiers) or

decrease them in others (negative modifiers). In either case, a dice roll of 6 always succeeds assuming the unit had a value of at least 6 to start with, and a roll of 1 always fails and results in a casualty.

Shaken Units

1. Once a unit has suffered casualties equal to its Stamina value it is shaken. This value is usually 6 for standard sized units and 4 for small units.

2. A unit can suffer more casualties than its Stamina value, up to a maximum of double, but these 'excess' casualties are only recorded for purposes of taking break tests. Once any required break tests have been taken, excess casualties are either removed or redistributed to supporting friends in the case of units engaged in hand-to-hand combat.

3. Units that accumulate casualties equal to double their Stamina value are automatically shattered. These units are deemed to be broken and are removed as destroyed without the need for a break test. This applies both in respect to casualties from ranged attacks and hand-to-hand fighting.

Hand-to-Hand Fighting

1. A combat engagement is initiated when one unit charges another, usually in the Command part of the turn as a result of an initiative move or order. Charges can also occur following combat as part of a sweeping advance as noted later.

2. A combat engagement consists of mutually fighting units plus their respective supports. In most cases an engagement will therefore consist of one fighting unit on each side plus a number of supports. It is possible to have multiple

combats where one side has units with significantly shorter frontages (e.g. elephants).

3. All fighting and supporting units are engaged in combat and are therefore unable to move during the Command part of the turn or make ranged attacks during the Ranged Attacks part of the turn. Special rules may include exceptions, specifically Feigned Flight which allows units to move out of a combat engagement.

CHARGE MOVES IN GENERAL

1. A charge move is a move intended to bring a unit into contact with the enemy. Often a unit will move several times during the turn as a result of an order, but only the final move into contact is a charge move.

2. A unit given a charge order must move towards the intended target as quickly and directly as possible. This applies to all the moves made that turn and not just the charge move itself.

3. Where a unit intends to charge the enemy by means of an order the player must state his intention to charge and must indicate the target or targets of the charge. Where a charge is executed on initiative it is still necessary to declare this before moving.

4. A charge intention can result from a blundered order regardless of the wishes of the player.

5. The following units are unable to charge and may be unable to receive orders or move at all in some cases.

   • Units that are already engaged in combat.
   • Disordered units.
   • Shaken units (i.e. units that have suffered casualties equal to their Stamina value).
   • Units in column or square formation. Note that units in column can be ordered to change formation and then charge. Units in square are limited to one move and so are unable to do so.
   • Artillery units.
   • Units in open order are not allowed to charge formed units of infantry or cavalry. Units capable of doing so can change formation and charge. Open order units can charge enemy in buildings or fortifications.
   • Cavalry and chariots are not allowed to charge home onto the front of a pike phalanx unless the phalanx is shaken and/or disordered, except in the case of a scythed chariot where special rules apply.

MAKING A CHARGE WITH FORMED UNITS

1. A formed unit can only make a charge move against an enemy it can see, which is within charge range, and which lies directly in front of the unit's centre-front or leader position.

2. The charge range of a formed unit is measured from the centre-front position to the closest part of the enemy. If within range the unit can charge regardless of the distance moved by individual models.

3. If the chargers lie to the front quarter of the target they will charge to the front, if to the side they charge to the flank, and if behind they charge to the rear. However, note that a unit given a charge order will always move towards the enemy in the most direct manner, it is not permitted to move from the front of an enemy unit and charge its flank or rear even where two or three moves are available.

4. Move the charging unit so that it brings its own centre-front position and as great a portion of the frontages of both units into contact as possible. Where a charge is mounted to the enemy's flank or rear then the charger must contact as great a portion of the appropriate unit facing. The charger always moves the least distance required to accomplish this in the most direct manner.

5. Two (or more) on one combats are allowed where the centre-front positions of several units can successfully charge and contact the same enemy unit one after the other.

6. Where units are already engaged, a second (or subsequent) charger is allowed to draw line-of-sight through friendly engaged troops onto the target.

7. Where two enemy units are positioned next to each other, such that charging one will bring the adjacent unit into touch, then the obligation for the charger to maximise frontal contact extends to the adjacent unit. If the result is to bring the adjacent unit into the engagement as a fighting unit, then it may react as if charged

MAKING A CHARGE WITH OPEN ORDER UNITS

1. Units in open order are not allowed to charge formed infantry or cavalry. They are unable to charge other units if doing so would bring formed enemy infantry or cavalry into the engagement as fighting units.

2. The charge range of an open order unit is measured from the closest part of the charger to the closest part of the target that it can see. If within range the whole unit can charge regardless of the distance moved by individual models.

3. When an open order unit charges its models are brought forward to form an approximate line in as satisfying a manner as possible.

4. As with other units, those in open order will charge to the front if positioned to the enemy's front quarter, to the flank if positioned to the side, and to the rear if positioned behind.

MORALE SAVE MODIFIERS		
Dice Score	Situation	
+1	**Square or Wedge.** Troops in square or wedge formation derive extra protection from their overlapping shields, whilst their close mass makes it practically impossible for individuals to shy from the fight. Add +1 to the morale value of such troops.	
+1	**Cover.** The unit is within woodland, behind hedgerows or low walls, or in other situations where it is felt it should rightly benefit from the physical protection and reassurance of cover. Add +1 to the morale value of such troops.	
+2	**Testudo.** Troops in testudo formation derive extra protection from their overlapping shields and the rigidity of their ranks prevents flight. Add +2 to the morale value of such troops.	
+2	**Buildings.** If a unit is occupying a substantial building it benefits further from their cover. Add +2 to the morale value of such troops.	
+3	**Fortification.** If a unit is sheltering behind even more considerable fortifications it will be protected from missile fire. Add +3 to the morale value of such troops.	
-1	**Hit by Light Artillery.** If a unit is hit by light artillery then deduct –1 from its morale value to represent both the penetrating power and demoralising effect of artillery fire.	
-2	**Hit by Medium or Heavy Artillery.** If a unit is hit by medium or heavy artillery then deduct –2 from its morale value to represent both the penetrating power and demoralising effect of artillery fire.	
-2	**Column.** If a unit is attacked whilst in column formation it is unprepared for combat and will quickly fall into disarray. To represent this deduct –2 from the morale value of such troops.	

CHARGE RESPONSES

1. Units that are charged must declare their responses as soon as it is established a charge has been made and before moving the chargers, or as soon as practical where adjacent units are brought into an engagement as fighting units.

2. The following charge responses are permitted where appropriate.
   - **Stand.** The default response. Units in open order will form an approximate line as already noted.
   - **Closing shots.** Enemy armed with long ranged weapons make closing shots upon the charger. Work this out once the chargers are in contact.
   - **Evade.** Open order units that are not disordered can attempt to evade from a charge as noted below.
   - **Countercharge.** A cavalry or chariot unit charged to its front can countercharge assuming it would otherwise be allowed to charge.
   - **Turn to face.** A cavalry or elephant unit charged to the flank or rear can pivot to face a charging enemy as noted below.

3. **Evades.** Units in open order are allowed to evade from chargers, and do so by moving directly away by one, two or three moves after giving an order in the usual way. This is worked out before the chargers make their moves once it is established they would otherwise charge home successfully. Evading units always move at least once, even if their order is failed – i.e. they get a free move. Evaders are automatically destroyed if they fail to outpace their chargers.

4. **Countercharge.** Where a countercharge is permitted both chargers and counterchargers move simultaneously and meet at a point equidistant between them. Both units are treated as having charged, and both receive the appropriate combat bonuses and any special rules pertinent to charging. If cavalry or chariots countercharge against formed infantry units, then the infantry automatically become disordered and receive no 'to hit' bonus for charging. Where units countercharge, then any other cavalry or chariot units already positioned such as they could support them can be included in the countercharge and can join the ensuing engagement as supports.

5. **Turn to face.** An unengaged, non-disordered, formed cavalry or elephant unit that is charged to the flank or rear can respond by pivoting to face the chargers assuming there is room for it to do so. This move is made at the same time as the charge and is automatic.

FIGHTING – WORKING OUT COMBAT ENGAGEMENTS

1. Regardless of which side's turn it is both sides take part in hand-to-hand fighting. All units that are fighting will fight, and all units that are supporting will contribute to the engagement as supports. As both side's fight, each turn of hand-to-hand fighting is referred to as a round: a round is fought in red's turn, a round is fought in blue's turn, then red's turn again, and so on.

2. During each round it is usual to work out all the current engagements one at a time, completing each engagement and taking any break tests required before moving on to another. The player whose turn it is can decide the sequence in which the engagements are resolved.

HAND-TO-HAND COMBAT FORMATION MODIFIERS

Combat Value	Formation Modifiers
1 Dice	**Column.** Units in column have a combat value of one dice regardless of their size.
2 Dice/Face	**Square.** Units in square are limited to a maximum of two dice for any face up to their full combat value in total.
2 Dice/Face	**Buildings.** Units occupying buildings are limited to a maximum of two dice from any face up to their combat value in total.

HAND-TO-HAND COMBAT ATTACKS

1. All attacks are assumed to be simultaneous, but for the sake of simplicity it is usual for one side to make all of its attacks and then the other. Units fight as they are at the start of the round, so it makes no difference which side goes first.

2. In hand-to-hand combat, units that are fighting use their clash combat attack value in the initial round of any engagement, and their sustained combat value in any subsequent round of any engagement. Units that are supporting use their short ranged attack value. The term combat value refers to all of these values, including supporting attacks made in hand-to-hand combat. In all cases these values indicate the number of dice rolled.

WORKING OUT HAND-TO-HAND COMBAT ATTACKS

1. Roll the number of dice equivalent to the attacking unit's combat value. Any dice scoring 4, 5 or 6 once any modifiers have been taken into account are 'hits'. Dice failing to score hits are 'misses'.

2. Regardless of any modifiers that apply, dice rolls of 1 are always misses and dice rolls of 6 are always hits.

3. If a unit is engaged in more than one direction then its attacks are distributed as follows. If fighting to the front at least half of its attacks must be made against the enemy to its front, dividing such attacks equally where two or more enemies are fighting to the front. No more than half a unit's attacks can be allocated to each flank. If not engaged to the front all of a unit's attacks can be allocated to its rear: if fighting to the front then any attacks not made to the front can be made to the rear if desired.

4. Supporting units make their attacks against the same target as the unit they are supporting. A unit can potentially support two fighting units, in which case it divides its attacks between them.

5. The following modifiers apply to the dice scores rolled. Note that Charging and Winning modifiers apply only to fighting units as indicated, i.e. they do not apply to supporting units. This may mean it is necessary to roll supporting attacks separately as they may require a different score to hit.

MORALE SAVES IN HAND-TO-HAND COMBAT

1. Morale saves for hits inflicted in hand-to-hand combat are worked out in the same way as those inflicted by ranged attacks.

SUPPORTS

1. Units positioned alongside or behind fighting units support by making their short ranged number of attacks.

2. Units that cannot be supported in hand-to-hand combat are listed below.
   - Units in open order
   - Artillery
   - Wagons and baggage
   - Units in buildings except from troops within the same building
   - Units in squares
   - Units in testudo
   - Units in wedge except by enclosed friends
   - Cavalry cannot be supported by elephants
   - Scythed chariots

CLOSE RANKS

1. Shield-armed heavy infantry can close ranks at the start of any combat round with -1 'to hit' and +1 'to save'.

COMBAT RESULTS

1. Combat results are worked out for each engagement as soon as all units taking part have fought including any supports and any commanders where they are present.

2. Add up the total number of casualties inflicted by each side that round. Do not including casualties inflicted by closing or traversing shots prior to the combat. Include commanders if they are killed or wounded during the round.

3. The side that has inflicted the most casualties has won and the other side is defeated. Where both sides score the same the result is a draw.

4. If a fighting unit has suffered a total number of casualties equal to double its stamina value that unit is shattered and is removed immediately and treated as broken. No break test is required for such units.

5. Aside from shattered units, defeated fighting units must take a break test. The break test result is modified by the difference in casualties inflicted by each side during the round, so make a note of this before reallocating casualties.

6. All excess casualties inflicted on fighting units are reallocated to supporting units. Excess casualties are reallocated as equally as possible between the fighting unit's supports, starting with supports that are touching the enemy. Any casualties remaining in excess of a unit's Stamina value once casualties are reallocated are discarded.

7. Break tests are taken by defeated fighting units. This can result in fighting units breaking, in which case they are removed, and each supporting units must then take a separate break test. Otherwise, both fighting and supporting units must act as indicated by the break test result.

8. Fighting units that are shaken must also take a break test if the result of the combat is a draw. This can mean both sides have to test and both can potentially be broken.

9. Units that remain engaged once hand-to-hand fighting is complete will remain where they are. Combat will resume in the next hand-to-hand combat round.

BREAK TESTS

1. A break test is required in the Ranged Attacks part of the turn as follows:
   - If a unit is shaken by ranged attacks.
   - If a unit that is already shaken suffers further casualties form ranged attacks.
   - On the roll of a 6 'to hit' by ranged attacks requiring better than 6.
   - On two rolls of a 6 'to hit' by ranged attacks requiring 6's.

2. A break test is required following ranged attacks in other parts of the turn as follows:
   - If a unit is shaken by closing or traversing shots.
   - On the roll of a 6 'to hit' by closing/traversing shots requiring better than 6.
   - On the roll of two 6's 'to hit' by closing/traversing shots requiring 6's.

3. A break test is required in hand-to-hand combat as follows:
   - If a fighting unit is defeated in hand-to-hand combat.
   - If a fighting unit that is already shaken draws hand-to-hand combat.
   - If a unit is supporting a fighting unit that breaks or is shattered.

4. Break tests are taken by rolling two dice and adding the scores to get a result between 2 and 12. The following modifiers apply.
   - For break tests from ranged attacks deduct any excess casualties scored on the unit.
   - For break tests from hand-to-hand fighting deduct the difference in casualties scored from the loser's dice roll. This applies both to fighting units and to supports if they have to test following a fighting unit breaking.

5. Units retreating as a result of ranged attacks move one move away from the closest enemy attackers. Note that the proximity rule will oblige them to

continue to face their enemy if within 12". Units unable to clear the position of friends with a single move will move as far as required to do so, and then become disordered. Units unable to make their move because of impenetrable terrain or engaged units move as far as they can and become disordered.

6. Units giving ground in hand-to-hand combat move 6" directly away from their enemy. Artillery and baggage units obliged to give ground are automatically destroyed. A defeated fighting unit that is unable to give ground because of terrain, the presence of opposing units, friends who do not move out of the way, or engaged troops is destroyed. A supporting unit unable to give ground in the same situation will move as far as it can, but is not otherwise penalised.

7. Friendly non-engaged and non-disordered troops in the path of units giving ground can move out of the way by up to one move in order to make a path for them. If they do this, the unit giving ground is automatically disordered and the moving unit is disordered on the dice roll of a 1, 2 or 3. If friends are unable or unwilling to move out of the way the unit giving ground is destroyed.

8. Uphill advantage. A unit defeated by an enemy with uphill advantage treats any result of 'Hold your ground' as 'Retreat in good order'.

9. Artillery units that give ground are automatically destroyed whether fighting or supporting.

DISORDER

1. Disorder can result from:
   - A break test from ranged attacks.
   - A break test from hand-to-hand combat.
   - A test for moving through or out of the way of other units
   - Units forcing friends to move out of the way when giving ground.
   - Formed infantry units countercharged by cavalry or chariots.
   - Retreating units obliged to retreat two or

Dice Score	Situation
	'TO HIT' MODIFIERS FOR HAND-TO-HAND COMBAT
+1	**Charging.** If a fighting unit has charged or countercharged into combat the bonus applies in the first round of fighting.
+1	**Winning.** If a fighting unit fought and won the previous round of the same combat engagement then this bonus applies during the following round of fighting.
+1	**Uphill.** If the unit is uphill of its opponent and has neither charged/countercharged this turn, nor moved following the previous round of the same engagement, then this bonus applies in the current round. If a unit moves following combat results the bonus is lost in the next round regardless of whether the unit won or lost the fight.
-1	**Shaken and/or disordered.** This applies if the attacking unit is either shaken, disordered, or both.
-1	**Open Order.** This applies if the attacking unit is in open order formation.
-1	**Flank/Rear.** This applies to all of a unit's attacks if it is engaged to either flank or to the rear, including to any attacks made to its front.

three moves to clear friends, or unable to retreat due to impassable terrain, enemy, combatants, etc.

- As defined by special rules: specifically units defeated by scythed chariots, and chariots/cavalry failing a test versus long spears or disordered pikes.

2. Disordered units cannot move in the Command part of the turn either by initiative or by orders except as noted below.

- Open order units can use initiative to move away from enemy/towards own table edge.
- Units from broken divisions receive a free move to 'retire' even where no order is issued.

MOVEMENT OF VICTORIOUS UNITS FOLLOWING COMBAT

1. If all of the enemy in contact with a victorious fighting unit give ground or are destroyed, then the victors can make one move if they wish. They can do this even if disordered.

2. A move can take a unit forward to maintain contact with an enemy who has given ground. Combat continues in the following round and the victors count the +1 bonus for winning the previous round.

3. Otherwise, a fighting unit can move as it wishes within the constraints of the proximity rule, which will usually oblige it to continue to face the enemy.

4. Supporting units do whatever the unit they are supporting does in so far as they can, and will continue to support where possible. This can potentially bring a supporting unit into a fighting position – this is allowed.

5. If all the enemies fighting a victorious unit are destroyed, and no other enemies remain in contact, victors who are neither shaken nor disordered are allowed to make a sweeping advance. A sweeping advance is up to two normal moves into the unit's front quarter. This can be a charge against another enemy in which case the move is termed a sweeping charge.

6. Where a sweeping charge enables a unit to rejoin the same engagement (by charging a unit that was previously supporting, for example) the combat continues in the following round and the victorious unit counts as charging in that round.

7. Where a sweeping advance initiates a new engagement against a previously unengaged enemy, then a new combat is worked out immediately. The victorious unit counts as charging. Should this engagement also result in the destruction of the enemy note that no second sweeping advance is permitted: only one sweeping advance is allowed in a round.

8. Where a sweeping charge carries a victorious unit into another as yet unfought engagement, the victorious unit

joins the engagement and fights again this round, counting as charging.

9. Where a sweeping charge carries a victorious unit into another already fought engagement, the victorious unit joins the engagement and fights from the following round counting as charging in that round.

10. A sweeping charge is a charge, and targets are allowed the usual charge response where appropriate. This may result in closing shots from a charged unit or traversing shots from units nearby.

11. The movement of victorious units may be blocked by incidental contact to the unit's front. In this case units must give ground. Note that artillery units cannot block and are therefore destroyed.

RULES FOR BREAK TESTS AND HAND-TO-HAND COMBAT

1. Open order units that have closed their ranks to fight hand-to-hand combat automatically disperse into regular open order if they are no longer engaged once hand-to-hand combat is over.

2. Squares. Units in square formation ignore break test results of Retreat and Give Ground and treat all such results as Hold Your Ground.

3. Buildings. Units in buildings ignore break test results of Retreat and Give Ground and treat all such results as Hold Your Ground.

4. Units fighting against troops in buildings can occupy the buildings if the enemy are destroyed. Supporting troops can make one move in any fashion.

COMMANDERS

1. The army's general is allowed to re-roll the dice when making a test to issue an order, and can do so whatever the result including a blunder. The re-rolled score stands even if it is a worse result that the initial roll. The general is allowed one re-roll in each turn.

2. Commanders who fall casualty are replaced with a 'reserve'. Reserve commanders have a Leadership rating of 1 lower down to a minimum value of 5. The reserve commander is placed within 12" of any unit in his division.

3. If a commander is within 12" of a unit from his own division he can issue it a Follow Me! order. Whether successful or not, a Follow Me! instruction always ends orders from that commander for that turn. If successfully issued, the commander moves to join the unit and can then make three moves as the player wishes within the usual constraints of the rules.

4. If a commander is within 12" of a unit from his division that has suffered two or more casualties, he can issue it a Rally! order. Whether successful or not a Rally!

instruction always ends orders from that commander for that turn. If successfully issued, the commander moves to join the unit and the unit removes one casualty.

5. A commander who has not already joined a unit can join any unit within his division within 12" that is fighting hand-to-hand combat. He can do this at any point prior to hand-to-hand combat being worked out, and can do so even during the opposing side's turn.

6. A commander who is joined with a unit that is engaged in combat must remain with it until it is no longer engaged or until he is wounded or slain.

7. A commander model moved over by an enemy unit must immediately join a friendly unit within one move's distance. If unable to do so he is captured and removed as a casualty.

8. If a commander has joined a unit that is subsequently shattered or broken roll a dice. 1-2 = slain (removed as casualty), 3-4 = wounded (see below), 5-6 = unharmed. Wounded and unharmed commanders must make an immediate move to join a friendly unit and if unable to do so are captured.

9. If a commander has joined a unit that is shaken by ranged attacks, or suffers further ranged casualties if already shaken, the opposing player rolls two dice. The commander is deemed to have been hit on the score of a 12. Roll a further dice to determine what happens to him. 1-3 = slain (removed as casualty), 4-6 = wounded (see below).

10. If a commander is with a fighting unit in hand-to-hand combat then he risks being slain or wounded regardless of whether the combat is won or lost. Once other attacks have been resolved the opposing player rolls two dice to determine if the commander is hit. He adds +1 to the total for each attack the commander has made above 1 (i.e. 1 attack add nothing, 2 attacks add +1 and three attacks add +2). On a total of 12 or more the commander is hit. This scores an extra casualty against that side's combat result regardless of whether the commander is slain or wounded. Roll a dice. 1-3 = slain (remove as casualty) and 4-6 = wounded (see below).

11. A commander who has been wounded can no longer make any attacks in hand-to-hand fighting and cannot join a unit that is fighting hand-to-hand combat. If he is already with a unit that is fighting hand-to-hand combat he must remain with it until it is no longer engaged. Wounded commanders can otherwise move and issue orders as normal.

VICTORY AND DEFEAT

1. An army is defeated once more than half of its divisions are broken.

2. A division is broken once more than half

		BREAK TESTS	
Dice Score	**Unit**	**RANGED ATTACKS**	**HAND-TO-HAND**
10 or more	Infantry	Hold your ground without penalty	Hold your ground without penalty
	Cavalry	Hold your ground without penalty	Hold your ground without penalty
	Skirmishers	Hold your ground without penalty	Hold your ground without penalty
9	Infantry	Hold your ground without penalty	Hold your ground without penalty
	Cavalry	Hold your ground without penalty	Give ground in good order together with supports
	Skirmishers	Retreat in good order	Give ground disordered
8	Infantry	Hold your ground without penalty	Hold your ground without penalty
	Cavalry	Hold your ground without penalty	Give ground in good order together with supports
	Skirmishers	Retreat disordered	Break if shaken, otherwise Give ground disordered
7	Infantry	Hold your ground without penalty	Give ground in good order together with supports
	Cavalry	Retreat in good order	Give ground disordered, together with supports
	Skirmishers	Retreat disordered	Break
6	Infantry	Hold your ground disordered or Retreat in good order	Give ground in good order together with supports
	Cavalry	Retreat disordered	Give ground disordered, together with supports
	Skirmishers	Retreat disordered	Break
5	Infantry	Hold your ground disordered or Retreat in good order	Give ground disordered, together with supports
	Cavalry	Retreat disordered	Break if shaken, otherwise Give ground together with supports – all disordered
	Skirmishers	Break if shaken, otherwise Retreat disordered	Break
4	Infantry	Retreat disordered	Break if shaken, otherwise Give ground together with supports – all disordered
	Cavalry	Break if shaken, otherwise Retreat disordered	Break if shaken, otherwise Give ground together with supports – all disordered
	Skirmishers	Break if the unit has suffered any casualties, otherwise Retreat disordered	Break
3	Infantry	Break if shaken, otherwise Retreat disordered	Break if shaken, otherwise Give ground together with supports – all disordered
	Cavalry	Break if shaken, otherwise Retreat disordered	Break
	Skirmishers	Break	Break
2 or less	Infantry	Break if unit has suffered any casualties, otherwise Retreat disordered	Break
	Cavalry	Break if unit has suffered any casualties, otherwise Retreat disordered	Break
	Skirmishers	Break	Break

of its units are either destroyed or have left the table whilst shaken. A division is also broken if all of its remaining units are shaken at the end of its side's Command part of the turn. The following units do not count when making this calculation unless such units make up the majority type in the division.

- Skirmishers
- Light artillery
- Tiny units
- Light infantry/light cavalry and others where agreed prior to the game

3. Once a division is broken no units that are shaken, or which subsequently

become shaken, are allowed to rally. They remain shaken from thereon.

4. Broken divisions must attempt to quit the field as expediently as practical. Unengaged units from broken divisions will 'retire' moving once even where no order is issued and even where a unit is disordered. Units failing an order also move once (free move).

5. Units from broken divisions are not allowed to charge the enemy, though they can countercharge if otherwise allowed to do so.

APPENDIX 5: RESOURCES

Publishing this book would not have been possible without a host of enthusiastic, talented individuals:

Miniatures and terrain courtesy of the collections of: *Alan Perry, Michael Perry, Rick Priestley, John Stallard, Paul Sawyer, Kevin Dallimore, Bennett Blalock-Doane, Dave Bodley, Sascha Herm, Mark Bedford, Paul Cubbin, Dale Yates, Great Escape Games, Mark Sims, Dr Phil Hendry, Steve May, Paul Darnell, Warwick Kinrade*

Playtesting: *Alan Perry, Michael Perry, Paul Sawyer, John Stallard, Alessio Cavatore, Steve Morgan, Andy Bartlett, Duncan McFarlane, Peter Brown, Dr Phil Hendry, Nigel Stillman, Jervis Johnson, Steve May*

Miniatures painted by: *Rick Priestley, Paul Sawyer, Dr Phil Hendry, Mark Bedford, Dale Yates, Darren Linington, Darren Harding, Andrew Chesney, Sascha Herm, Alan Perry, Michael Perry, Steve May, Bruno Allanson, Colin and Duncan Patten, Mystic Spirals, Darrell Hindley, Mike Collington*

We hope you've enjoyed the photographs of our collections of painted armies. The models featured in Hail Caesar come from a number of manufacturers and suppliers including the following:

Warlord Games
www.warlordgames.co.uk
Unit U-15, Lenton Business Centre, Lenton Boulevard, Nottingham NG7 2BY, UK.
Email: *info@warlordgames.co.uk*

Perry Miniatures
www.perry-miniatures.com
PO Box 6512, Nottingham, NG7 1UJ, UK.   Email: *perryminiatures@aol.com*

Immortal Miniatures
www.immortal miniatures.com
PO Box 9713, Nottingham NG8 9GR, UK.   Email: *info@immortalminiatures.com*

Grand Manner
www.grandmanner.co.uk
Unit B, Harolds Court, Saxon Business Park, Hanbury Road, Bromsgrove, Worcestershire, B60 4FL, UK.
Email: *grandmanner@live.co.uk*

Gripping Beast
www.grippingbeast.com
Unit 8, Briar Close Business Park, Evesham, Worcestershire WR11 4JT, UK.
Email: *grippingbeast@btconnect.com*

Wargames Foundry
www.wargamesfoundry.com
24-34 St. Marks Street, Nottingham NG3 1DE, UK.
Email: *sales@wargamesfoundry.com*

RANGED ATTACKS 'TO HIT' MODIFIERS

Dice Score	Situation
-1	Attackers are shaken and/or disordered
-1	The target is partly obscured, in open order, artillery or baggage
-1	The target is formed and either cataphracts or the front of heavy infantry
-1	Closing Shots
-1	Traversing Shots
-1	Long Range Shots – this applies to all shots at ranges over 12"

MORALE SAVE MODIFIERS

Dice Score	Situation
+1	Square or Wedge
+1	Cover
+2	Testudo
+2	Buildings
+3	Fortification
-1	Hit by Light Artillery
-2	Hit by Medium or Heavy Artillery
-2	Column

HAND-TO-HAND 'TO HIT' MODIFIERS

Dice Score	Situation
+1	Charging/Countercharging – fighting units only
+1	Winning – fighting units only
+1	Uphill
-1	Shaken and/or disordered
-1	Open Order
-1	Engaged to the Flank/Rear

BLUNDER TABLE

1 Uncontrolled flight! Face to rear and make 2 moves. Take 1 casualty.

2 Back! Make 1 move backwards whilst continuing to face.

3 Drift left. The unit makes 1 move to its left.

4 Drift right. The unit makes 1 move to its right.

5 Forward! The unit makes 1 move to its front and charges if possible.

6 Uncontrolled Advance! The unit makes 3 moves to its front and charges if possible.

MOVEMENT

Infantry, Elephants, Wagons and Baggage, Man-portable Artillery, Cataphract Cavalry, and Heavy Chariots	6"
Light Chariots and other formed Cavalry	9"
Light Cavalry in open order and Horse Archers	12"
Commanders	24"

FORMATION MODIFIERS

Column	Ranged Attacks 0, Hand-to-Hand Attacks 1
Testudo	Ranged Attacks 0
Square	Ranged Attacks 1, Hand-to-Hand Attacks 2 per face
Buildings	Ranged Attacks 2 per face, Hand-to-Hand Attacks 2 per face

RANGED ATTACK DISTANCES

Javelins, Darts and other thrown weapons	6"
Bows, Crossbows and Staffslings	18"
Slings	12"
Light Artillery	24"
Medium Artillery	36"
Heavy Artillery	48"

· HAIL CAESAR ·
™

QUICK REFERENCE SHEET

BREAK TESTS

TEST WHEN:

› A unit is shaken by ranged attacks including by closing/traversing shots.

› A shaken unit takes further casualties from ranged attacks.

› On the roll of a 6 'to hit' by ranged attacks requiring better than 6 to hit.

› On two rolls of 6 'to hit' by ranged attacks requiring 6 to hit.

› If a fighting unit is defeated in hand-to-hand combat.

› If a fighting unit that is already shaken draws a hand-to-hand combat.

› If a unit is supporting a fighting unit that breaks or is shattered.

BREAK TEST MODIFIERS (2D6):

› For Break tests due to ranged attacks deduct excess casualties suffered by the unit from the dice score.

› For Break tests due to hand-to-hand combat deduct the difference in casualties suffered from the dice score.

DICE SCORE	UNIT	RANGED ATTACKS	HAND-TO-HAND
10 or more	Infantry	Hold your ground without penalty	Hold your ground without penalty
	Cavalry	Hold your ground without penalty	Hold your ground without penalty
	Skirmishers	Hold your ground without penalty	Hold your ground without penalty
9	Infantry	Hold your ground without penalty	Hold your ground without penalty
	Cavalry	Hold your ground without penalty	Give ground in good order together with supports
	Skirmishers	Retreat in good order	Give ground disordered
8	Infantry	Hold your ground without penalty	Hold your ground without penalty
	Cavalry	Hold your ground without penalty	Give ground in good order together with supports
	Skirmishers	Retreat disordered	Break if shaken, otherwise Give ground disordered
7	Infantry	Hold your ground without penalty	Give ground in good order together with supports
	Cavalry	Retreat in good order	Give ground disordered, together with supports
	Skirmishers	Retreat disordered	Break
6	Infantry	Hold your ground disordered or Retreat in good order	Give ground in good order together with supports
	Cavalry	Retreat disordered	Give ground disordered, together with supports
	Skirmishers	Retreat disordered	Break
5	Infantry	Hold your ground disordered or Retreat in good order	Give ground disordered, together with supports
	Cavalry	Retreat disordered	Break if shaken, otherwise Give ground together with supports – all disordered
	Skirmishers	Break if shaken, otherwise Retreat disordered	Break
4	Infantry	Retreat disordered	Break if shaken, otherwise Give ground together with supports – all disordered
	Cavalry	Break if shaken, otherwise Retreat disordered	Break if shaken, otherwise Give ground together with supports – all disordered
	Skirmishers	Break if the unit has suffered any casualties, otherwise Retreat disordered	Break
3	Infantry	Break if shaken, otherwise Retreat disordered	Break if shaken, otherwise Give ground together with supports – all disordered
	Cavalry	Break if shaken, otherwise Retreat disordered	Break
	Skirmishers	Break	Break
2 or less	Infantry	Break if unit has suffered any casualties, otherwise Retreat disordered	Break
	Cavalry	Break if unit has suffered any casualties, otherwise Retreat disordered	Break
	Skirmishers	Break	Break

· HAIL CAESAR ·
QUICK REFERENCE SHEET

UNITS ON FOOT							
Type	Combat				Morale Save	Stamina	Useful Rule
	Clash	Sustained	Short Range	Long Range			
Heavy Infantry	7	7	3	0	4+	6	
Heavy Infantry with Long Spear	7	7	3/0	0	4+	6	Long Spear
Heavy Infantry Pikemen	7	7	3/0	0	4+	6	Phalanx, Pike
Heavy Infantry with Double-Handed Weapon	8	7	2/0	0	4+	6	Double Handed
Medium Infantry	6	6	3	0	5+	6	
Medium Infantry with Long Spear	7	7	3/0	0	5+	6	Long Spear
Medium Infantry Pikemen	6	6	3/0	0	5+	6	Phalanx, Pike
Medium Infantry with Double Handed Weapon	7	6	2/0	0	5+	6	Double Handed
Medium Infantry Archers	5	5	3	3	5+	6	
Medium Infantry with Spear and Bow	6	6	3	3	5+	6	
Medium Infantry Warband	7,8 or 9	6	2	0	5+	6	Wild Fighters
Light Infantry	5	5	3	0	6+	6	
Light Infantry Archers (standard unit)	4	4	3	3	0	6	
Armoured Light Infantry Archers (standard unit)	4	4	3	3	6+	6	
Light Infantry Archers (small unit)	3	3	2	2	0	4	
Armoured Light Infantry Archers (small unit)	3	3	2	2	6+	4	
Skirmishers (standard unit)	5	4	3	0	0	6	
Skirmishers with ranged weapons (standard unit)	4	4	3	3	0	6	
Skirmishers (small unit)	3	2	2	0	0	4	
Skirmishers with ranged weapons (small unit)	2	2	2	2	0	4	

Note. This list provides examples of values and commonly employed useful rules, and can be varied and extended should players wish to do so. Troops equipped with swords, javelins, and light thrusting or throwing spears are the standard type, hence weapons are not indicated. Other troops, for example those with heavy throwing weapons (Pila) have the same values as common troops of their type.

· HAIL CAESAR ·
™

QUICK REFERENCE SHEET

Type	Combat				Morale Save	Stamina	Useful Rule
	Clash	Sustained	Short Range	Long Range			
Cataphract Cavalry	9	6	3	0	4+	6	
Cataphract Cavalry with Kontos	9	6	3/0	0	4+	6	Kontos
Cataphract Cavalry (Bow-Armed) or Kontos and Bow	9	6	3	2	4+	6	Kontos
Heavy Cavalry	9	6	3	0	4+	6	
Heavy Cavalry with Kontos or Lance	9	6	3/0	0	4+	6	Kontos, Lance
Heavy Cavalry (Bow-Armed) or Kontos and Bow	9	6	3	2	4+	6	Kontos
Medium Cavalry	8	5	3	0	5+	6	
Light Cavalry (standard unit)	7	5	3	0	6+	6	
Light Cavalry (Bow-Armed) (standard unit)	7	5	3	3	6+	6	
Light Cavalry (small unit)	5	3	2	0	6+	4	Feigned Flight
Light Cavalry (Bow-Armed) (small unit)	5	3	2	2	6+	4	Feigned Flight
Horse Archers (standard unit)	6	4	3	3	6+	6	Parthian Shot
Horse Archers (small unit)	4	2	2	2	6+	4	Parthian Shot
Light Chariots	6	6	3	0	4+	6	
Light Chariots (Bow-Armed)	6	6	3	3	4+	6	
British/Celtic Light Chariots	6	5	4	0	4+	6	Feigned Flight
Heavy Chariots	9	5	3	0	3+	6	
Heavy Chariots (Bow-Armed)	9	5	3	3	3+	6	
Heavy Scythed Chariots (small unit)	7	0	0	0	3+	4	Scythed Chariots
Elephant	4	3	1	0	4+	6	Elephant
Elephant with Bow-Armed Crew	4	3	1	1	4+	6	Elephant
Light Artillery	1	1	2	2	0	3	
Medium Artillery	1	1	0	3	0	3	
Heavy Artillery	1	1	0	3	0	3	
Wagons/Baggage	3	1	1	0	0	6	

MOUNTED UNITS